José María Arguedas
Reconsiderations for Latin American Cultural Studies

This series of publications on Africa, Latin America, and Southeast Asia is designed to present significant research, translation, and opinion to area specialists and to a wide community of persons interested in world affairs. The editor seeks manuscripts of quality on any subject and can generally make a decision regarding publication within three months of receipt of the original work. Production methods generally permit a work to appear within one year of acceptance. The editor works closely with authors to produce a high quality book. The series appears in a paperback format and is distributed worldwide. For more information, contact the executive editor at Ohio University Press, Scott Quadrangle, University Terrace, Athens, Ohio 45701.

Executive editor: Gillian Berchowitz
AREA CONSULTANTS
Africa: Diane Ciekawy
Latin America: Thomas Walker
Southeast Asia: William H. Frederick

The Monographs in International Studies series is published for the Center for International Studies by the Ohio University Press. The views expressed in individual monographs are those of the authors and should not be considered to represent the policies or beliefs of the Center for International Studies, the Ohio University Press, or Ohio University.

José María Arguedas

Reconsiderations for Latin American Cultural Studies

Edited by

Ciro A. Sandoval and
Sandra M. Boschetto-Sandoval

Ohio University Center for International Studies
Monographs in International Studies
Latin American Series Number 29
Athens • *1998*

The books in the Center for International Studies Monograph Series
are printed on acid-free paper ∞

Library of Congress Cataloging-in-Publication Data

José María Arguedas: reconsiderations for Latin American cultural studies /
edited by Ciro A. Sandoval and Sandra M. Boschetto-Sandoval.
    p. cm. -- (Monographs in international studies. Latin America
series: no. 29)
    Includes bibliographical references.
    ISBN 0-89680-200-0 (paper : alk. paper)
    1. Arguedas, José María -- Political and social views. 2. Quechua Indians
in literature. 3. Acculturation in literature.
I. Sandoval, Ciro A. II.Boschetto-Sandoval, Sandra M. III. Series.
PQ8497.A65Z679 1997   97-27131
863--cd21   CIP

This series of publications on Africa, Latin America, and Southeast Asia is designed to
present significant research, translation, and opinion to area specialists and to a wide
community of persons interested in world affairs. The editor seeks manuscripts of
quality on any subject and can generally make a decision regarding publication within
three months of receipt of the original work. Production methods generally permit a
work to appear within one year of acceptance. The editor works closely with authors to
produce a high quality book. The series appears in a paperback format and is distributed worldwide. For more information, contact the executive editor at Ohio University
Press, Scott Quadrangle, University Terrace, Athens, Ohio 45701.

Executive editor: Gillian Berchowitz
AREA CONSULTANTS
Africa: Diane Ciekawy
Latin America: Thomas Walker
Southeast Asia: James L. Cobban

The Monographs in International Studies series is published for the Center for International Studies by the Ohio University Press. The views expressed in individual
monographs are those of the authors and should not be considered to represent the
policies or beliefs of the Center for International Studies, the Ohio University Press, or
Ohio University.

061899-2775X8

Contents

PART TWO
Transliterary Reconsiderations, 85

PART THREE
The Intersection of Subjectivities, 185

CONTENTS

Foreword

Antonio Melis

The essays included in this reconsideration of the work of José María Arguedas eloquently attest to the recent turnaround that has taken place in the critical appreciation of this Peruvian writer. During his lifetime, and even those years immediately following his tragic death, a profound misunderstanding limited scholarly and critical reflection on his work. With notable exceptions, many commentators have appraised his narrative texts as the ultimate gesture of a pathetic former *indigenismo* (indigenous literary movement). On the formal level, his literature has often been considered a prolongation—albeit at the height of the twentieth century—of the realistic and naturalistic currents of the nineteenth century.

Of course, the intent here is not so much to mount a case against the obvious lack of comprehension of Arguedas's contributions. The history of literature in all countries and in all eras presents many similar instances of misinterpretation. Rather, a much more interesting approach involves a focus on Arguedas himself. I am inclined to believe, first of all, that the misunderstandings generated around the significance and influence of Arguedas's work are tied to very specific cultural circumstances. His years of literary maturity coincide to a large extent with the development and influence of the so-called Latin American literary boom. The poet Emilio Adolfo Westphalen, a close friend of the author, said on the occasion of a literary debate that this new movement reflected a self-serving exaltation of its European success and that perhaps the phenomenon had more to do with the marketing of books than with literature. Nevertheless, alongside this view, it is important to underscore that the boom years coincided to a great extent, with the rise of a particularly aggressive form of literary theory and criticism, and with a clearly hegemonic slant. With French structuralism and modern semiotics not only did a new way of reading literary works progressively emerge, but also a new set of interpretive parameters. A new circle of relations, regrettably not always fortunate, arose between criticism and literary creation. Furthermore, an exclusionist trend began to take shape, one that in fact marginalized the writers who did not fit the new trend's procrustean paradigms.

Arguedas's reaction to this situation was fairly complex. On the one hand, he tended to accentuate polemically the very features for which he is reproached: for example, the attitude perceived at a deeper level in some of his responses during the famous Primer Encuentro de Narradores Peruanos (First meeting of Peruvian writers) held in Arequipa in 1965. While writers such as Sebastián Salazar Bondy confronted Arguedas with what Bondy called a verbal reality, Arguedas argued, in a quasi-candid way, for the identifying correspondence of word and thing. At the time, it was indeed difficult to capture the authentic undertones of such provocative assertions. Perhaps it would have helped in such a task to align these arguments alongside the message ensuing from the gestation of his narrative work, as well as with the Quechua poems he had begun to publish at that same time.

Nevertheless, naive exasperation was not Arguedas's only response in the face of his detractors and inquisitors. With the phenomenal achievement of *El zorro de arriba y el zorro de abajo* (1971, posthumous) (The fox from above and the fox from below), the author accomplishes not only what I call a countervindicating response implicit in his work, but also a convergence of two profound forces.

On the one hand, he attempts to carry his perceived identification of life with art to unforeseen and disquieting limits. The shot that brings both novel and life to an abrupt conclusion represents a dramatic irruption of the subject's reality, as well as the interruption of alternating play between narrative and journal segments. On the other hand, in the same novel, Arguedas constructs his formidable literary response to modernization. He creates a new type of narration, not only through the insertion of his journals, but also by the incorporation into the novel of the mythic perspectives inspired by the Huarochirí legend and manuscript. The final result, objectively speaking, is one of the most audacious and experimental texts in contemporary Latin American literature. Ironically, for these very reasons, when it first appeared, *El zorro* was misread and poorly received by certain critical circles.

The essays herein included explore new directions in the study of Arguedas's transdisciplinary work, as pioneered by such well-established Arguedistas as Alberto Escobar, Antonio Cornejo Polar, William Rowe, and Martin Lienhard. These contributions are worth highlighting here in their essential and singular insights on the work of this Peruvian writer and poet.

To begin with, the writings of Arguedas should be considered as an integrated totality (i.e., without the constraint of barriers such as genre). For that matter, it is counterproductive to draw a finalized portrait of the author, his life, and his work that includes abstract and forced separation between intellectual work, the Andean world, and historical circumstances. It goes without saying that there are continuous and fertile exchanges between Arguedas's ethnoanthropological investigations and literary creations, exchanges that open the way to fruitful and reciprocal illuminations. These interrelations allow his readers to perceive an incontrovertible fact: the presence of a permanent tension between tradition and modernity that permeates Arguedas's work. Equally there exists a lucid and documented vision of the dynamic tension that permeates the Andean world. This tension simultaneously produced changes and readjustments in Arguedas's work as it was influenced by modernizing trends. In Arguedas's view, indigenous Andean culture was not a static reality, but rather one that was itself pregnant with ideas of change, hence one in a process of continuous redefinition with regard to its complex relationships to tradition and modernity. Therefore, the tendency to view Arguedas's world as "archaic utopia" is not tenable. Rather, Arguedas read and interpreted modernity from within Andean cultural reality.

Another important aspect of this new investigation is the recognition of the significance of Arguedas's poetic production, which had previously gone unnoticed. Though it is not relatively extensive, poetry occupies a decisive niche in Arguedas's later production. Indeed, his poems bespeak the major themes that pervade his work, as embodied in a new powerful synthesis. At the same time, his poetry exhibits an original linguistic experimentation that confirms Arguedas's constant, almost obsessive preoccupation with language as a vehicle of representation of specific realities. This fact explains Arguedas's choice of the Quechua language for the first time as a literary and poetic vehicle, even though signs of his deliberate use of it can be found in Arguedas's earlier work. Nevertheless, in his poetry, Arguedas rejected the use of codified Quechua, as legitimated by more recent literary traditions of academic and purist orientation. This latter trend, Arguedas thought, viewed language as fossilized and incapable of expressing the new Andean reality. He therefore set out to construct a variation of Quechua that opened onto two new directions: on the one hand, he accepted its contamination by Spanish for he understood that contamination to be an irreversible fact triggered by unavoidable contact that favored linguistic and cultural osmosis and hybridization. On the other hand, as Arguedas clarified, he inserted Quechua variation into his regional *chanka*—for eminently stylistic purposes—the contributions of other regional variations of Quechua language. Arguedas was able to pursue in this way the creation of a veritable koine or patois capable of fostering mutual understanding among the different regional linguistic variations.

To point to another element that continues to draw critical attention, we must mention music as an authentic axis of the Arguedean opus. Its importance is manifest not only in Arguedas's personal testimonies, but also in critical studies of his work. In Pedro Lastra's affectionate testimony, music accompanies the daily life of the writer, and a song may even insinuate itself into an academic lecture as complement and culmination of the same. In William Rowe's view, the function of music is an indispensable element of Arguedas's vision of the world. Music is not only that which is produced by people in order to accompany all significant moments of their lives. It also constitutes the very presence of nature itself. Between these two manifestations, then, a network of correspondences is set in motion, one that shapes a system of cultural signs (a semiosis). Arguedas's world was full of open-ended meanings, and music played a decisive role in it. As our British colleague and critic underscores, music functions in Arguedas's work as a form of alternative knowledge, and at the same time, as a transformational force.

Another manifestation of Arguedas's countervindication is given by the new appreciation of his work as a means to uncovering the very depths of Peruvian reality. During his lifetime, Arguedas's work was subjected on various occasions to the scrutiny of the social sciences. The most notable example in this terrain is the bitter polemic that arose around his vision of Andean society, and that percolates through the pages of his novel *Todas las sangres* (All bloods, 1964). That vision was contested—mainly from within the paradigms of the social sciences—in the roundtable discussion organized by the Institute of Peruvian Studies (1965) shortly before the previously mentioned Primer Encuentro in Arequipa. The criticism launched against this vision as reflected in *Todas las sangres* directly contributed to the writer's personal crisis, to an extent that he would later question whether in fact he had "lived in vain." Nevertheless, he also found the strength to react affirmatively in the face of this situation and to pose new approaches to modernization. *El zorro de arriba y el zorro de abajo* epitomizes Arguedas's questioning of new ways of integrating contested realities. In this text, Arguedas boldly identified both Peru and himself as points of departure for this integration, noting that the Indian was transplanted onto a context (i.e., that of the port town of Chimbote) where modernity is expressed in degrading and alienating ways. At the same time that he detected Chimbote's hellish reality, he struggled to recover signs of possible redemption. A parallelism is thus established between the author's personal tragedy and the collective tragedy of the Andean peoples. Nevertheless, at the end of the novel, the author's tragic destiny is abruptly severed from that of Peru. Perhaps, the words of hope for the future of Peru written in his farewell represent the great writer's final message.

The essays included in this anthology open a new page in the investigation on the work of Arguedas. They uncover other forms of Arguedas's countervindication, forms that allow for different premonitions, perceptions, and directions of study. The timely compilation of these essays anticipates new critical reassessments on the work of this writer. Antonio Cornejo Polar, a pioneer in the interpretation of Arguedas's legacy, clears new ground with his illuminating presentation of the migrant's point of view. Migration as both personal and social phenomenon marks Arguedas's text. Cornejo Polar's essay captures its significance as "enunciative locus" from which to articulate a truly syncretic *mestizaje*.

On the literary, cultural, and political terrains Arguedas's works acquire an increasingly prophetic dimension. Martin Lienhard, to whom we also owe one of the most lucid and innovative interpretations of Arguedas's *El zorro*, highlights the creative force of Arguedas's poetic vein in that it is imbued with the vision of the Andean indigenous world so dear to him. Here, then, a clear connection exists between the flourishing of Arguedas's poetry, exclusively written in Quechua language, and the process of socioeconomic and political mobilization that continues to shape the Peru of today. Lienhard's essay emphasizes, in fact, that Arguedas's poetry distances itself as far from the recent tradition of Quechua poetry written in its autochthonous language as it does from present Quechua poetry written in Spanish. This fact, along with Quechua poetry's marginalization within the hegemonic canon, is one of the reasons why Arguedas's poetry is not as well known. A characteristic feature of his poetry is the revindication of Andean cultural roots, although in different forms, as an instrument capable of addressing the demands of new audiences in search of identities. This approach is exemplified, for instance, in Arguedas's poem "Tupac Amaru Kamaq Taitanchisman," which can be considered the poet's point of departure for his poetic explorations.

As for the other essays in this compilation, they analyze the work of Arguedas in the light of new interpretive hypotheses appearing in recent years. Julio Ortega had already applied the postulates of the Russian Tartu cultural school to his analysis of *Deep Rivers* in 1982. His essay here, a variation of a chapter from that study, points to new linguistic apertures of literary interpretation as well as to the integration of Arguedas's ethnoanthropological views. Priscilla Archibald in her essay also takes up this latter perspective but from the point of view of the ideologies dominant among the social sciences of his time. Thus, there reappear in this collection certain convergences characteristic of Arguedas's early career. More important, there also appear clear divergences with respect to the problems and issues postulated by theories of irreversible modernity. Furthermore, there appears the clear rejection of the writer in the face of any attempt to fetishize the Andean past at the cost of ignoring the reality of cultural *mestizaje*.

Alita Kelley's essay invokes the concept of postmodernity, while Rita De Grandis's contribution introduces the important notion of the postcolonial condition. But the overriding significance of these approximations is the validation of a new interpretive slant for Arguedean studies. Arguedas can, therefore, no longer be encased within the molds of a given critical methodology. On the contrary, Arguedas has been transformed into a cornerstone that allows present audiences to ascertain the potentiality and consistency of his new interpretive hypotheses.

The linguistic dimension of Arguedas's work reappears in John Landreau's essay, especially in reference to the interpretation and translation of the "otherness" of a cultural universe. Through processes of translation and interpretation, the autobiographical element, so present in Arguedas's work, acquires a collective, universal dimension. In the light of this central issue—translation as interpretation—Arguedas's polemical and supposed lack of technique is re-examined anew. Arguedas's use of oral Quechua tradition, for example, reveals alternative ways of knowing, very much in line with modern literary and critical practices.

The problem of alterity and alternative ways of knowing is also taken up by Ciro A. Sandoval and Sandra M. Boschetto-Sandoval in their essay on Arguedas's testimonial novel, *El Sexto* (The Sexto prison, 1961). This novel, one that has not been afforded much critical attention until now, analyzes the traumatic experience of imprisonment, an experience that provides the momentum to examine anew the Andean problematic in terms of indigenous culture and its validity in the face of modernizing postulates and rationalizing ideologies, which also indirectly led to Arguedas's imprisonment. In an analectic frame (by opposition to a dialectic one), the technologizing of knowledge (of a specific scientific cut) is countered by a more universally encompassing vision, one that thrusts its roots into nature itself, and that Arguedas believed could bring about the redemption of both modern Andean culture and Peru.

In Claudette Kemper Columbus's contribution, the dialogues between the foxes in *El zorro* in the fishmeal factory of Chimbote can be viewed as a reaffirmation and renewal of the presence of a "trickster." In its joining together of both cyclical and linear time, the folkloric backdrop of Arguedas's work is underscored. Above all, what is emphasized is the author's creative power.

Finally, Luis Jiménez in his essay brings to bear a Bakhtinian perspective on the "carnivalesque" manifestation of the two oppositional but central female characters in *Deep Rivers*: the feeble-minded "opa" Marcelina, and the heroine Doña Felipa. On the one hand, we uncover the "festive" but violent space of the latrines in the boarding school where adolescent sexual initiation takes place. On the other, the rebellious episode of the "chicheras" amply expresses an inversion of hierarchical social and cultural values.

The work of this Peruvian writer in the context of these multiple perspectives appears profoundly contestatory. Indeed, the new approximations herein included trace the writer's different texts in this same vein. Perhaps this situation represents the most engaging manifestation of what I have called Arguedas's countervindication, and one readily embodied in the author's compelling opus.

Translated by Ciro A. Sandoval and Sandra M. Boschetto-Sandoval

Acknowledgments

While we cannot thank individually all those who gave us thoughtful encouragement on this manuscript, we do want to make special mention of a few. We owe more gratitude than we can express to Antonio Cornejo Polar and Alita Kelley, whose ever-tireless collaborative spirit and assistance with countless details made this project possible. To Alita Kelley also for her diligent professional translation of several of the manuscripts, we are most grateful. To Pedro Lastra, who graciously extended addresses, phone numbers, and sympathetic guidance, as well as to Monica Barnes for her thorough reading of the manuscripts, special thanks. To Alberto Escobar, Frances Barraclough, and Carolina Teillier for their invaluable help with bibliographic references and photographs, our sincere appreciation. To Marc Zimmerman and Antonio Melis, who offered encouragement, support, and, above all, humor, we acknowledge our appreciation. To Deborah Schueller, whose wit and computer wizardry helped speed along manuscript processing, we are most grateful.

Finally, as academics who share enthusiasm for Latin America and its cultures, this project has special significance, but especially for a Latin American whose recollection of his father's love of the land in the highlands of Colombia fanned the fire of our mutual endeavor. It is to Avelino, therefore, that we dedicate this book.

Introduction

Ciro A. Sandoval

A writer, a man writing, is the scribe of all nature; he is
the corn and the grass, and the atmosphere writing.

—H. D. Thoreau, *A Writer's Journal*

The Man, His Place, and His Time

José María Arguedas Altamirano (1911–1969) was born into a world
shaped by particular historical circumstances, at the crossroads of
modernization's thrust into Peru. These circumstances would in turn
shape his character and his destiny as one of the most creative and
influential writers of both the Andean world and of Latin America as
a whole. He was born in the southern Andean town of Andahuaylas
to an itinerant lawyer from Cuzco, the capital of Tahuantinsuyu (the
Indian name for the Inca empire). As a young boy, Arguedas accompanied his father on many of his travels through various towns in the
southern Peruvian Andes. Arguedas would later portray its landscape and people in a masterful language, rendering transparent their
poetical, lyrical, and mythico-scientific visions. He once remarked:

> I journeyed the country fields, [and] performed the tasks of the
> "campesinos" under the infinite protection of the Quechua com-
> moners. My protectors showered me with a deep and brave tender-
> ness, . . . the purest love, which makes the individual who has

acquired it absolutely immune to skepticism. [introduction to *Yawar Fiesta*, 3)[1]

On another occasion Arguedas recalls that he was the product of his stepmother:

> My mother died when I was two and a half. My father married a second time—a woman who had three sons ... [and] who owned half the town; she had many indigenous servants, as well as the traditional contempt and ignorance of what an Indian was, and because she despised and hated me as much as [her] Indians, she decided that I was to live with them in the kitchen, eat and sleep there. [*Páginas escogidas*, 247]

These biographical sketches allow us to glimpse the ambivalence, both positive and negative reflections, that branded Arguedas's life from its early stages. These indelible scars would motivate his coming to terms with reality and creativity in a never-ceasing struggle with language, a struggle that embodied his very life and that one also traces from his early writings:

> I began writing after reading my first stories about the Indians; they were described in so false a way by writers I respected, who taught me what I know. . . . López Albújar knew the Indians only from his desk, as a criminal judge, and Mr. Ventura García Calderón, I do not know how he had heard of them. In these narratives the Indian was so distorted and the landscape so sugar-coated, so lacking in feeling, so ... strange that I said to myself: "No, I have to write it as it is, because I have enjoyed knowing it, because I have suffered it," and I wrote those first stories that were published in that little book I called *Agua* [Water]. [*Páginas escogidas*, 251]

As his friend Emilio Westphalen explained, "Arguedas's destiny was a special one: he happened to suffer in his own flesh, from within ... the basic cultural dichotomy of the country [indigenous versus nonindigenous cultures]" (introduction to *Páginas escogidas*, n.p.). The fact that Arguedas had not been born into that indigenous world to which he felt he belonged, if not by physical circumstance, then by emotional attachment, was a source of constant anxiety. That frustration would later progress to the painful realization that the dream of rescuing his beloved Andean world and culture through the creation of a national mestizo culture was doomed. The culture he envisioned, in which Indian, white Western European, and modern industrialized worlds could fuse into a new kind of *raza cósmica* (a cosmic race, to borrow from José Vasconcelos) was but a utopia made of language. Had this utopian wishful thinking materialized, Arguedas would most likely have preferred it to arise from an inverse conquest, the forging of a *mestizaje* (racial and cultural crossing) in reverse. Arguedas recalled, for example, one of the leaders of Pichqachuri (one of the four *ayllu*s, or Indian communities, of Puquio, a province capital) telling him once that his community was slow in progressing because it lacked *mistis* (whites, mestizos, and foreigners). The elders of the community were, therefore, set on having their sons undergo racial and cultural inmixing.[2] Arguedas believed that this transculturation was important because it pointed to the possibility that mestizos could come into existence in the communities of Pichqachuri and Qayao (Puquio muncipality) through a conscious transformation "launched by the Indians themselves, [and] not following the traditional, inverted process of impoverishment of *mistis* or as a consequence of illegitimate miscegenation" (*Páginas escogidas*, 187, 196).

As novelist, storyteller, folklorist, ethnographer, and educator, Arguedas wrote extensively. Yet, as he himself tells us in the *First Journal* (1968), he never thought of himself as a professional writer, one, that is, who sees writing as a profession (qtd. in Fell 1990, 18). Rather, Arguedas saw his writing as the very embodiment of his life, and as a means of testifying to the reality he knew and lived. In other words, he took writing as an author takes it, one for whom neither style nor form, nor canons, nor writing trends were the main concern, as Roland Barthes explains (1992, 143–50). As an author, Arguedas's concern was the totality of human culture. This also helps explain why he sought complementary venues of exploration in folklore, anthropology, and ethnography.

His yearning for humanistic and cultural totality finds expression in the continuous expansion of his writing from the local to the global; from the small indigenous communities, villages, and towns of the Andean sierra, to the larger coastal cities, from within the national Peruvian cosmos outward to the rest of the geographical and cultural world. As he illustrates with reference to his novel *Todas las sangres* (All bloods, 1964): "It would not have been possible for me to outline its course had I not first interpreted in *Agua* [Water, 1935] the life of an [Andean] village; that of a provincial capital in *Yawar Fiesta* [1941]; that of a wider and more complex human territory in *Deep Rivers* [1958]" (introduction to *Páginas escogidas*, n.p.). We can thus view his world as a subsystem within a wider global and universal system, with all things interconnected in different ways and at different levels. No more eloquent example of this weblike vision is found than the one reflected in his controversial novel *Todas las sangres*, which he places in the following perspective:

> I have had the good fortune of traversing during my lifetime almost all levels and hierarchies in Peru; I have even been Director of Culture. . . . I tried to write a novel in which I could portray all these hierarchies, with all that they reflect of promise and of burden. [In the novel] there are three characters . . . two of which are fundamental . . . two inherit large feudal estates, two brothers [that] hate each other . . . one of them has an absolute, feudal mentality; the other, educated in the United States and in Lima . . . wants to make of Peru a country very much like North America; the other one wants to hold it back as a traditional country. . . . Between these two, like a formidable wedge, stands an Indian that suffered all that an Indian can in Lima [Peru's capital], the honorable Rendón Wilka. [*Páginas escogidas*, 253]

The agitation of different social strata is the most conspicuously present mark of Arguedas's aesthetic, essayistic, and critical production. Bear in mind here that the term *indio*, which is used to mean the peasant of Quechua and Aymara origin in the Andean world of Peru and Bolivia, carries strong negative connotations for both mestizos and whites. It was because of this that in the early 1960s the populist regime of Velasco Ibarra attempted, with some success, to replace it with the term *campesino*, to mean highland people, and for whom Ibarra's government had plans of integration into the Peruvian mainstream. Despite this, *indio* (Indian) has prevailed, even to the present, as a term signifying those peoples who speak native languages, dress in native garb, and stubbornly hold to a way of life dubbed native, and to a status that no one else aspires to.

The Peru into which Arguedas was born, that he celebrated and agonized for as a "happy demon" who spoke "in Christian and in Indian, in Spanish and in Quechua," that made him "happy" precisely because he "felt Peru in Quechua and in Spanish (*Final Journal*, 1969; qtd. in Fell 1990, 437) was still suffering the aftermath of the War of the Pacific (1879–1883) in which Peru lost to Chile its southern nitrate-producing regions of Tarapaca in 1883 and Arica in 1929. The reader suffers this postwar depression in Arguedas's celebrated novel *Deep Rivers* (1958), which portrays Peru in the grip of a new paradigm of development, modernization, and turmoil.

Arguedas was born at the end of the so-called Aristocratic Republic (1895–1914), which arose from the alliance between the government of José Nicolás de Piérola and his former opposition party, the Civilistas. The end of the Aristocratic Republican period also marks the beginning of Peru's economic instability on the brink of World War I. At the time of Arguedas's birth, Peru was dragging under the burden of new elites emerging from the ruins of the War of the Pacific, elites who coalesced to form the powerful oligarchy founded on the reemergence of sugar, cotton, and mining exports, and on the entrance of Peru into the international economy. It was also a Peru undergoing changes in its work force, as its peasantry migrated not only to industrial enclaves that had arisen in Lima but also throughout other areas of the country. Traditional haciendas and small-scale mining gave way to modern agro-industrial plantations, mining enclaves, and new proletarians as well.

This political, economic, social, and cultural whirlwind would have far-reaching consequences, tarnishing Arguedas's hopes for the formation of a national as well as universal culture. This because there was no hope of a democratic process that discounted violence in a country where the oligarchy was so powerful. These consequences became clear at the outbreak of the military coup motivated by the millionaire businessman Guillermo Billinghurst, who first forced the Republican congress to elect him, then entered into a series of bitter conflicts with it. After threatening to arm the workers and dissolve the congress, Billinghurst provoked Colonel Oscar Raimundo Benavides (1914–1915; 1933–1936; 1936–1939) to seize power. This new coup would mark the beginning of a long-term alliance between the military and the oligarchy until the 1968 revolution of General Juan Velasco Alvarado (1968–1975), just one year before Arguedas's death.

As for other changes in the political and social arena after World War I, radical new ideologies spreading from the Mexican and Russian revolutions (1910 and 1917) fueled growing unrest. In the meantime, *indigenista* (indigenous) movements attracted the attention of the first wave of indigenous writers, particularly middle-class mestizos who were interested in retracing their roots in this changing Peru and who wanted to celebrate the glorious Inca past. New indigenous awareness was galvanized by a series of native uprisings in the southern Andes, where communities were disrupted and dislocated by the opening of new international markets, the reorganization of the wool industry, and the expansion of other trades as demands from urban coastal areas for products from the sierra increased. The postwar worker-student alliance generated a new era of radical thinkers and reformers such as Victor Raúl Haya de la Torre of the University of San Marcos, who later founded the revolutionary and influential political leftist party APRA (American Popular and Revolutionary Alliance) while in exile in Mexico in 1924. Outside the academy, José Carlos Mariátegui, a brilliant Lima journalist, founded the Socialist Party as well as a liberal and widely read popular opinion magazine, *Amauta*, also a prestigious publishing house, which published extensively on economics, literature, and politics. Mariátegui's celebrated collection of essays dealing with these issues, *Seven Essays on the Interpretation of Peruvian Reality* (1928), would exert a tremendous influence on the thinking and writing of José María Arguedas. Especially influential was Mariátegui's socialist argument that Peruvian Marxism could be welded to an indigenous Andean revolutionary tradition, to include not only *indigenismo*, with its emphasis on the proud history of resistance of the Andean peasantry, but labor as well.

After 1930 both the military and the oligarchy, now firmly allied, became, along with APRA, the most important actors in Peru's political, social, and economic scenario until the 1960s. During this time, which would last to the end of Arguedas's life, the military often acted at the behest of the oligarchy to suppress the "unruly" masses represented by APRA and by the PCP (Communist Party of Peru). As expected, this oligarchic-military alliance provoked bloody uprisings of the APRA, such as the one in Trujillo (1932) in which some sixty army officers were executed by the insurgents. This violent act resulted in the first use of aerial bombing in the history of South America and was responsible for the death of some one thousand APRA members and sympathizers.

By maintaining its long-term export-oriented model of growth (led by cotton and new industrial metals such as lead and zinc) essentially unaltered, Peru was, in the 1930s, one of the countries in the continent least affected by the world economic depression. Yet, despite the measures taken by the presidency of Sánchez Cerro to reorganize its debt-ridden economy—including the invitation of North American consultant Edwin Kemmener, whose advice helped usher in Peru's return to the gold standard—the country was unable to forestall a moratorium on its U.S. $180-million debt in 1931. As a consequence, the country was barred from U.S. markets for the next thirty years.

The APRA party of the 1930s was essentially nationalist, populist, and reformist in its ideology and platform. Although certainly radical from the perspective of the oligarchy, the APRA platform focused on correcting the historical inequality of wealth and income in Peru, as well as on reducing and controlling large-scale foreign investments in the country (indeed very high in comparison with other Latin American and Andean countries). At the same time, Peru's richest, most powerful forty families perceived a direct challenge to their traditional privileges and absolute right to rule, which they were not willing to sacrifice without resistance. The oligarchy intensified its attacks in the face of APRA polemicist rhetoric, contributing thereby to the unleashing of violent assassinations, widespread imprisonment, and torture of Apristas and their followers. These events would later inform the main political corpus of Arguedas's testimonial novel *El Sexto* (The Sexto prison, 1961).

At the end of the Benavides presidency in 1939, Manuel Prado y Ugarteche, a prominent Lima banker, won the presidency and gradually moved to soften official opposition to APRA, as Haya de la Torre moved to moderate the party's platform in response to the changing national and international environment brought on by World War II. Consistent with this new environment and his reformed ideology, Haya de la Torre no longer proposed to radically redistribute income but instead to create new wealth and to replace the earlier radical "anti-imperialism" with more favorable calls for democracy, foreign investment, and hemispheric harmony. In response, the Prado government legalized the APRA party, thus allowing it to enter the political arena after thirteen years of underground activity.

In 1945, José Luis Bustamante (1945–1948) was elected president on the basis of his alliance with the now legal APRA. Nevertheless, this alliance would also cause problems for the government as it tried to respond to a more reformist, populist-oriented agenda, including a general fiscal expansion, higher wages, and controls on prices and exchange rates. These policies came at a time when Peru's exports were sagging after World War II. As a result, inflation and unrest began to mount, destabilizing the government.

After the 1947 assassination by Aprista militants of Francisco Graña Garland, director of the conservative newspaper *La Prensa*, and the naval mutiny organized by Aprista elements in 1948, the oligarchy pressed the military to overthrow the government and install General Manuel Odría as president (1948–1956). Odría imposed a personalistic dictatorship and returned to the familiar pattern of repression of the left, while astutely shielding himself by establishing a paternalistic relationship with labor and the urban poor through a series of charity and welfare measures. Odría could initiate these measures because his government had installed itself at a time when prices for the country's diverse commodities were rising on the world market due to the outbreak of the Korean War in 1950. Greater political stability also brought increased national and foreign investment. In general, the economy experienced a period of strong export growth. However, not all Peruvians benefited from these favorable events in capitalist development, for they were confined mainly to the more modernized coastal region, a fact that accentuated the dualistic social structure of the country by widening the gap between the sierra and the coast. To be sure, the sierra has been losing economic ground to the modernizing forces operating on the coast since 1920. As expected, this phenomenon provoked an intense social mobilization of the rural population to the coast, as well as a series of confrontations between peasants and landowners during the 1950s and 1960s. All this was exacerbated by a rapid increase in Peru's urban population, which provided abundant and cheap labor, locking the arable land into feudal-like *latifundios* (large estates owned as private property), thus causing the demographic equality of land ownership to deteriorate and to increase peasant pressure on the land. Peru's land tenure system remains to this day one of the most unequal in Latin America. In the meantime, those peasants who chose not to migrate to urban centers did not remain passive in the face of their worsening circumstances but became increasingly organized and militant.

The postwar period of industrialization, urbanization, and economic growth also created a new middle and professional class that helped to alter the political panorama by creating two new political parties: Acción Popular (Popular Action), or AP, and Partido Demócrata Cristiano (Christian Democratic Party), or PDC. These parties emerged in the 1950s and 1960s to challenge the oligarchy as well as the left (especially the APRA), with its emphasis on modernization and development within a somewhat more activist framework.

In light of these events, APRA accelerated its rightward tendency and entered into a new alliance with its old enemy, the oligarchy, in exchange for new legal recognition. As a result of this suspect alliance, many of APRA's former party members flocked to support the charismatic reformist and founder of AP (Popular Action), Fernando Belaúnde Terry (1963–1968). Belaúnde ushered in a modest agrarian reform, colonization projects in the montaña (high jungle), and construction of the North–South Jungle Border Highway, running the entire length of the country. All this at a time when U.S. president John F. Kennedy was launching his Alliance for Progress campaign in Latin America, thereby contributing to widespread expectations for progress.

In 1969, the year of Arguedas's death, the Agrarian Reform Law was watered down in Congress by a conservative coalition between APRA and Odría's National Union Party (UNO). This coalition prompted the rise of guerrilla movements led by rebellious Apristas. Belaúnde lost his reformist zeal and called on the army to put down the guerrillas, opting for a more technocratic orientation and large numbers of construction projects, including irrigation, transportation, and housing, while at the same time investing heavily in education. Such initiatives were made possible, in part, by the economic boost provided by the dramatic expansion of the fishmeal industry that flourished in these years. The new industry, aided by new technologies and abundant fishing areas, was also favored by marine currents that brought an abundance of plankton to the Peruvian marine platform. By 1962 Peru became the world's leading fishmeal producer, with fishmeal accounting for one third of the nation's exports. Nevertheless, this bonanza would be of little help to Belaúnde. In 1967, faced with a growing balance-of-payments problem, he was forced to devaluate the sol, the county's monetary unit. Eventually, in 1968 he capitulated to foreign investments in a final controversial settlement with the International Petroleum Company (IPC) over La Brea y Paiñis oil field in Northern Peru. With growing public discontent, General Velasco Alvarado overthrew the Belaúnde government in 1968, launching thereby an expected series of reforms.[3]

The Scribe of All Nature

Historically and culturally positioned at the crossroads of indigenous and industrial global environments, Arguedas's "poetic,"[4] ideological, and cultural writing enacts a countercolonizing, counterassimilating scheme that is now gaining wider popular reception and critical attention, both within and outside Spanish-speaking countries. José María Arguedas, as "educated third,"[5] or "cultural mestizo" whose education partakes of both indigenous and white, Western European worlds is uniquely positioned to enlighten different audiences, not only on the possibilities pertaining to an as yet incomplete Latin American cultural *mestizaje*, but on other transculturations as well. For these reasons, Arguedas stands as an authoritative voice for modern cultural history; a heartening symbol of cultural alternative within a fractured and complex world. As several of his readers, critics, and commentators (among them William Rowe) have suggested, the literary work of Arguedas, to name but one of his diverse facets, can claim universal validity because it openly dramatizes the conflict between traditional and modern democratic capitalistic cultures. Arguedas calls attention to the possibility that it is not in the interest of modern capitalism, as a cultural system, to foment and preserve the best of humanistic culture.[6] On the contrary, it blindly contributes to dismantling it.

To read Arguedas implies not only new ways of confronting very specific locally defined problems and issues, such as internal sociocultural, economic disruption(s) caused by modernization processes. It implies the necessity, as well, of revising our ways of reading, thinking, and portraying the world in a more holistic, *systemic* way, which is to say, as a system of multiple interconnections. Thus, Arguedas's work serves as a *locus* whereby to play out new openings onto social, aesthetic, and cultural paradigms. Arguedas's work calls for new ways in which to read and to theorize about literature (Cornejo-Polar et al. 1984, 27), and especially literature from the emerging world (Third and Fourth, Indigenous worlds). Indeed, to read Arguedas in the context of what is currently taking place in the world is to focus our attention on important global issues, whether technological, political, economic, or ethical, issues that most often impact on indigenous peoples and nations on the verge of final silencing or assimilation into mainstream structures. To paraphrase the Mexican essayist, poet, and Nobel laureate Octavio Paz, with every culture that disappears from the face of the earth so too does another possibility for human survival (Azcuy 1986, preliminary aphorisms, n.p.).

Within the current process of globalization, traditional binary structural oppositions such as "the local" and "the global" have progressively blurred to the point of rendering them less discernible or even recognizable. Thus, it no longer makes sense within the Peruvian landscape, to characterize Indians as opposed to *mistis*. Rather, it is more appropriate to think of entire ethnias or nations confronting cultural and economic usurpation (Cornejo-Polar et al.

1984); this is because such nations do not always fit within the frontiers defined and created by modern states. It is within this context that Arguedas inserts the problematic of indigeneous nations and cultures, first, within his beloved Peru, then within the Third World vis-à-vis global imperialisms.

Thus, Arguedas's work acquires a distinctly universal character. This universality, however, should not be viewed in purely Western ideological terms. As Cornejo-Polar points out, Arguedas's universality arises from within a culture that is historically rooted in concrete Andean experience, an experience that is as universal as "the Greek, the Chinese, or the Hindu, [and that] can be fully adopted as the patrimony of humanity . . ." (1984, 33). In this sense, Arguedas partakes of universal isomorphic cultural practices, such as those embodied in mythological paradigms; models as valid as those postulated through science and philosophy.

This helps us understand the extraordinary cultural intertextuality called for when reading Arguedas. Intellectual disciplinary endeavors cannot be defined in terms of absolute parameters or borders. It is arbitrary, therefore, to study Arguedas's literary work as independent or disconnected from his work as ethnographer, folklorist, compiler, translator, and interpreter of legends, myths, songs, and especially from his deep preoccupation with the study of autochthonous creativity and culture. If Arguedas is important, it is because he attempted a sociology of art and culture through literary, anthropological, ethnographic, linguistic, and folkloric venues. All these endeavors simultaneously unfold in Arguedas and mutually complement and interconnect at different levels.

Arguedas's life and work represent a drama of the unspeakable, of the undecidable, of the culturally and linguistically untranslatable, a drama that began for him as a struggle with language, and its ability to reflect an authentic reality:

Men legitimately express themselves in the language they have created. That language, like the men who created it, is son of the earth and of the landscape within which its creators were born. . . . In that sense, [Quechua] is the pure and genuine language of the men of the Ande[s]. And because of that . . . the [Quechua] *huayno* [typical musical Inca composition] is more beautiful than the Castilian [Spanish] or than the mixed [mestizo] one. . . . In the [Quechua] *huayno* the Andean landscape lives, as it is felt, suffered and carried in the soul by the man of the Ande[s]. [*Nosotros los maestros*, 35]

As a bilingual educated mestizo (educated third), speaking both Quechua and Spanish, Arguedas confronted the problem of communicating a lived reality to an audience unfamiliar with it, an audience to whom this reality was strange. This audience was mainly of Spanish Creole descent, people who had settled primarily in the coastal regions of Peru, neither speaking nor understanding Quechua.

Integration and disintegration, the construction of cosmos within the experience of chaos itself, both individual and textual, are constants in Arguedas's aesthetic and ideological undertaking. This is perhaps why Arguedas in *El zorro de arriba y el zorro de abajo* (The fox from above and the fox from below) compares himself to a tree that far extends its branches "tanteando y anhelante" (groping and yearning) (92). This is why for Arguedas, to write is not merely to designate, to refer, or to represent, but rather to bring things into presence, to unveil them, as Heidegger would say.[7] The difficulty of endowing the non-Quechua word with the essence of things—as only this language can—would ultimately lead Arguedas to a tragic impasse: the realization of an impossible translation of the being or essence of things (*Seiendes*) into modern languages, including scientific ones, and technolects (to borrow a term from Serres). Not unlike Socrates' skeptical posture on the written word's ability to portray reality as it is, Arguedas's writing displays a clear suspicion of written logocentrism.

Critics have noted, for example, that Arguedas writes from a "poetics of orality" (Rowe 1989, 6). In fact, Arguedas consistently signals in his work the very close relationship between the sound and the meaning of words in the Quechua language, hence of its possibility to communicate to the reader an alternative cultural perspective, quite unlike that of modern, positivistic, or dominant ways of thinking and writing. As Walter J. Ong has noted, sound is sensitive to the secrets of the heart and displays a forceful capacity for synthesis that cannot be discounted from a magical perception of reality.[8] Magic in Arguedas breaks with homogeneity as embedded in modern democratic capitalistic systems, in the imposition of standardizing consumerism, and in ways of seeing nature and the world that threaten to obliterate cultural diversity. For Arguedas, writing was more than a means of deferring personal and cultural demise; it was both an ethical and political act and responsibility: to disseminate a vision of the indigenous world beyond its borders in the hope of bringing forth both internal and external change, change that would allow for the indigenous world to merge into mainstream culture without losing its traditional values and identity.

Given this context, possibilities arise for the intertwining of myth and history as forms of consciousness, the creation of hybrid paradigms as alternatives toward modernity (crossings between the traditional and the modern, the local and the global) as a response to the inevitable globalizing processes that science and technology have unleashed. By reenacting popular memory, while at the same time considering outside modernizing trends, Arguedas's hope was that the cultural traumas of invasion and usurpation, unleashed by sixteenth-century European discoveries and expansionist economies, could be reassessed in new ways, opening up more positive perspectives for the future. Hence, the importance of retracing the points whereby modern industrial technology and culture come together with magic, nature, and preindustrialized culture.

Within this framework, a crucial characteristic of Arguedas's work is his preoccupation with social immobility and individual solitude that Indian communities still confront in present times, either in their natural habitats or in industrial ones because of cultural dislocations and displacements brought on by impinging forces of moderniza-tion. This perspective explains Arguedas's reluctance to relinquish a utopian mode of thinking, a method that also allows us to compare and evaluate our own models (scientific, technological, cultural, and sociological). To be sure, Inca forms of organization provided the basic economic, social, and cultural model for such celebrated utopias as Thomas More's *Utopia* (1516) and Edward Bellamy's *Looking Backward* (1888) (Morgan 1946).

Arguedas saw the problematic of indigenous culture as essentially "transcultural," with a special role assigned to the mestizo, a figure Angel Rama calls "the compassionate heir" by opposition to the mere "renegade" (202). In his role of compassionate heir, the mestizo fulfills within himself the necessary transmutations that insure both his own as well as ancestral survival. In this regard, the mestizo echoes the goal assigned to Virgil's Aeneas in the renewal or founda-tion of human civilization, and to that of Demetrio Rendón Wilka in Arguedas's controversial novel *Todas las sangres* (1964).

The above may serve not only to call attention to Arguedas's com-mitment to indigenous issues but to underscore his originality and his divergence from traditional *indigenista* writing. Unlike the first *indigenista* writers, who wrote about indigenous peoples from afar (merely through reading and hearing about them), and with a pater-nalistic, condescending attitude, Arguedas's originality as an *indi-genista* author stems from his firsthand knowledge of these peoples, speaking and writing from within, in an authentic, autonomous, tes-timonial and metatestimonial voice. Also distinguishable is Ar-guedas's representation of the mestizo as bridge between indigenous and white Western European worlds. For this Peruvian author, who saw *himself* as mestizo, *mestizaje* represented more than racial or blood crossings. For Arguedas, as for the French philosopher Michel Serres, *mestizaje* is also a cultural process involving the reassessment of values, and the voluntary adaptation of individuals, institutions and societies to their particular environments and social contexts.

As a polifacetic cultural mestizo (educated third), Arguedas could see that Peru had been mistakenly classified after World War II as a country undergoing transition from a traditional, nonindustrial society to a modern industrial one. Nothing could be farther from Arguedas's perceptions on the matter. In his view, this alleged process of transition was not to be understood simply as a replacement of one structure for another. Rather, Peruvian society was still *in a process of reformulation and reconsideration of both traditional and new*, communal and institutional social structures. This process is tellingly illustrated in his ethnographic study of the Mantaro River Valley (1953), where he uncovers one of the most radical processes of transculturation of the indigenous population of Peru (*Formación de una cultura nacional indoamericana*, 28–33, 80–148)[9] In this context Arguedas's paradigm of "modernization from within" not only confronted social scientists of the time with an alternative model of societal development. More important, Arguedas's conception concerning societies *of* transition have only recently begun to be recognized as a way of describing a much-debated, distinct Latin American approach to entering modernity.

In our times of crisis, wherein nature and indigenous cultures lie at the brink of obliteration by modern technological constructions, as these push outward, increasing their radius of influence and dislocation—whether of place or cultural heritage, real or abstract—dislocation and loss of identity is traced to the theoretical construction of a subject as mere discursive category without ontological foundation. How did Arguedas sort out this problematic within his poetic, ideological endeavor? We can attempt to answer this question by postulating Arguedas's desire to give legitimate voice to "otherness." Arguedas's consideration of the "other" (whether indigenous, mestizo, or white), however, must not be understood as difference, but rather as a constitutional element of the whole.[10] There is no better reflection of this posture than Arguedas's proclaiming himself to be "nonacculturated," a statement meant not to portray an isolated difference but rather to defiantly reaffirm his connection to the Andean peasantry, to that class that Michel Serres also calls "universal" (1985, 1991). The words of José de la Riva-Agüero, in this context, sound disturbingly Arguedean and prophetic: "The destiny of Peru is inseparable from that of the Indian: it either falls or is redeemed with him, but Peru cannot abandon him without committing suicide" (1969; qtd. in Tord 1978, 25).

Arguedas's work is undeniably innovative, and tellurically Latin American. Unfortunately, where Arguedas needed political and literary support, he met with incomprehension, discrepancy, and personal attack. When questioned about his "political radicalization," he noted, "When I started writing, I was very radical, toward 1931–32. Then, I began giving in, to the point wherein I came to believe in a pacifist revolution. I once again understand that the selfishness and sensuality of those who profit from others' work cannot be destroyed by good intentions alone" (1968; qtd. in Forgues 1989, 425). Hence, his ambiguous relation to political faction, as expressed in his own words: "I still believe that to belong to a party in [Latin America] marginalizes the intellectual; it turns him into a target of prejudicial enmity... (letter to Marie Gutton, September 26, 1967; qtd. in Forgues 1989, 444).

As Arguedas well knew, to go outside a familiar worldview into another may be possible for individuals only in a theoretical way. The rupture with parochialism carries inherent dangers, including the precipitation of interpretive crisis. Arguedas's final words to his students and colleagues that fateful day in November 1969 are symbolic of this painful reflection, of a man caught between the worlds he could not bring into a democratic dialogue, except perhaps through imagination and his readers' good will.

Notes

1. All translations are my own, unless otherwise indicated.
2. Arguedas also notes that Don Nieves Quispe (another indigenous

elder) decreed that all native children become mestizos so that the official authority and direction of the community be assumed by the mestizo descendants of Indians rather than by exclusive right of the traditional mestizos (*Páginas escogidas*, 196).

3. For an expanded historical view of Peru, see Hudson 1993.

4. Here I use the word *poetic* in connection with the general meaning assigned to the Greek term *poiesis*: production as social creativity.

5. Paraphrasing Michel Serres (*Le tiers-instruit*, 1991), I use the term "educated third" as a value of cultural adaptation, cultural sharing, and the creational process that ensues from it. Arguedas was aware, as José Uriel García put it, that "There is no doubt that the world[s] of the Indian, the mestizo, and the creole still exist, even more the creative impulse, the spiritual force, tied to the blood that corresponds to each type. However, all that they produce is simply traditional and the man who overcomes those individual simplicities, he who can become the synthesis of each one of them, will be the creator of the future" (1937, 6–7).

6. The term *culture* has now acquired a more ample sense, as tackled by the new cultural studies movement, and as brought to the fore by the Marxist thinker and social critic Raymond Williams. As Williams explains, *culture* is all-encompassing; it incorporates not only those classical meanings as implied in the active cultivation of the mind, but also those in the cultivation of the land. *Culture*, therefore, also has economic implications. In our own time, "culture" must coexist "often uneasily with the anthropological, and extended sociological use to indicate the 'whole way of life' of a distinct people or other social group" (1981, 11).

7. Arguedas's struggle is in translating into Spanish an indigenous reading of nature, a reading that, to paraphrase Serres, is also tantamount to the reading of atoms that make up the codes of universal substances and entities, and as written in universal memory (Serres 1982).

8. By way of example, see chapter 6 ("Zumbayllú") in *Deep Rivers* (1978),wherein Arguedas provides a thorough explanation of the suffix *-yllu* as living, magical entity or spirit. See also "Acerca del intenso significado de dos voces quechuas" (Concerning the intense meaning of two Quechua voices) in *Indios, mestizos y señores*, pp. 147–49.

9. See for instance in this volume "Cambio de cultura en las comunidades indígenas económicamente fuertes" (Cultural exchange in economically viable indigenous communities), 28-33; and "Evolucíon de las

comunidades indígenas: El Valle del Mantaro y la ciudad de Huancayo: un caso de fusión de culturas no comprometida por las accíon de las instituciones de origen colonial" (The evolution of indigenous communities, Valley of Mantaro and the city of Huancayo: a case of cultural fusion uncompromised by the action of colonial institutions), 80-147.

    10. Tzvetan Todorov in *The Conquest of America* (1984) explores the concept of "otherness" from the perspective of the conquest in the chapter "Typology of Relations to the Other." For Todorov this notion of the other develops at three levels: axiological (value judgment), praxiological (identification or nonidentification with the other), and epistemic (mutual knowledge or disavowal of knowledge). All three levels apply in their positive connotations to Arguedas's relations to indigenous communities. Thus, for example, at the axiological level, the other is not "bad" or inferior in relation to the one who judges (Arguedas himself). At the praxiological level, Arguedas embraces the other's values and identifies with them. At the epistemic level, Arguedas declares himself bound to the other in mutual knowledge.

Works Cited

Arguedas, José María. 1972. *Páginas escogidas* (Selected pages). Lima: Editorial Universo.

———. 1972. *El zorro de arriba y el zorro de abajo* (The fox from above and the fox from below). Buenos Aires: Biblioteca Clásica y Contemporánea.

———. 1975. *Formación de una cultura nacional indoamericana* (The formation of a national Indoamerican culture). Mexico City: Siglo XXI Editores.

———. 1978. *Deep Rivers*. Trans. Frances Horning Barraclough. Austin: University of Texas Press.

———. 1986. *Nosotros los maestros* (We the teachers). Lima: Editorial Horizonte.

———. 1989. *Indios, mestizos y señores:* (Indians, mestizos, and gentlemen). 3d ed. Lima: Editorial Horizonte.

———. 1993. *Yawar Fiesta*. Lima: Editorial Horizonte.

Azcuy, Eduardo A. 1986. *Identidad cultural y cambio tecnológico en América Latina* (Cultural identity and technological change in Latin America). Buenos Aires: Editorial Fundación Ross.

Barthes, Roland. 1972. "Authors and Writers." In *Critical Essays*, 143–50. Evanston, Ill.: Northwestern University Press.

Cornejo-Polar, Antonio, Alberto Escobar, Martin Lienhard, and William Rowe. 1984. *Vigencia y universalidad de José María Arguedas* (The force and universality of José María Arguedas). Lima: Editorial Horizonte.

Fell, Eve-Marie, ed. 1990. *José María Arguedas: El zorro de arriba y el zorro de abajo* (The fox from above and the fox from below). Nanterre, France: Centre de Recherches Latino-Américaines.

Forgues, Roland. 1989. *José María Arguedas: Del pensamiento dialéctico al pensamiento trágico: Historia de una utopía*. (José María Arguedas: From dialectic thought to tragic thought: The history of a utopia). Lima: Editorial Horizonte.

García, Uriel J. 1937. *El nuevo indio: Ensayos indianistas sobre la sierra surperuana* (The new Indian: Essays on the Indian of the southern Peruvian mountain range). Cuzco: H. G. Rosas Sucesores.

Hudson, Rex A., ed. 1993. *Peru: A Country Study*. 4th ed. Washington, D.C.: Federal Research Division, Library of Congress.

Morgan, Arthur E. 1946. *Nowhere Was Somewhere: How History Makes Utopias and How Utopias Make History*. Chapel Hill: University of North Carolina Press.

Ong, Walter J. 1982. "Oral Memory, the Story Line and Characterization." In *Orality and Literacy: The Technologizing of the Word*, 139–55. London: Methuen.

Rama, Angel. 1987. *Transculturación narrativa en América Latina* (Narrative transculturation in Latin America). Mexico City: Siglo XXI Editores.

Rowe, William. 1989. "*Yawar Fiesta*: José María Arguedas." *Third World Quarterly* 11 (no. 4): 274–78.

Serres, Michel. 1982. "The Origin of Language: Biology, Information Theory, and Thermodynamics." In *Hermes: Literature, Science, Philosophy*, ed. Josué V. Harari and David F. Bell, 71–83. Baltimore: Johns Hopkins University Press.

———. 1985. "Visite." In *Le cinq sens* (The five senses), 255–340. Paris: Bernard Grasset.

———. 1991. *Le tiers-instruit* (The educated third). Paris: François Bourin.

Todorov, Tzvetan. 1984. *The Conquest of America: The Question of the Other*. Trans. Richard Howard. New York: Harper Collins.

Tord, Luis Enrique. 1978. *El indio en los ensayistas peruanos, 1848–1948* (The Indian in Peruvian essayists, 1848–1948). Lima: Editoriales Unidas.

Vasconcelos, José. 1992. *La raza cósmica: Misión de la raza iberoamericana, Argentina y Brasil* (The cosmic race: The mission of the Iberian-American race, Argentina and Brazil). Mexico City: Espasa-Calpe Mexicana.

Williams, Raymond. 1981. *The Sociology of Culture*. Chicago: University of Chicago Press.

Part One

The Convergence of Cultural Discourses

Nestor García Canclini in *Hybrid Cultures: Strategies for Entering and Leaving Modernity* (Minneapolis: University of Minnesota, 1995) has suggested that to study culture is to occupy oneself with junctures between and mixtures of disciplines. Indeed, not unlike Arguedas's "migrant condition," as described by Antonio Cornejo Polar in our section on "The Intersection of Subjectivities," Canclini describes an ideal nomadic condition for the human sciences, a disciplinary *"mestizaje"* capable of a de-absolutizing transformation of the social. The essays in this section draw on sociohistorical, anthropological, political, and "ethnoliterary" conjunctions in Arguedas's textual production.

Priscilla Archibald reviews the modernizing processes and theories (starting in the 1920s) that generated "the most dramatic remaking of Peruvian society since the conquest." She contrasts the "presumptuous" anthropological interventions of the times with Arguedas's own anthropological "interpretive horizon," as framed in historical and cultural specificity, and a decentering praxis.

1

Archibald's analysis of Arguedas's attempts to address the complexities that lie between Andean and Western cultural production and exchanges lead her to note that "a regionalist alibi can make for a particularly contestatory form of cosmopolitanism."

William Rowe reevaluates Arguedas's poetic and literary endeavor through the more ethnographic lenses of music, song, and dance, "in such a way that its profoundly transformative nature is made manifest." Sound, and the "transindividual" cosmic awareness that it opens up, is Arguedas's way of conveying his perception of the Andean utopian cosmos, of a knowledge that transcends postmodern alienation by uniting "being and the world."

Rita De Grandis, in turn, takes to reevaluating Arguedas's "indigenized" theory and "ethnoliterature" as counterdiscursive practices—"as a vital cultural means of identity preservation"—within the converging notions of postmodernism and postcolonialism. Taking as her point of departure Arguedas's attempt to theorize from what she considers to be a "neocolonial subject position," De Grandis examines Arguedas's short story "Rasu-Ñiti's Agony" (1962) and his transcription of the oral Quechua narrative "The *Pongo*'s Dream" (1965) in order to demonstrate how "ethnoliterary" propositions and "indigenized theory" point in Arguedas's works to the creation "of a new aesthetic model which corresponds to colonial dualism." Alita Kelley's analysis follows in the steps of both Rowe and De Grandis, as she examines Arguedas's literary voice "possessed of a lyricism born of the Quechua tradition." In her examination of Arguedas's textual and thematic experimental techniques, as well as his "will to depict the moments of union with the natural world," Kelley places Arguedas's literary project within the "constant" modernist tradition, while underscoring Arguedas's difficulty in coming to terms with the postmodern viewpoint.

Andean Anthropology in the Era of Development Theory

The Work of José María Arguedas

Priscilla Archibald

The modernizing process that began in the 1920s with the presidency of Augusto B. Leguía took on a new character in the economic boom following World War II, when industrialization was heralded as the solution to Peru's problems. Industry now received the privilege that agriculture had previously enjoyed. The strategy of industrialization known as Import Substitution Industry was implemented, and legislation in the form of the Law of Industrial Promotion made industry particularly attractive to foreign investors. This aggressive modernizing policy reshuffled economic and political terrain. Between the early fifties and late sixties, manufacturing and agriculture's portions of the GNP were practically inverted, with new urban elites displacing the traditionally hegemonic agro-export bourgeoisie (Yepes 1992, 69). These changes had enormous consequences for Andeans, who faced increasing impoverishment and marginalization with the decline of the agricultural sector. Andean emigration to coastal cities took place in overwhelming numbers. Lima's population more than quadrupled throughout the fifties and sixties;

Chimbote, a typical coastal town and a site of the booming fish flour industry, grew from 5,000 to 100,000 overnight. The modernizing drive of the fifties generated perhaps the most dramatic remaking of Peruvian society since the conquest. In only two decades Peru was transformed from a millennially rural society to a predominantly urban one.

Theories of modernization likewise engendered new attitudes and policies regarding Andean populations:

> Peru has entered a new stage of indigenous politics. The state, services, and agencies of international technical help, as well as specialized institutions, all converge at the initiation of this period, which is characterized by accomplishments, with the conscious help of those directly benefited, the peasants. [Valcárcel 1964, 9][1]

Thus wrote Luis Valcárcel in the late 1950s, when a new collaboration between anthropologists and governmental agencies once again set about defining Andeans' relation to nationhood and modernity. Valcárcel is describing the advent of applied anthropology in Peru, an offshoot of the development theories which took shape after World War II. According to Arturo Escobar, strategies of development generated networks of power and knowledge dedicated to the emerging category of the Third World. A new professionalism and specialized knowledges, the creation of international institutions such as the International Monetary Fund (IMF) and the World Bank were elements of the discourse of underdevelopment that became the dominant, indeed inescapable way peripheral nations were apprehended. As Escobar remarks, "'Development,' as a mode of thinking and a source of practices . . . became an omnipresent reality" (430). The near impossibility of thinking alternatively perhaps accounts for Luis Valcárcel's excitement over the new approaches. Valcárcel is often regarded as the father of Peruvian anthropology, having founded the Institute of Ethnology at San Marcos University in the early fifties. There could be no more unlikely spokesman, however, for the pragmatism of the fifties than Valcárcel, author of *Tempestad en los Andes* (Tempest in the Andes). The speculative and romantic character of *indigenismo*, which his work represents in the extreme, was soundly rejected by the new professionals: "they are moving away from generalization and utopian thinking. . ." (Valcárcel 1964, 9). These professionals likewise abandoned the spirit of social critique and social imagination which accompanied the earlier more speculative endeavors.

Postwar North American expansion was an integral part of the global transformations that gave rise to development strategies. The unrivaled dominance of North America as a global actor was quite evident in the early days of Peruvian anthropology. North American anthropologists were at least as numerous as their Peruvian counterparts and certainly more visible. The empirical orientation of the North American social sciences was adopted, and in general the influence of these early anthropologists was, to put it mildly, extremely heavy handed. Cornell University alone sponsored nearly 20 percent of the projects undertaken between 1945 and 1965, including, in the words of Dr. Carlos Monge Medrano, "the miracle of Vicos"—the singularly most important project of the era.[2]

In 1952 Cornell University in collaboration with the Instituto Indigenista rented the Vicos Hacienda in northeastern Peru for an initial period of five years. Vicos was the pilot project for an experiment in "rapid modernization" whose ultimate goal was the integration of indigenous populations within national society. Its apparent success spawned several similar projects throughout the Andes, and its philosophy of acculturation served as the anthropological model for the fifties. Keeping in mind Escobar's description of development discourse as a network of institutions and knowledge, it should not seem surprising that shortly after the creation of the U.S. Peace Corps, volunteers arrived in Vicos. In effect, the anthropologists from Cornell became the new overseers of the Indians and mestizos who worked on Vicos. Using methods of applied anthropology, which included direct intervention as well as observation, the intention was to liberate these workers from their habitual servitude to a state of productive self-sufficiency. *Science* was the buzzword in applied anthropology, and Allan R. Holmberg, the leader of the project, had a clear understanding of the scientific methods behind the Vicos project of "induced change." And it seems he was not altogether wrong about those methods, since nearly every aspect of life at Vicos underwent transformation.

The process of inducing change, however, generally strikes one as a crude behaviorism whose methods function by virtue of neglecting larger cultural and historical issues. Holmberg compares the experiment at Vicos to a laboratory, in which one manipulates complex blocks of reality. Science, while never impartial, was in this case synonymous with a policy of active modernization and served as an alibi to neutralize more critical reflection. The blatant ethnocentrism behind the Vicos project was not the product of a more naive era, but a product of the acritical posture put into play with development discourse. Much had to be unlearned or relearned from José Carlos Mariátegui's day. Notwithstanding the persuasiveness of development theory, what could pass as science seems nevertheless remarkable. In a jointly written article which set out to analyze the cultural changes accomplished at Vicos, the authors do not hesitate to equate modernization with Westernization. They then contrast the feudal inequality that had existed at Vicos with "fundamental postulates of modern Western civilization" ("postulados fundamentales de la moderna civilización occidental") and examine to what extent the latter had been achieved at Vicos (Holmberg 1966, 61). The way irrepressible good intentions accompany the cultural presumptuousness of the anthropologists at Vicos is in the unmistakable cultural style of the United States, a singularly powerful provincialism in the postwar era.

It must be granted however, that significant gains were realized by the "vicosinos." Agricultural productivity soared, a school was built that became the model for the region, basic needs such as sanitary facilities were met, and most important, the people of Vicos were eventually able to buy the land on which they had worked for centuries as peons. Perhaps there is some truth, then, to the anthropologists' claim that Vicos represents an example of agrarian reform (Dobyns 1970, 22). Still, agrarian reform is a bit of an overstatement in this case. It might be more appropriate to say that Vicos won the lottery, a prize with considerable strings attached. Typically, agrarian reform involves some attention to larger social structures, national if not international. At Vicos, activity that intruded upon the narrowly defined laboratory was taken into account only with a mind to its removal.

The project at Vicos was not regarded as an extreme or unusual application of anthropological methods then in vogue. Quite the contrary, it was the example after which much activity was modeled. More moderate or less interventionist approaches were no more oriented toward a broader social critique. A collection of ethnographic writings, *Estudios sobre la cultura actual del Perú* (Studies on the contemporary culture of Peru) contains some of the earliest examples of professional anthropology in Peru. In the prologue, Arguedas surprisingly praises the collection, which included many of the most prominent anthropologists of the day, for being the first truly "objective" study of Andean society. These works display a significant break with earlier *indigenista* writers. Instead of subjective or poetic reflection they are based on fieldwork, observation and contact. Objectivity, in this case, however, generally sanctioned or, more precisely, enacted a retreat from social critique. The goal of indigenous acculturation to the *national* economy, *national* society, or *national* culture is reiterated throughout these and all the works of the fifties. The nation, so deeply problematized by the social thinkers of the twenties and thirties, functions here as the constant by which indigenous lack may be accounted for and indigenous progress measured. Sociologist Pedro Morande writes how in the new spirit of academic professionalism, thinkers of prior generations were dismissed as amateurs, prescientific dilettantes (9). Certainly Mariátegui's meaningful deferral of Peruvian nationhood, which addressed both indigenous exploitation and global capitalism, found little echo in the mantra of progress and modernization. The concepts and methodologies put into play with modernization theory—such as the focus on a present without history or culture—is well suited to the rhythm of North American hegemony. The product of a period of tremendous optimism, however, the largely rhetorical character of the category of the nation will become evident with the dismal failure of industrialization, and the demographic transformations that will change Peru beyond recognition.

José María Arguedas, Anthropologist

José María Arguedas began his anthropological career at this rather inauspicious time. During the fifties Arguedas was one of the first to enroll in the doctoral program at the Institute of Ethnology at San Marcos University, where he wrote most of the essays that have been posthumously collected in *Formación de una cultura nacional indoamericana* (Formation of an Indoamerican national culture). Initially he embraced the presence and new scientific attitudes of North American anthropologists. Proponents of applied anthropology are cited as authorities in many of his articles, and he even accompanied Holmberg on a visit to Vicos before that project was underway. One of the documents from Vicos includes a photograph of scholars who were present at the project's initiation, and in the front row, far left, is José María. His deferential attitude in this instance is certainly surprising, since from the start Arguedas's ideas are thoroughly at odds with anthropological practices based on modernizing premises.

The reader who stumbles upon Arguedas's ethnography "Puquio, una cultura en proceso de cambio" (Puquio: A culture in the process of change) in its original place of publication, the collection *Estudios sobre la cultura actual del Perú*, might likewise feel a sense of incongruity. The text deals with an Andean town after the construction of a highway in 1926 transformed it into an active trading center. By the objective criteria of the day life in Puquio was much improved. Social stratification had become less rigid, antagonism between mestizos and Indians softened considerably, and with the exception of one *ayllu* and the aristocrats, the majority of whom had left Puquio, most had experienced economic gain. The text, however, conveys a sense of enormous loss. Arguedas studies the different beliefs and myths of Puquio's four indigenous *ayllu*s, in order to lament their eventual disappearance. The younger Indians, he contends, no longer have an interest in the cultural practices and knowledge of prior generations. They are not familiar with Inkarrí, the myth of Andean redemption. One can even detect in Arguedas's study a certain nostalgia for the aristocrats and for colonial traditions displaced by the new entrepreneurial spirit. Arguedas conveys the intricacies of both indigenous and colonial traditions, practices that continue to evoke the history that made them. It is this evocation of historical meaningfulness that makes the abrupt replacement of Andean traditions with another called modernity seem so tragic.

In a prologue to Arguedas's doctoral thesis, "Las comunidades de España y del Perú" (The communities of Spain and Peru), Jesus Contreras praises the author's attention to history, a welcome change, he writes, from the "presentista o ahistórica" (presentist or ahistorical) orientation of anthropologists working along the lines of modernization theory (16). This attention to history is one of the distinguishing features of Arguedas's anthropological production. Many of the essays in *Formación de una cultura nacional indoamericana* are historical narratives. The text "Cambio de cultura en las comunidades indígenas economicamente fuertes" (Cultural change in economically strong indigenous communities), which attempts to recuperate the unwritten history of Mantaro through clues in colonial documents, resembles ethnohistory. Even subject matter seemingly less given to historical investigation is animated by an impression of the irrevocable imprint of historical actors and events. Arguedas begins an ethnography about the geographical conditions of the sierra with the words of a famous conquistador:

> No description of Peru seems to us more beautiful or more exact than that written by Pedro de Cieza de León in the dedication of his book *The Chronicle of Peru*, to the "very noble and powerful Señor Don Felipe" . . . : Who can describe what different types of things are found in Peru, the towering mountains and deep valleys where multiple rivers, expansive and of such great depth, are discovered and conquered. . . the differences between towns and peoples with diverse costumes, rites, strange ceremonies; so many birds and animals, trees and fish so different and unknown? ("La sierra en el proceso de la cultura peruana," *Formación de una cultura nacional,* 9).

Arguedas refers again and again to Cieza de León, weaving the text of human history with geography—a landscape inextricably meshed with the voices of the colonial encounter.

The project of modernization generally inspired the opposite tendency. Historical and cultural specificity were at best a distraction. Following the example of Bolivia, many anthropologists advocated replacing the term *indio* with *campesino*, which they considered a more exact social identification and less given to erroneous historical connotations. It is precisely its evocation of the "errors" of history, Arguedas argues, that makes the term *indio* so meaningful: "This culture, which we call Indian because no other term exists that names it with the same clarity, is the result of the long process of evolution . . . since the time that it felt the impact of the Spanish invasion" ("El complejo cultural en el Perú," *Formación de una cultura nacional,* 2). As John Murra remarks, this position was generally considered sentimental, a throwback to the "pre-scientific" essayists of the twenties (8). Yet Arguedas was not the romantic traditionalist that this pragmatic dichotomy between word and deed implies. His attention to history, to culture, and to language itself did not elide questions of change, but was very much part of his vision of an alternative Andean future.

If development theory chose to ignore historical considerations, it was predicated on a very precise version of history. In *Europe and the People without History*, Eric Wolfe discusses the origin of the terms traditional and modern as they are used within social science (3–23). With the impact of capitalism and industrialization new types of social formations emerged in nineteenth-century Europe. Thinkers conceptualized the transformation in various ways: from community to society, folk to urban culture, collectivization to individualization, or from the sacred to the secular. The change was registered as a crisis and was by no means acritically embraced. Indeed the concept of the organic traditional community served as a perpetual critique of the emerging order. Foreseeing an inevitable replacement of the sacred and moral with utilitarian and technical values, Max Weber described with great ambivalence what he saw as the inexorable movement toward a rationalized modernity. According to Wolfe, by the mid-twentieth century Weber's prognosis was read prescriptively, becoming the basis of modernization theory. Within this teleology of progress the notion of the traditional loses its critical function and assumes a wholly pejorative meaning, representing merely a lack of modernity. It was then, not simply a Eurocentric text that brought the Third World into view after World War II, but an actively Westernizing one. According to this scheme of things, what seemed relevant to know about the people of Vicos was, as one anthropologist put it, that they represent an enormous anachronism. To learn that Vicos was one of the sites where the Inkarrí myth was discovered it is necessary to look to less orthodox sources. This particular instance of anthropological inattention or dismissal is quite noteworthy. Prophesying the restoration of an Inca deity that will bring about the end of indigenous subjugation, the Inkarrí myth has played a motivating and mobilizing role throughout Andean history, and dramatizes the social and political potential of cultural expression.[3]

When Arguedas anticipates that his Andean students will one day contribute an original version of the conquest, historical interpretation is acknowledged as an important site of ideological battle. If always true, it is all the more so for those thought to possess no history at all. Development ideology proceeded with a notion of the traditional as unchanging, ahistorical repetition, whereas modernity was defined as flux, change, and progress. Throughout *Formación de una cultura nacional* a countermyth takes shape. Arguedas argues that the radical discontinuities and contradictions that Andeans have known since the conquest have produced a fiercely creative and adaptive culture. Far from ahistorical, negotiating at the crossroads of various and overlapping traditions, the Andean emerges in these pages as the ultimate historical subject.

During the fifties, acculturation or Westernization had little pretense to social theory, so readily was it accepted as a historical given. Arguedas's insistence that Andean acculturation to Western modernity was in fact not inevitable but ideological was at the time quite startling. His studies of the region of Mantaro represent perhaps most concisely his alternative to developmentalist vision.[4] These studies suggest that as historical agents Andeans can lay claim to their own version of the future, define modernity in their own way, loosening the teleology of history that had constricted social imagination. Largely mestizo, Mantaro symbolized possibility because it achieved a productive economy without breaking from its Andean cultural roots. Contact and commerce with Lima invigorated rather than drained Mantaro's economy and population. Arguedas found "traditional" culture to be flourishing. New songs and dances integrated Western elements while still retaining what he regarded as cultural authenticity and traditionalism. Although atypical because of its historic development—Mantaro was not a colonial center—it became an important symbol for Arguedas. As a meaningful Andean insertion into modernity, the region represents an alternative to the theory of acculturation, and the traditional-modern binarism. If the Andean region had long been viewed through this binary optic, it gains a new type of operative import during the development era. Once the traditional and the modern are no longer regarded as mutually exclusive states, heavy-handed projects like the one at Vicos are far more difficult to legitimize.

Additionally, these ethnographic essays might be viewed as new nationalist narratives, particularly in their transcendence of the binarism that constricted nationalist vision. Much like Mariátegui, Arguedas reminds us of the relationship of so-called traditional and modern societies made nearly invisible by the privileged narrative of their historical asynchronicity, or by privilege itself. Quite often in Arguedas's writing it is a use of language (preferring the term *Indian* over *peasant*) or a question of style (weaving Cieza de León's description of the sierra into his own) that persuades us with a vision of the future, and of the past, that is ideologically nearly unthinkable. In so outsmarting the reified categories of modernization theory, whose echoes have far from disappeared, Arguedas restores a practice of critical thinking that still has the ability to startle. The emancipatory potential Arguedas attributes to anthropological knowledge was eclipsed by a code of disciplinary professionalism that contained anthropology's interpretive horizons. It is in part through the poetic character of his work that Arguedas subverts this professionalism, and like some of the earlier *indigenista* writers whose ideas science was thought to transcend, arrives at a social critique that is poised on utopian thinking.

Making too much or too little of a name are opposite ways of attributing lack. When Valcárcel writes, "La raza permanece idéntica a si misma" (The race remains identical to itself), or when Holmberg advocates replacing *indio* with the more specifically economic term, *campesino*, historical content is effaced. It was not on account of an essential referentiality that Arguedas argued for the meaningfulness of the term *indio*. What term more poignantly conveys the arbitrariness of the signifier than *indio*, the product of geographical fantasy and political ambition. According to anthropologist Michael Taussig this linguistic arbitrariness is perpetually signified in the less stable social narratives of colonial societies, offering a glimpse of the heterogeneous origins occluded in proper identities.

Arguedas challenges the different essentializing visions of *indigenismo* and modernization theory. His concept of a differential indigenous culture counters a myth of authenticity, yet his insistence on cultural strength and integrity also disputes the idea that indigenous identity can be reduced to the history of indigenous exploitation. Where these perspectives would see either a redemptive or a static traditionalism, Arguedas sees perpetual change, and where developmentalists see only lack Arguedas sees cause for affirmation: "The vitality of pre-Hispanic culture has been verified by its capacity for change, for the assimilation of foreign elements . . . everything has changed since the times of the Conquest; but it has remained, throughout so many important changes, *different* from the West . . ." ("El complejo cultural en el Perú," *Formación*, 2; emphasis mine). This description of Andean society and history contradicts dominant descriptions in nearly every way imaginable. Perhaps most important, and most significant insofar as it suggests a new cultural paradigm, for Arguedas the virtue of indigenous culture lies in its capacity for perpetual self-recreation amid radical discontinuity. While historical Andean figures like Guaman Poma or Tupac Amaru certainly confirm Arguedas's conception of Andean history, it is important to underscore that his interpretation is also a very timely and strategic response to the increasingly formidable presence of Westernizing forces.

Beyond Nativism

One of the most interesting aspects of Arguedas's writings is his attention to colonial traditions, decentering the privileged status of the Indian in Andean studies. Typically, in both scientific and romantic texts, the *misti* is acknowledged only insofar as he is the agent of indigenous exploitation. As the subject of anthropological study rather than the object of moral denunciation, the *misti* emerges as an infinitely fascinating character. Like the Indian, Arguedas claims he is the product of a long process of transculturation that Indianized his culture, customs, and language. Particularly in his studies of folklore, Arguedas deals with the complex and interrelated development of indigenous and *misti* cultural practices. The way certain musical instruments came to be played only by Indians and others only by *mistis*, their different repertoire of songs, or different forms of religious worship are products of historical negotiations that do not reflect a specifically autochthonous or Spanish origin. *Huaynos* are sung by *mistis* just as Indians have produced Christian hymns. Arguedas's compelling presentation of colonial traditions is related to yet another remaking of the Andean (and the West): "The Andes defended and continue defending, like a giant shield, not only the autochthonous culture of Peru but all tradition, *and that now includes the colonial tradition*" ("La sierra en el proceso de la cultura peruana," *Formación* 20; emphasis mine). Arguedas's fondness for colonial traditions increasingly marginalized by a liberal modernity is a salient aspect of many of his novels. As the very ambivalent attitude toward *mistis* in *Yawar fiesta* suggests however, the revindication of cultural traditions inextricably tied to the cruelties of colonial history is deeply problematic. A fictional resolution to this impossible nostalgia is represented by the character of Don Bruno in the novel *Todas las sangres* (All bloods), a reformed *misti* who embraces those he had formerly abused. Arguedas's attention to the *misti* introduces an important ideological transformation. It highlights the constitutive relationship between *mistis* and Indians, problematizing the prelapsarian subject at the center of earlier nationalist writing.

The most prominent social actor in Arguedas's anthropological work, however, is the mestizo. After attending the First International Congress of Peruvianists in 1952, Arguedas expressed disappointment with its limited focus on *lo indigenista* (the indigenous) and *lo hispanista* (the Hispanic). Once again the mestizo was left to the margins of Andean history, figuring ambiguously in the shadows of the two primary Andean actors. This omission comments on the mestizo's illegitimacy, and on the persistence of the polarizing terms of colonial ideology. Whether because of their historically compromised role (loyal to neither *misti* nor *indio*) or for notions of racial purity, mestizos came to represent something like an Andean antihero. Luis Valcárcel is perhaps the strongest proponent of this point of view, and one suspects that his racial essentialism is hardly secondary to his status as the founder of Peruvian anthropology. While Valcárcel's aggression against the mestizo is far from typical, the general lack of studies addressing the mestizo reflects the same racial categories that inform Valcárcel's sentiments. Rather like underground figures, Arguedas comments that mestizos inspired debate and controversy, but no official study. Arguedas stresses the urgency of the issue with unusual severity: "The study of the mestizo is one of the most important investigations that anthropology is obligated to undertake in Peru" ("El complejo cultural en el Peru," *Formación*, 2). Arguedas's apprehension of the increasingly pivotal social role played by the mestizo certainly counts among his most important anthropological contributions. While a singularly important corrective to scientific procedure, Arguedas's attention to the mestizo or decentering of nativist logic contributes perhaps more significantly in the way of a decolonizing ideology.

Arguedas attributes the growth of mestizo populations to republican transformations that made a knowledge of Spanish and Western social practices more and more indispensable. As the title of one of his essays suggests, "Entre el kechwa y el castellano la angustia del mestizo" (Between Quechua and Spanish, the anguish of the mestizo) *mestizaje* is less a homogenizing identity than a deeply contradictory one. Situated between an ever more aggressive West and a native Andean culture, the mestizo attempts to incorporate the former without sacrificing his own cultural roots. Particularly in his pedagogical and folklore essays Arguedas examines the way this radical incongruity stimulates ingenious production: the linguistic and cultural complexity of mestizos' performance in a contest of insults with *mistis* and *indios*; a new Andean *retablo* (altarpiece) geared toward the market in Lima that somehow retains a genuinely religious content; or the appropriation of the refined poet José María Eguren by young Andean students learning Spanish. The innovations of the mestizo, irreverent toward a rigid traditionalism, likewise disabuse one of any illusion that there is but one version of the future.

Arguedas's evolving sense of the mestizo's importance generated considerable transformations in his vision of nationhood. Arguedas advocated not simply the study of the mestizo as an important Andean actor, but a process of *mestizaje* as well. Surely this would surprise or even scandalize many who credit Arguedas with a more conventional notion of cultural authenticity and a tragic sense of nostalgia. For Arguedas what distinguishes the mestizo from the Indian is the mestizo's greater contact with "modernity." He believed that the Indians' more protective, inward-looking stance vis-à-vis the West could only result in poverty and cultural disintegration. For Arguedas the potential of *mestizaje* is best represented by the region of Mantaro, where simple resistance is replaced with a far more creative response to global capitalism's undeniable power. The ambiguity traditionally attributed to the mestizo is present in Arguedas's account as well. "Unstable and dynamic," the mestizo is situated between innovation and dislocation, between new expression and painful disarticulation, between poverty and entrepreneurialism. It is of course misleading to refer to a singular mestizo. As Arguedas insists there are infinite grades of *mestizaje*. The social reality of urban mestizos, for example, is quite distinct from that of *indomestizos* of the small Andean town. Yet this very elusiveness with respect to a stable social or political identity is also what makes *mestizaje* such a subversive historical phenomenon and for Arguedas, the potential agent of Andean redemption.

A Cultural Politics

The active role that Arguedas played in establishing anthropology in Peru and in reshaping official policy toward Andean culture makes it all the more surprising that his nonliterary work has met with such complete neglect. The considerable time Arguedas devoted to anthropological activities hardly suggests that he regarded these endeavors to be of secondary importance. Aside from his investigations, teaching positions, and editorial work for several publications, Arguedas served in a number of governmental offices: Director (Conservador General) of Folklore in the Ministry of Education; Director of the Section of Fine Arts (later renamed the Section of Folklore) in the Ministry of Education; Director of the Institute of Ethnology at the Museum of Culture; Director of the House of Culture (Casa de la Cultura); and Director of the National Museum of History. Given general knowledge about Arguedas, few would guess that the author of *Yawar fiesta* and *Los ríos profundos* (Deep rivers) was so seriously involved in nonliterary domains. If the privileging of Arguedas's creative work enhances certain illusions about his literary vocation, it greatly distorts the nature of his Andean revindication. Just as Néstor García Canclini comments that the traditional is constructed across a wide variety of disciplines, so in turn is Arguedas's revindication of Andean society.

The cultural orientation of Arguedas's anthropological work may have contributed to the critical neglect that it has received. Arguedas collected Andean myths and stories, wrote about the songs and dances of Indians, mestizos and *mistis*, analyzed the historical development of Andean artisanry, and in general highlighted culture in the study of social organization and transformation. Like the developmentalist Carlos Monge, he had a sense of the miracle of Vicos (*milagro de Vicos*) but his had to do with the Adaneva myth he discovered there. Aside from his love for Andean artistic production, Arguedas believed that a great deal could be learned about Andean society through the study of folklore. *Folklore* is an unfortunate word choice in this case (although Arguedas himself used it), implying as it does a fetishistic attitude toward traditional cultural production. Angel Rama renames these "folklore" studies a sociology of Latin American art, and one could additionally redesignate Arguedas from *folklorista* to culture critic, since not only the sociological but also the artistic value of Andean cultural production is a matter of concern in his work (Rama 1989, xxii).

While Arguedas approached the collection of oral literature with a certain urgency, believing that otherwise many Andean myths and tales would disappear without leaving a trace, this nostalgic response to historical change was reserved quite uniquely for oral cultural expression. He reacted strongly to adulterated versions of Andean tales that purified them of what were regarded as extraneous, nonindigenous elements. Instead of the inevitable dissolution of traditional culture in the face of Westernization, Arguedas believed that "popular art can change and does change over time . . . its authors assimilate foreign influences with a quickness that is perhaps greater than supposed . . ." ("Puquio, una cultura en proceso de cambio," 70). Again a conception of Andean culture based on a folkloric nostalgia for origins is replaced in his writings with a sense of the Andeans' great capacity for historical change. In markedly post-Hispanic oral literature such as Quechua Catholic hymns, the Inkarrí and Adaneva myths, and oral stories such as *El sueño del pongo* (The Indian servant's dream), which he eventually transformed into a short story, Arguedas stresses the presence of Andean historical imagination.

Oral literature seems to be a predicate vehicle for what many contemporary scholars, following Flores Galindo, refer to as the Andean utopia. Far from the ahistoricity that supposedly characterizes myth, examples of the Andean utopia like the Inkarrí—a prophesy of the restoration of an indigenous dynasty that recurs throughout Andean history in varying forms—possesses a rather radical historicity. On one occasion Arguedas even adopts the figure of Inkarrí into his own analytical work. Lamenting the disintegration of indigenous cultural lifeways, he ends his ethnography on Puquio in a most unlikely way: "Inkarrí returns, and we cannot help fearing that he may be powerless to reassemble the individualisms that have developed, perhaps irremediably. Unless he can detain the Sun, . . . all is possible where such a wise and resistant creature is concerned" ("Puquio, una cultura en proceso de cambio," 79). Arguedas takes the figure of the Inkarrí to heart, invoking its power to transform historical fortunes in an otherwise quite orthodox ethnography! As is often the case with Arguedas, his work in this instance defies precise classification, challenging one to reflect on the categories that make the production of anthropological knowledge possible.

If structural anthropology later redeemed the study of myth, it did so as an ahistorical, self-referential construct, ultimately keeping in place the same teleological underpinnings that informed earlier empiricists. As noted, the character of much Andean oral literature, most specifically the recurring strain of an Andean utopia that thematizes issues of time and change, hardly lends itself to this type of interpretation. Arguedas's analytical orientation resembles more recent attempts like Flores Galindo's *Buscando un Inca* (Searching for an Inca) and the essays collected in Jonathan Hill's anthology *Rethinking History and Myth* to reconstrue the myth and history divide. What is questioned in Arguedas's work is less the difference than the mutually exclusive character of myth and history. One recalls the *zumbayllu* chapter of his novel *Los ríos profundos*, where mythic and historical consciousness are interwoven, or *El zorro de arriba y el zorro de abajo* (The fox from above and the fox from below), which draws heavily from the collection of Andean myths that Arguedas translated as *Dioses y hombres de Huarochirí* (Gods and men of Huarochirí). The anthropologist Terence Turner's belief that "history and myth, far from contradictory modes associated with different evolutionary stages of social development, are not merely compatible but complementary forms of consciousness" is exemplified throughout much of Arguedas's work (252). Whether in his appeal to Inkarrí as an anthropologist, or in his celebration of technology in the poem "Oda al jet" (Ode to the jet), or in the example of a syllabus from a course Arguedas taught on contemporary narrative, where oral "folkloric" stories are indiscriminately included with texts by canonical writers like López Albújar and Ciro Alegría, Arguedas's challenge toward dominant historical narratives has sometimes made his project undecipherable to Western critics ("Estudio de la cultura peruana en la literatura oral y escrita," *Nosotros los maestros*, 193).

Arguedas's studies of Andean cultural production stress the vanguard role of mestizos. He cites the increasing presence of *huaynos* by known authors, musical groups that transgress traditional repertoires based on class divisions (even to a jazz "Inca-style"), and poets publishing in Quechua as examples of mestizo negotiations between Andean and Western culture. A long essay devoted to the work of sculptor-painter Joaquín López discusses one particularly ingenious example of mestizo creativity ("Notas elementales sobre el arte popular religioso y la cultura mestiza de Huamanga," 148–72). A creator of the San Marcos *retablos*, López's work was much in demand in metropolitan centers. According to Arguedas, not only are mestizos best able to take advantage of the growing international market for Andean goods, but are more likely to maintain artistic integrity. He analyzes the transformations which Joaquín López "dared" to make in the *retablo*'s traditional design, and notes that despite the change from a magical-religious context to a secular one, these *retablos* remarkably still possess a deep religiosity. By contrast, one of the most popular pieces of indigenous artisanry, the "toro de Pucará" (Pucará bull) fared less well in the transition. "That bull has died," remarks Arguedas, its magical content replaced by ever more absurd commercial figurines ("Salvación del arte popular," 255). According to Arguedas both Indians, who remain isolated from Western culture and tied to more traditional styles of production, as well as *mistis*, who are unaware of López's fame in the capital and generally dismissive of mestizo art, are disinclined to address the social order which increasingly marginalizes them.

A detailed sociological analysis of *retablos* that double as religious art and collectable artifact that is also an aesthetic evaluation, this essay by Arguedas is itself, like López's work, without precedent yet deeply respectful of tradition. Conforming to what Rama describes as a sociology of art, it is also a cultural critique. Beyond cultural artifacts, the artistic value of these Andean cultural objects is a privileged issue. What Arguedas regarded as an increasing trend toward individual authorship of once anonymous or collective cultural practices is evident in his own work. The names and work of sculptor-painter Joaquín López, musician Raúl García, or storyteller Carmen Taripha are imprinted on the reader's imagination. Less a loss of cultural integrity, this illustrates the same type of transculturation that Arguedas praises in his essays.

James Clifford's call for "a genuinely comparative, and non-teleological, cultural studies, a field no longer limited to 'advanced,' 'late capitalist' societies," could find no more exemplary model than these studies by José María Arguedas (96–112). If they strike us as unexpected victories it is precisely because the relationship between decolonizing and late capitalist societies leaves little ground for "genuinely comparative . . . cultural studies." Clifford perhaps underplays the difficulty of arriving at such cultural comparisons. The distortions produced by the hegemonic gaze—including the misreadings of much of Arguedas's work—comment on the improbability of "cross-cultural" exchange between the "traditional" and the "modern." Furthermore, the postmodern dismantling of binarisms like *traditional* and *modern* that are central to First World hegemony increasingly disappoints. Instead of a critique, postmodernism, as Frederic Jameson has suggested, is the perfect cultural vehicle for a globalizing market. Be that as it may, as the examples of Joaquín Lopéz, Carmen Taripha, and Arguedas himself demonstrate, to suppose that the market has the final or only word on Andean cultural production would certainly be a hasty conclusion.

Arguedas addresses the complexity that lies between Andean and Western exchange, restoring a sense of the social heterogeneity that dominant narratives and practices mask. Whether inadvertently or deliberately, Arguedas frequently illustrates just how contingent knowledge and vision are on social position and positioning. If this leads him to praise Joaquín Lopéz's ability to produce against the grain—or to produce meaningful work in spite of the market—he inversely chastizes anthropologists for believing that scientific conventions offer a transparent view onto the Andean world. Arguedas's most explicit critique of anthropology occurs in the poem "Llamado a algunos doctores" (Appeal to certain intellectuals), which he originally wrote in Quechua. In this poem, the absence of comparative or simple ground between the West and the Andean region is thematized in a way that indicts the anthropologist or at least destabilizes his confidence. More broadly it critiques the position of the Westerner. A tone of mockery runs through the first part of the poem, which belittles the so-called legitimate methods of scientific inquiry: "Take out your telescope, your best eyeglasses. Look, if you can." Similar to the contemporary feminist discourse on science, anthropology's largely visualist orientation comes under harsh criticism. It is only the practitioners of anthropology that seem to benefit or multiply from the scientific endeavors undertaken in the Andes: "They say that some doctors affirm that about us; doctors who reproduce in our own land, who get fat here or return yellow." Instead of the predictable condemnation of anthropology, however, on nationalist or nativist grounds the poem is a challenge to anthropologists to become familiar with the Andean world in a far more intimate way: "Don't run from me doctor, come close! Take a good look, recognize me. How long do I have to wait for you?" In his desire for transparent communication, Arguedas ironically highlights the systemic inequality that underlies much of the anthropological encounter. The poem also anticipates contemporary anthropological works like Renato Rosaldo's *Culture and Truth: The Remaking of Social Analysis*, whose critique of objectivity explores subjectivity as not only an inevitable but a potentially productive component of anthropological investigation.

To suppose that Arguedas's proximity to the lifeways he writes about gives his work an unquestioned authenticity does not begin to address the complexity of his writing. The posture of naivete *(lo ingenuo)* that Arguedas is sometimes credited with, and which the poem "Llamado a algunos doctores" might be thought to possess, is itself evidence of the intersection of metropolitan discourses with Andean self-definitions. Like the anthropologists in his poem, Arguedas was involved in questions of knowledge and power, with the difference that he was keenly and often painfully aware of his involvement in these issues. As the principal metropolitan discourse about the Andean subaltern, Arguedas's engagement with the discipline of anthropology was most certainly overdetermined. Yet, like other mestizo artists, he manages to retain a large degree of autonomy or integrity through the way that he practices that discipline. Defining the character of Arguedas's anthropological production, whether he be called an anthropologist, native anthropologist, *indigenista*, or folklorist—to mention a few—presents enormous difficulties. Arguedas insinuates knowledge not adequately accounted for by established intellectual norms; mixing romance and science, he does not hesitate to transgress those norms. This unclassifiable character of his writing inadvertently reveals the ideological underpinnings of anthropological convention, redefining that discipline as a site of negotiation and struggle in the context of the Andes.

Culture or Commodity?

Believing that it possessed a great deal of nationalist potential, Arguedas undertook the dissemination of Andean culture with tremendous enthusiasm, promoting the trend of Andean art appreciation that began in the twenties. He recorded songs, documented stories, judged dance competitions, sponsored musical events, and wrote scores of newspaper articles with the aim of educating coastal Peruvians about Andean cultural traditions. His efforts assumed the character of a cultural politics, challenging the text-bound and exclusively Western character of "national" culture. As the director of the Casa de la Cultura from 1963 to 1964, he transformed the elitist and Western orientation of that national institution into a popular, predominantly Andean one. Arguedas acknowledged that the transformations in conditions of production and circulation, which the transition from a local to a national market entailed, necessarily involved a loss of sorts or at least a change of dramatic proportions. Yet, he believed that a more protective attitude toward Andean cultural traditions would finally lead to a far more definitive loss. Arguedas's vision of a remaking of the Peruvian cultural patrimony—where local ritualized practices would be adopted to a national, secular setting—demonstrated tremendous faith in the Andean capacity for transculturation. Retrospectively, one cannot help but suspect that Arguedas underestimated the power of the market with its appropriation of the traditional as an ever more commodified site of authenticity.

Arguedas himself grew alarmed by the distortions that passed as Andean art in Lima. Where he once praised mestizos' abilities to respond to the international interest in Andean goods, he later unequivocally came to regard tourism as the enemy of all cultural integrity. Arguedas fought against governmental attempts to gratify tourists' desire for a traditionalist authenticity by prohibiting the sale of Western goods in the local *ferias* (markets). In "El monstruoso contrasentido" ("The monstruous contradiction in terms"), an article published in 1962, Arguedas expresses outrage at the cultural caricatures produced by a fetishized traditionalism, particularly the cult of the *incaico* (215–19). Beribboned dancers and singers performed Inca-style, transforming infinitely rich post-Hispanic traditions into empty stylizations. The sense of productivity that Arguedas's cultural writings convey evaporates in the spectacle's depthless appeal. Commenting on the undignified commercialization of traditionalism, Arguedas nearly repented of his promotion of Andean culture: "We have been interested and even active witnesses—and are nearly repentant of that—to, first, the discovery and then the great diffusion and the disorders and transformations that, particularly in Lima, these arts have undergone" ("Notas sobre el folklore peruano," *Formación,* 209).

That it is difficult (for the First World at least) to think beyond traditionalist images, whether in fascination or despair, does not presuppose that they fully account for the social and cultural resourcefulness of Andeans. Particularly during the last few years of his life, Arguedas countered the hegemonic positioning of Andeans with a quite distinct vision of Andeans' participation in modernity. Responding to the massive Andean emigration to coastal cities, these writings represent a significant revision of many of the ideas expressed in his earlier work. While many critics have contended that Arguedas's worldview crumbled with the demographic transformations of the fifties and sixties, there is in fact little in his writing that supports this point of view. Not only was Arguedas quite receptive to the Andean presence in the city, but the incomparable analytical breadth and ideological clarity of his late writings suggest a renewed rather than defeated social vision. Néstor García Canclini comments, "It seems that we anthropologists have more difficulties entering modernity than the social groups that we study" (230). The same could certainly be said as well of literary critics who address Andean society, and misreadings of Arguedas's late writing point to critics' discomfort with Andean transformations. Canclini's question, "How does one study the millions of Indians and peasants that migrate to the capitals . . . ?" though directed specifically to questions of ethnographic style, is likewise relevant for literary studies (230). If the tired images of traditionalism no longer captivate, neither have they been reformulated. As the renewed interest in Arguedas suggests, many scholars are turning to his work for clues in addressing the changed and quite volatile dimensions of contemporary Peruvian society.

Arguedas's conception of Andean cultural authenticity underwent great transformation throughout the forties, fifties, and sixties. In an article written in 1944, "En defensa del folklore musical andino" ("In defense of Andean musical folklore"), Arguedas claimed in a critique of Lima artist Ima Sumac: "only the native-born artist, he who inherits the genius of folklore, can interpret it and transmit it to others" (233). Twenty-four years later, cultural authenticity is no longer located in regionalism, and if Arguedas had rarely essentialized Andean identity, now his work pointedly de-essentializes ethnicity. He writes about the brilliant performance of Juan Aguilar, a young black man who learned Andean music from the radio and whose talent for dance was discovered while he was working in the dressing rooms of the coliseums. In Lima, Andean cultural events took place in the coliseums, often by performers like Juan Aguilar, who never having left the city nevertheless remained faithful to the spirit and history of Andean dance. Arguedas enthusiastically writes: "The coliseums are forges, genuine forges. Coast and sierra are fused by fire, and integrate, grow stronger" ("Simbolismo y poesía de dos canciones populares quechuas," *Señores e indios,* 247).

Developments like the coliseums prompted Arguedas to redefine his understanding of folklore. Contradicting his earlier view that folklore was limited to oral, traditional cultures he writes, "the popular is also folkloric." If empty spectacles like the performances of Ima Sumac represent one Andean crossing with modernity, Juan Aguilar represents a quite different one. Arguedas was increasingly interested in this second type of cultural crossbreeding, which intersected with metropolitan forces but was not coopted by them. Ironically, he comments on the powers of Andean transculturation at a conference devoted to Urgent Anthropology, a branch that stressed the need to rescue ethnic groups from extinction due to Western penetration.

Arguedas's faith that Andeans could appropriate the instruments meant for their own subjugation contradicts the general premises of the conference: "Among those instruments employed to condition the mentality of the masses and uproot their particular national tradition, the most effective (radio, TV, etc.) convert into powerful vehicles of transmission and contagion, in the affirmation of the typical and the uncolonizable" ("La cultura: Un patrimonio difícil de colonizar," 188).

The resurgence of Quechua as a national language was instrumental to Arguedas's renewed social vision: "The most recent census seems to demonstrate that, for example, in Peru, instead of dying out, the Quechua language is growing stronger, gaining prestige . . ." (ibid.). After the deeply nostalgic novel *Todas las sangres* (All bloods), in which Arguedas's interpretation of the wave of peasant land repossessions in the early sixties is at the service of a quite conservative vision of cultural continuity, he wrote a series of poems in Quechua, which have since been translated and collected in the edition *Katatay*. The contestatory nature of these poems should shatter any conviction about the ideological disillusionment that supposedly marked Arguedas's final days. Along with poems dedicated to traditional figures in Andean history and mythology, titles such as "Oda al Jet" ("Ode to the Jet"), "Llamado a algunos doctores," ("Appeal to certain intellectuals"), "A Cuba" ("To Cuba"), "Ofrenda al pueblo de Vietnam" ("Offering to the people of Vietnam") indicate a radically transformed conception of Andean identity. The poems' contestatory tone and expansive, cosmopolitan rather than defensive attitude toward Andean identity displays a new cultural and ideological confidence.

Various developments such as the growing legitimacy of Quechua as a national rather than merely regional language as well as the impact of the Andean presence in coastal cities generated a more fluid sense of community. In *Cultura andina y forma novelesca* (Andean culture and the novelesque Form) Martin Lienhard discusses how

Arguedas's artistic practice of translating Andean culture for uninitiated Westerners is replaced by the presence of mixed and intersecting codes. In Arguedas's final novel, *El zorro de arriba y el zorro de abajo,* references to Andean myths and cultural traditions are not explained to the Western reader, and passages in Quechua are left untranslated. This final novel deals with the dislocated inhabitants of Chimbote, a port city whose population grew from 5,000 to 100,000 in less than a decade. In a letter to John Murra, Arguedas writes about the combination of disquieting social forces and cultural vitality that characterize Chimbote: "If I manage to get better I will write a narrative about Chimbote and Supe that will be like sipping the substance of the seething Peru of these days from a very strong liquor, its ebullition and the burning materials with which the liquor is forming" ("Documentos anotados," 378). The attitude expressed in this quote could hardly be characterized as nostalgia.

Few shared Arguedas's enthusiasm for the new Andean cosmopolitanism. During the sixties the settlements of Andean emigrants that began to circle Lima were referred to as *cinturones de miseria* (poverty belts). Arguedas by contrast comments, "We prefer to call them 'belts of fire of the renovation, of the resurrection and of the insurgency of "Authentic Peru"' " ("Folklore y educación," *Formación,* 17). Where Arguedas celebrates renovation, others see only the coopted, colonized, and impoverished. Although the horrific conditions of the *barriadas* (shanty towns) certainly did, as the renamed *pueblos jóvenes* (young towns) do now, give cause for alarm, the invisibility of the contestatory character of Andean urban society to sociologists and anthropologists in the sixties was indicative of their complicity with the powers of domination. Arguedas comments that this instance is no exception to the given that domination generates resistance:

> Like all inhumane enterprises, this one does not have a guarantee of
> success, indeed particularly not in countries like Peru, where the very
> instruments that fortify economic and political domination bring

: vitable opening of new channels for the greater diffusion
ial cultural expression and its nationalizing influence. ["La
in patrimonio difícil de colonizar," 187]

/ its many disturbing consequences, for Arguedas the Andean transformation of urban spaces also generated the possibility of
a new nationalist imagination that was no longer founded on cultural
or ethnic essentialisms, yet still managed to resist metropolitan appropriation. This approach toward the social forces at play in the sixties gives Arguedas's work a remarkable relevance to contemporary
Peru. The Andean "invasion" of previously criollo cities like Lima
has dislocated Andeans and criollos alike, disarticulating cultural
practices while creating new forms of cultural and social crossbreeding. If these social developments make it meaningless to speak of Andean society in terms of a discrete regionalism, as the example of
Arguedas suggests, it is nevertheless quite possible, indeed perhaps
crucial, to speak of a specifically Andean cosmopolitanism. In the
essay "Traveling Cultures" James Clifford explores ways of thinking
about contemporary experiences of dislocation. His term *discrepant
cosmopolitanisms* is particularly helpful in accounting for the contradictory yet often overlapping ways that dislocation is experienced in
late-twentieth-century Peru. Rather than simply "inverting the strategies of cultural localization," Clifford points to the specific and varying causes—poverty, war, travel, business, government policy—that
work to dissolve regional or national identities, and make for quite
varied positionings in a more global network of power and connections. While the momentum of transnationalism may seem undeniable, the powers of the regional imagination have not yet been
thoroughly exhausted. For emigrants in Lima regional identity often
continues to structure one's reality in a fundamental way, determin-
ing one's friends, home, work, and cultural affiliations. And, as Arguedas's claim, "I am a provincial of this world" suggests, a regionalist
alibi can make for a particularly contestatory form of cosmopolitanism.

Notes

1. All translations are mine with the exception of the following article: José María Arguedas, "Puquio: A Culture in Process of Change," in *Yawar Fiesta.* Trans. Frances Horming Barraclough. (Austin: University of Texas Press, 1985).

2. Statistics are from the following sources:

Henry F. Dobyns, *Comunidades campesinas del Perú (Peasant communities of Peru)* (Lima: Editorial Estudios Andinos, 1970), p. 19.

Carlos Monge Medrano, Introduction to *Vicos: método y práctica de antropología aplicada* (Vicos: Methods and practice of applied anthropology) (Lima: Editorial Estudios Andinos, 1966), p. 12.

3. Alberto Flores Galindo, *Buscando un Inca* (Searching for an Inca*)*, 2d ed. (Lima: Editorial Horizonte, 1986). In this book Flores Galindo explores the important role of the myth of the Inkarrí throughout Andean history.

4. José María Arguedas, "Cambio de cultura en las comunidades indígenas económicamente fuertes" (Cultural change in economically strong indigenous communities) and "Evolución de las comunidades indígenas" (Evolution of indigenous communities), in *Formación de una cultura nacional indoamericana* (Formation of an Indoamerican national culture), 5th ed. (Mexico City: Siglo XXI Editores, 1975), pp. 28–33, 80–147.

Works Cited

Arguedas, José María. 1964. *Estudios sobre la cultura actual del Perú* (Studies on the contemporary culture of Peru). Lima: Universidad Nacional Mayor de San Marcos.

———. 1966. *Dioses y hombres de Huarochirí: Narración quechua recogida por Francisco de Avila (1598?)* (Gods and men of Huarochirí: A Quechua narrative collected by Francisco de Avila [1598?]). Ed. and trans. J. M. Arguedas. Lima: National Museum of History and Institute of Peruvian Studies.

———. 1968. "Las comunidades de España y el Perú" (The communities of Spain and Peru). Ph.D. dissertation, National University of San Marcos.

———. 1975. "Cambio de cultura en las comunidades indígenas economicamente fuertes" (Cultural change in economically strong indigenous communities). In *Formación de una culura nacional indoamericana* (Formation of an Indoamerican national culture). 5th ed. Mexico City: Siglo XXI Editores.

———. 1975. "La cultura: Un patrimonio difícil de colonizar" (Culture: A patrimony that is difficult to colonize). In *Formación de una culura nacional indoamericana* (Formation of an Indoamerican national culture). 5th ed. Mexico City: Siglo XXI Editores.

———. 1975. *Formación de una cultura nacional indoamericana* (Formation of an Indoamerican national culture). 5th ed. Mexico City: Siglo XXI Editores.

———. 1975. "Notas elementales sobre el arte popular religioso y la cultura mestiza de Huamanga" (Elemental notes about popular religious art and the mestizo culture of Huamanga). In *Formación de una cultura nacional indoamericana* (Formation of an Indoamerican national culture). 5th ed. Mexico City: Siglo XXI Editores.

———. 1976. "En Defensa del folklore musical andino" (In defense of Andean musical folklore). In *Señores e indios: Acerca de la cultura quechua* (Lords and Indians: Concerning Quechua culture). Montevideo: Arca Editorial.

———. 1976. "El monstruoso contrasentido" (The monstruous contradiction in terms). In *Señores e indios: Acerca de la cultura quechua* (Lords and Indians: Concerning Quechua culture). Montevideo: Arca Editorial.

———. 1984. *Katatay.* Lima: Editorial Horizonte.

———. 1985. "Puquio, a Culture in Process of Change." In *Yawar Fiesta.* Trans. Frances Horning Barraclough. Austin: University of Texas Press.

———. 1986. "Entre el kechwa y el castellano: La angustia del mestizo." (Between Quechua and Spanish: The Anguish of the mestizo). In *Nosotros los maestros* (We the teachers). Lima: Editorial Horizonte.

———. 1986. *Nosotros los maestros* (We the teachers). Lima: Editorial Horizonte.

———. 1990. "Documentos Anotados" (Annotated documents). In *El zorro de arriba y el zorro de abajo* (The fox from above and the fox from below), ed. Eve-Marie Fell. Nanterre: Centre de Recherches Latino-Américaines.

Clifford, James. 1992. "Traveling Cultures." In *Cultural Studies*. Ed. Lawrence Grossberg, Cary Nelson, and Paula A. Treichler. New York: Routledge.

Contreras, Jesus. 1987. "El lugar de José María Arguedas en la etnología de España y de los Andes" (The place of José María Arguedas in the ethnology of Spain and the Andes). In *Las comunidades de España y del Perú* (The communities of Spain and Peru). Madrid: Ediciones Cultura Hispánica del Instituto de Cooperación Iberoamericana, y Ministerio de Agricultura, Pesca y Alimentación.

Dobyns, Henry F. 1970. *Comunidades campesinas del Perú* (Peasant communities of Peru). Lima: Editorial Estudios Andinos.

Escobar, Arturo. 1992. "Imagining a Post-Development Era? Critical Thought, Development, and Social Movements." *Social Text* 31–32:20–56.

Flores Galindo, Alberto. 1986. *Buscando un Inca* (Searching for an Inca). 2d ed. Lima: Editorial Horizonte.

García Canclini, Nestor. 1990. *Culturas híbridas: Estrategias para entrar y salir de la modernidad* (Hybrid cultures: Strategies for entering and leaving modernity). Mexico City: Editorial Grijalbo.

Hill, Jonathan, ed. 1988. *Rethinking History and Myth: Indigenous South American Perspectives on the Past.* Urbana: University of Illinois Press.

Holmberg, Allan R. 1966. "El procedimiento de investigación y desarrollo para el estudio del cambio cultural" (The procedures of investigation and development in the study of cultural change). In *Vicos: Método y práctica de antropología aplicada* (Vicos: Method and practice in applied anthropology), ed. Allan R. Holmberg. Lima: Editorial Estudios Andinos.

Lienhard, Martin. 1990. *Cultura andina y forma novelesca: Zorros y danzantes en la última novela de Arguedas* (Andean culture and the novelesque form: Foxes and minstrels in Arguedas's final novel). Lima: Editorial Horizonte.

Medrano, Carlos Monge. 1966. "Introduction to *Vicos: Método y práctica de antropología aplicada* (Vicos: Method and practice in applied anthropology). Ed. Allan R. Holmberg. Lima: Editorial Estudios Andinos.

Morande, Pedro. 1984. *Cultura y modernización en América Latina: Ensayo sociologico acerca de la crisis del desarollismo y de su superacíon* (Culture and modernization in Latin America). Santiago: Cuadernos del

Instituto de Sociología, Pontificia Universidad Católica de Chile.

Murra, John. 1987. "José María Arguedas: Dos imagenes" (José María Arguedas: Two images). In *Las comunidades de España y del Perú* (The communities of Spain and Peru) by José María Arguedas. Madrid: Ediciones Cultura Hispánica del Instituto de Cooperación Iberoamericana y Ministerio de Agricultura, Pesca y Alimentación.

Rama, Angel. 1989. Introduction to *Formación de una cultura nacional indoamericana* (Formation of an Indoamerican national culture) by José María Aguedas. 5th ed. Mexico City: Siglo XXI Editores.

Rosaldo, Renato. 1993. *Culture and Truth: The Remaking of Social Analysis.* 2d ed. Boston: Beacon Press.

Taussig, Michael. 1987. *Shamanism, Colonialism, and the Wild Man: A Study in Terror and Healing.* Chicago: University of Chicago Press.

Turner, Terence. 1988. "History, Myth, and Social Consciousness among the Kayapó of Central Brazil." In *Rethinking History and Myth: Indigenous South American Perspectives on the Past,* ed. Jonathan Hill. Urbana: University of Illinois Press.

Valcárcel, Luis E. 1964. "Indigenismo en el Perú." (*Indigenismo* in Peru). In *Estudios sobre la cultura actual del Perú* (Studies on the contemporary culture of Peru), ed. José María Arguedas. Lima: Universidad Nacional Mayor de San Marcos.

Wolf, Eric. 1982. *Europe and the People without History.* Berkeley: University of California Press.

Yepes, Ernesto. 1992. *La modernización en el Perú del siglo XX: Economía y política, ilusion y realidad* (Modernization in twentieth-century Peru: Economics and politics, illusion and reality). Lima: Mosca Azul Editores.

Arguedas

Music, Awareness, and Social Transformation

William Rowe

When a meeting of cultures occurs that is devoid of all intent at colonization and domination, the mutual transformation produced is of the greatest value.[1] In the scientific field a good deal has been said about the universality of Western science, but for the fifteen centuries prior to its rise, the flow of information was from East to West, a fact that tends to be forgotten, since it does not form part of the dominant schemas of our time. Joseph Needham, the English scientist and historian of Chinese science and pioneer critic of the false European universalism, has said that the basic fallacy of Eurocentrism is the supposition that the science and technology that had their start in post-Renaissance Europe are universal, as is everything else about European culture. Needham adds ironically that European music is music and all other music is anthropology (1983, 14–15).

José María Arguedas has shown that a strong process of transculturation can be produced even when, as is the case with the Peruvian Andes, most brutal domination exists. In this context, Angel Rama must also be mentioned for the outstanding role he has played in promulgating the study of Latin American literature from the perspective of transculturation, and for his strong commitment to the work of Arguedas.

In his speech on receiving the Garcilazo prize, Arguedas spoke of the importance for him of scientific socialism, insisting that it had "never killed the magic within [him]." His poem "Llamado a algunos doctores" (Appeal to certain intellectuals) mocks, from the position of traditional Andean knowledge, a scientific ideology that is incapable of recognizing Andean wisdom.

Arguedas believes that music, above all else, is the alternative to Western rationalism as a means for transmitting true knowledge. My purpose here is to outline the role of music in his work in such a way that its true nature is made manifest. Far from resembling merely descriptive theories of reality, it has a profoundly transformative underpinning, a belief that true knowledge cannot be separated from the need for social change. In other words, that the model of profound knowledge provided by the indigenous culture needs, for its fulfillment, to transcend the limitations of resistance and to translate itself into a revolutionary transformation of the whole.

As mentioned above, Arguedas looks to the Andean culture in order to depict an image of the nonalienated awareness that nourished his life and creative work. His approach to Andean culture is not merely functional, but rather utopian, though this should not be construed as meaning falsified, nor even depicted in the manner of the *indigenista* writers. This approach required his viewing the material and symbols of that culture from a utopian, transformative perspective and so depicts a culture both new and much needed.

Arguedas's decision to move to Sicuani from Lima at the end of the 1930s is significant in this context. The months he had spent in the jail known as El Sexto had convinced him that political struggle on the left at that time had become sterile. By living in the Vilcanota valley he would be able to draw from the living Andean culture, not as a means of evading historical conflict but of tackling it. It was in Sicuani that he began writing the articles on Andean culture that he sent to *La Prensa* in Buenos Aires. In these essays Arguedas's mature literary style of *Los ríos profundos* (Deep rivers) first manifests itself. The articles are of an ethnological nature, but, unlike much ethnography, are based on a passionate personal approach to the object being studied.

In those essays music is a constant theme, and the passages of greatest intensity are those where individual boundaries are broken by dance and song, in drunkenness and death rites. A foreshadowing of the character Ernesto of *Los ríos profundos* can be recognized in these articles. In what is perhaps the most important essay, "El carnaval de Tambobamba" (Carnival in Tambobamba) the effects of music and the breaking of personal limits fully coincide. The geographic space is the Apurímac valley—the "Holy Apurímac"—and the song whose text, translated into Spanish from Quechua by Arguedas, appears in the essay is sung in different versions in the area, but always to the same sad, beautiful melody.

The essay may be considered a paradigm of nature understood as language. The distinguishing trait of the landscape—and of the Andean landscape in general—is the clash of extremes, without mediation:

> Apurímac means "the mighty one who speaks." Because it can only be seen from the peaks, but its voice can be heard everywhere. It runs in the deepest gullies imaginable. On the mountain peaks that rise beside it, the perpetual snow shimmers. . . . From those peaks the river can be seen. It runs between dark forests of almost jungle-like trees. It has no banks; its two sides form a savage, mysterious abyss. [*Indios, mestizos, y señores,* 151]

There are no transitional, intermediate points in this meeting of opposites, and the voice of the river arises, articulating the totality of the world around:

> its deep sound issues from the bottom of the immense gully, never silent, a profound song of the incredible abyss. [*Indios,* 151]

This speaking or singing of the river constitutes a paradigm of the process of human awareness constructed from language. The sound of the river overlays the external world—"its solemn, eternal song covers all"—and, in bathing all, it penetrates the interiority of the person, giving form to everyday awareness:

> It is in the hearts of those who live in the valley, in their minds, their memories, their love and tears. [*Indios*, 152]

This passage exactly illustrates the analysis made by Voloshinov (or Bakhtin) of the concordance of interior awareness and the sign; according to Voloshinov, external signs renew themselves and become dynamic when submerged in the sea of internal signs: "every outer . . . sign, of whatever kind, is engulfed in and washed over by inner signs—by the consciousness. The outer sign originates from this sea of inner signs and continues to abide there" (1973, 33). Seen in another way, the transformation of the external world into meaningful material corresponds to the creation of an interior voice. Thus, according to Voloshinov: "all manifestations of ideological creativity—all other non-verbal signs (such as painting, music, ritual, and human acts)—are bathed by, suspended in . . . speech" (1973, 15). This conceptual key helps us understand how the voice of the holy speaker—an alternative translation of the word *Apurímac*—can be in all places:

> it is beneath the breast of the singing birds that live in the cornfields, woods, and bushes, . . . it is in the boughs of the trees that sing, too, with the winds at dawn; the voice of the river is the essence, poetry and mystery, heaven and earth, in these deep valleys, so rugged and beautiful. [*Indios*, 152]

The signs and concepts in this passage belong to the collective cultural code and function as an axis, midway between individual awareness and collective cultural awareness, and the speaking/singing of the river thus marks the mutual convergence of individual and social community. This trait is not merely thematic but forms an essential part of Arguedas's musical prose.

Let us now consider in some detail, the ways in which nature appears as if it were a language. Music is a privileged space in which matter is transformed into meaning. At the end of the text Arguedas refers to a chorus of human voices singing the carnival song in the plaza:

> the voice of the river mingled with the song, its very fruit, its entrails, its living image, its human voice, charged with pain and fury, greater and more powerful than its own river voice, giant river, river that dug an abyss in the hard rock for a thousand leagues. [*Indios,* 155]

As the world is being turned to music, the music itself—like the voice of the river—washes over the surrounding world in its totality, penetrating its most secret spaces. In another essay, "La muerte y los funerales" (Death and funerals), we find the following passage concerning a farewell lament to the dead man:

> the piercing voice of the women . . . like a sudden blaze reaches to the icy peaks of the mountains and enveloping sky, plains, and rivers. Nothing as far as the horizon remains untouched by the deathly essence of this chorus. [*Indios* 190]

In another essay he speaks thus of the songs known as *harauis*:

> The vibration of the final note drills into the heart, proving no element in the worlds of earth or sky remains untouched by the final cry. [*Señores e indios,* 178]

One is reminded of one of the final paragraphs of *Los ríos profundos*:

> The plague must, at that very moment, be almost frozen to death by the Indians' prayers, by their songs and the final wave of *harauis*, which must have penetrated to the rocks, reaching down even to the tiniest roots of the trees. [2]

So music serves as paradigm for the world become signification and for the ebb and flow of that signification, made cultural message, upon that world.

Let us now look at the text of the carnival song recorded by Arguedas himself, which tells of the death of a young man of

Tambobamba who drowned in the river. In this case the river is referred to as *yawar mayu* (river of blood), the Andean symbol of metamorphosis, of the breaking through borders both individual and collective. The following is from Arguedas's own translation into Spanish:

> The river of blood has brought a lover from Tambobamba.
> Only his *tinya* is floating, only his *charango* is floating,
> only his flute is floating.

The song ends with the triumphal cry: "*Wifalalalay wifala*. . . ." Arguedas comments:

> The song awakens an uncontainable despair, a sadness born of all the force of the spirit. It is like an insuperable desire to struggle and lose oneself. . . . It is an unbridling of sadness and fortitude. [*Indios*, 154]

The same emotional process dominates the final chapters of *Los ríos profundos* with exaltation and a rush of energy at the extreme moment of sorrow. The 1942 essay *(Indios, mestizos, y senores)* still lacks the representation of this energy let loose through rebellion and social transformation that can be found in Arguedas's great novels: *Los ríos profundos*, *Todas las sangres* (All bloods), and *El zorro de arriba y el zorro de abajo* (The fox from above and the fox from below). The song is still tragic, bearing the stamp of death, the existential limit to which the anonymous young victim had succumbed. We have reached the zone of recurrences that are not to be questioned, which is characteristic of peasant culture. By the time Arguedas wrote *Los ríos profundos* he had grown aware of the need for social revolt and in that and subsequent novels there is a feeling of social and political utopianism, when individual limits are broken, and this, at the same time, transforms Andean material culture into a new music.

The sound of the river becoming music produces, as I have already said, a totalizing effect. It is not a matter of representative totality—nothing, to be precise, is being represented—nor is it expressive (the natural world is not expressed, since it is already the material of signification); rather, it is a totalizing whole. There is also a key passage in *Los ríos profundos* in which, through the sound of the river Pachachaca, a space is opened where transformation can occur. The police are hunting down Doña Felipa, one of the *chicha* vendors whose rebellion has brought repression by the forces of the state:

> The firing continued. When the *guardias* reached the precipice on which one end of the bridge rests, they stopped to watch and listen. The Pachachaca roars in the silence, the noise of its waters spreads out like another universe within the universe, and beneath that surface one hears the insects, even a locust hopping about in the brush. [143]

We note first that this universe within the universe consists of sound; sound is the means through which the world is registered. It is not a question of the novelist using a framing device to exclude those aspects of reality he does not wish to appear within it, but of a sensory surface able to capture all reality, even its most hidden aspects. Arguedas presents it as a sensorial surface beneath which all can be heard. There is an element of paradox here, inasmuch as what is described is one sound that intensifies other sounds, such as the normally barely audible sounds of insects, and makes them emerge more clearly. It is a surface on which the nonverbal is recorded; one might almost say reality itself is recorded. It is not a question here of a graphic register of signification produced by the voice, but of finding a means to represent sound that, unlike alphabetical representation, will not be dependent on sounds emitted by the voice; this explains why, in Arguedas's work, the visual level so often approximates the sound level. On the other hand, the medium of sound is the paradigm for Arguedas's musical prose, eager to register all aspects of the world perceived in its totality, not merely the nonhuman (as evidenced by the references to insects), but including the entire social world in a way that is in direct opposition to the divisive effects of class ideologies. The sound of the river, therefore, interrupts the narrative telling of the hunting down of the *chicha* vendor, and the force is utopian; it involves a world in which the very senses work differently, and are beyond and against historical repression. There the magical dimension can be found, in its most important sense.

To sum up my thesis to this point and anticipate the rest of my argument, let us say that in the sound of the river, or, more exactly, under the cloak that the sound of the Pachachaca casts over all things, space becomes sound, and within that sound all reality is made manifest. Sound is also the means of conveying the utopian thrust in Arguedas's texts, as will be seen in a passage from *Todas las sangres,* the special value given to sound by Arguedas is in keeping with the dynamics of an oral culture. Finally, I will speak of Arguedas's last novel, *El zorro de arriba y el zorro de abajo,* in which the previous music with its tragic resonance is set aside and a new music, arising from a complex, open rejoicing is heard.

In *Todas las sangres* the major transformative passages receive their dynamism at the level of sound. We hear sound when the serpent Amaru is heard in the depths of the mine, or when Demetrio Rendón Willka rings the bells of the blazing church of San Pedro de Lahuaymarca:

> The voice of the bells, the hymn Demetrio played on them, tightened the bonds between the town and the mountains that protected it, between the chain of hills and the snow-capped peaks from which it had become separated. [*Obras completas*, 4:397]

As Don Bruno changes his attitude from upholding a feudal code to one of millenarianism, the sound of the skylark is heard:

> It covered the yard, the whole sky, with its song culled from the weeping of the smallest flowers, the rushing of the river, and the great cliff rising from the far bank, alert to all the sounds and voices of the earth. . . . The skylark flies and sings, not in the *pisonay* trees, but in the bleeding heart of Carhuamayo itself, as it caresses it, and in the unfathomable temples of the *patrón*, who shudders, suddenly. [1978, 44]

In Quechua the bird is known by the onomatopoeic name of *tuya*. In a 1942 article Arguedas wrote:

> The sweetest *waynos*, the most passionate love songs, and the saddest, have been addressed to the *tuya*. (*Indios*, 159)

It is for this reason that Ernesto in *Los ríos profundos* asks if the song of the skylark can be made of the same matter he is made of, and from the same widespread place from which he has been thrown into the world of men. The way in which sound and being unite through such onomatopoeia should never be overlooked; Ernesto's words reveal none of the alienation Mario Vargas Llosa attributes to him (1978, 9), but rather a searching for a way to be that differs from the one being imposed on the boy in Abancay, one that draws sustenance from the Quechua cultural code. We might speak, in this case, of an ontology based on sound.

A poem entitled "Canta la calandria" (The skylark sings) by the Argentinean poet Juan L. Ortiz begins:

> The skylark is singing . . . is singing . . .
> All creatures are singing, d'you hear them?
> It sings "to be" even in the "mystery"
> and estranged from itself. . . . [1970, 3:201]

Juan L. Ortiz was a provincial poet who lived in Paraná. When I visited him in 1974, he said that he knew that when José María Arguedas was being buried, the horses wept.

I have mentioned the tragic dimension that informs some traditional Andean music. In his 1961 article "La soledad cósmica en la poesía quechua" (Cosmic loneliness in Quechua poetry), Arguedas insists that "cosmic pain" should not be considered the trait most typical of Quechua poetry, but rather that this pain is a historical phenomenon born of conquest and oppression:

> It is a post-Columbian sentiment that has still not caused all sources of joy to dry up, as it is often accused of having done; when the

harsher forms of social oppression disappear, it soon ceases being the dominant mood. [2]

The conflict in *Los ríos profundos* is between the tragic alternative and letting loose the social forces capable of opposing oppression. The final pages point toward the utopian solution, from which, nonetheless, tragedy is never absent. In *Diamantes y pedernales* (Diamonds and flint), written during the same period, sorrow predominates. The struggle between the different social forces is presented in such a way that can only have a tragic outcome. Mariano, a musician, dies, victim of the violently contradictory urges of his *patrón*, Don Aparicio, a dissolute mestizo landowner similar to Don Bruno in *Todas las sangres* but without the millenarian outlook that causes the latter to change. Mariano's spirit, and one might say that of the text itself, is reflected in the following passage:

> Don Mariano sat himself down in the sunshine at the door of the tack room. Flies were playing in the damp spots on the ground, buzzing and chasing each other. A spider with a large body and short legs, lying in ambush, almost hidden behind a dusty stone, waved its tiny forelegs. Don Mariano listened to the animals and saw them misted by tears.
>
> "What am I crying about, *mamita*? What am I crying about?" he asked himself in Quechua.
>
> The world was making him weep, the whole world, the resplendent dwelling place who loved man, her child. [*Obras completas*, 2:36]

Mariano hears painful, tragic music through the almost imperceptible movements of the insects.

In *Todas las sangres*, within the text itself, the possibility of a conscious, political rejection of cosmic loneliness in its tragic guise is debated. "Let no Indian be born to a cold nest, without father nor mother" (*Obras*, 4:172), Rendón Willka insists, speaking of a common subject of Quechua poetry: the state of being orphaned. Instead of singing about the tragic limits of existence, thus fostering the social status quo, let autonomy be celebrated, and so, when the peasants from Paraybamba face the troops, they sing a work song, implying a return to the "sources of joy":

> The swallow moves its wings
> but not so much as you, my
> boy, my man.
> A silver needle, the fish
> crosses the waters
> of the lake, of the river,
> but not as much as you,
> my boy, my man. [*Obras,* 4:299]

It is in the story "La agonía de Rasu Ñiti" (The death agony of Rasu Ñiti) that human existence receives its most intense celebration in song. The whole world sings, we are told, in the sound of the dancer's scissors. The music even outdoes the song of the birds:

> The little birds sang joyfully, but compared with the voice of the steel and the figure of the *dansak'* their throats were a barely noticeable fili-gree of sound, as when man reigns and the glorious universe, it seems, is only there to adorn him, and give living juice to its lord. [*Obras,* 1:206]

It should be noted that, just as in the song of the Paraybamba peasants quoted above, the pattern of the carnival song from Tam-bobamba is broken and the nouman is no longer an immutable back-ground against which a person clashes and is destroyed. There the river carries the young singer to his death and only his musical in-struments remain; another might come after him, but he would suffer the same fate. In "The Death of Rasu Ñiti," on the other hand, the product of human culture is foregrounded and, as Antonio Cornejo-Polar has clearly stated, the renewal and continuity of the indigenous culture is being celebrated. While the musical form that accompanies the death of the *dansak'* is, as before, the *yawar mayu,* the same symbol is articulated in a modified way and there is a letting go, a dancing toward death itself, and from the death of Rasu Ñiti the new *dansak'* will receive his power:

> It was he, father Rasu Ñiti born again, with the tendons of a young animal and the fire of Wamani, the Condor mountain, its ages-old wind aflutter. [*Obras*, 1:209]

Yawar mayu represents death and fertility. It is, for example, the name of a song that is sung before ritual battles are enacted, and its connotations of sacrifice can also be sensed in the carnival song of Tambobamba. However, it seems correct to say that the more Arguedas developed his art, the more he tended to abandon this dimension. This tendency is particularly evident in *El zorro de arriba y el zorro de abajo*, but before we discuss that text, we will consider the way in which our comments thus far are characteristic of an oral culture.

We have spoken of music as a means of transmitting awareness of reality, and of ideological limitations arising from a tragic orientation historically produced. Let us first consider the way in which orality tackles the matter of cosmic awareness, and then come back to the ideological aspect. Knowledge/awareness is characterized differently in oral and in literate cultures. If we consider Plato as the first to classify knowledge within the literate culture of the West, we will see that in the break with orality, three key elements stand out. First, poetry and music must be taken out of the proposed epistemological program because they are found to be incompatible with the new philosophical education. Next, the new program must be based not on sensorial rhythm but on the suprasensuous, exemplified by geometry and mathematics: that is, that which can be understood is privileged over that which can be felt. Finally, the eye replaces the ear as the principal organ for learning and retaining information. The ear, as has been affirmed in studies on the transition from orality to literacy, is sensitive to interiorities and possesses a markedly synthetic capacity, while sight only captures the surface and is characterized by the way it dissects reality.

The falsely called primitive cultures should not be thought of as lacking the capacity for abstraction. Lévi-Strauss, among others, has refuted that attitude, although perhaps from a position that also smacks of rationalism. In the case of Arguedas's work, abstracting and giving form to that which has been abstracted clearly plays a part, but it is shown as a musical process and, unlike Plato's geometry, it does not depend on analytical and atemporal models. If, for Plato, the transition between poetry and true knowledge requires the abstraction of a unity from a multiplicity, a parallel can be found, to some degree, in the way in which Arguedas conceives of music, since it, too, is shown as a means of capturing the essence of reality, which is referred to many times as "juice" or "sap." In the passage quoted previously (from "La Agonía de Rasu Ñiti," *Obras,* 1:206), the voice of the scissors makes the universe offer up its "living juice" to humanity. Music in Arguedas's work can be felt; it mingles with social reality, it does not eschew emotion, it produces transparency, but not a disembodied transparency.

Of Arguedas's texts, *El zorro de arriba y el zorro de abajo* is undoubtedly the one that most fully develops the concept of music as a mode of knowledge. The character called Maxwell speaks of

> that silence of the high plateau that lets you hear the voice of the molecules in the grass and in the planets, and also your own palpitation, not of your heart, no, but of the whole of life, and through it, of the maze of all humanity. [255]

From "the magic world of sound" the spatial categories of Western science are subverted. The ego and the object are joined and become one same continuity, while in Western rationalism exactly the opposite occurs, and the analytical and atemporal qualities of the objects of knowledge separate the knower from what is known. The "magic juice of nature," as Arguedas calls it, is not an essence separate from the different elements, but an aggregate of the relations or vibrations that permit the whole to be thought as one totality, and this refers, not to the entirety of nature alone, but to that of society also.

Sight is assimilated into the process of sound and does not partake of cold, idealistic rationality; it plays a profoundly transformative role in an image of knowledge acquired in childhood, that of the *pariwanas*:

> They cast light from the heights; without consolation or reach, they illuminate all the eyes, even those of the lice that I had by the thousands, when I was a child, in my hair and in the seams of my clothing. [*Zorro,* 96]

Knowledge is contextualized and historicized; from his childhood in the Andes to his experiences in the modern city, Arguedas's trajectory repeats a key process of Peruvian history, the illumination of which, we are told, does not emerge from one lone, fixed point; it is produced in a multicentric manner that might be called pantheistic or magical, turning interiority toward the outside:

> those lice were illuminated, were made transparent, showed their little insides by the light of the wings of the *pariwana*, a light more intimate and yet more distant than that of the sun.

And, adds Arguedas, "this image turned all our life into music" (*Zorro* 96). Transparency is a constant trait in these musical passages. It is not a question of a merely subjective state. It must be remembered that it is the nontransparency of reality that makes possible ideology and domination. For that reason, we should read the transparency in these texts as a denial of domination.

The complexity of the process that we are indicating is in the sound being conceptualized in two simultaneous and different ways: as a surface on which reality is inscribed, and also as liquid that runs through the object. The two functions are summed up in the image that Maxwell gives to speak of his knowledge of Peruvian reality through Andean music:

> water in the background, a mirror backed with poor quality quicksilver so it reflects each thing as different, yet shows whatever it has in its nature that vibrates, is born and redeemed. [*Zorro*, 254]

It is in the incident in Arequipa involving a giant pine tree that music attains greatest reach as the principle of awareness. This is found in the *Third Diary* in *El zorro de arriba y el zorro de abajo*, in which Arguedas answers the polemic that Cortázar made against him in the Spanish edition of *Life* magazine (vol. 33, 1969). There he faces the difficulty of

> writing about what one knows only through adult fear and joy and not in the buzzing of a fly that one perceives almost as soon as one develops the capacity to hear. [*Zorro*, 98]

In the *Third Diary* he confronts the need to transcend the modalities of knowledge that were acquired in childhood and circumscribed by the limits of Andean traditional culture. When he hears the sound of the pine tree, it is not simply a matter of hearing the sounds of nature, but the production of a new music of space, as befits the most revolutionary text in Arguedas's literary and anthropological output.

The passage fills two pages of the *Diary* and begins by mentioning how happy he had been in Arequipa with his wife: "For the first time I felt no fear of the woman I loved, but, on the contrary, felt happiness" (*Zorro*, 205).

The theme of his relationship with his wife is related to changes at the deepest levels of Arguedas's being, changes against which the author is fighting and which feed into the text. In a letter written in 1968 he says:

> I have gone, truly, incredibly, from the age of myths to the light of the terrible twenty-first century. My wife is coated with steel, a strong yet tender woman of the twenty-first century.

In the face of such emotional surrender, the pine tree transmits a totalizing knowledge:

> It knows what the stars, what all types of roots and waters, insects, birds, and worms are made of; and this knowledge is transmitted directly in the sound that comes from its trunk . . . it transmits it like music, like wisdom, like consolation, like immortality. [*Zorro*, 206]

In different ways this passage transcends the sources of knowledge found previously in Arguedas's texts. It opens a transindividual and utopian space, and for this reason reaches farther than the image of the *pariwana*, which was enough for childhood. It also exceeds the limits of native music. It is a matter of a new music—"Music that neither Bach, Vivaldi, nor Wagner could have made so intense and transparent of understanding" (*Zorro*, 207)—the same music, that is, that the text itself generates, not "natural" but "created" and capable of competing with Bach, Vivaldi, etc., music in which precapitalist sounds and utopian postcapitalist sounds from the "age of myth" to the "twenty-first century" are found.

Another quality of the pine tree's music is that of being "oneirically penetrating of the matter of which all of us are made" (*Zorro*, 207). It might be said that rationalism divides the senses and forms hierarchies of them, giving greater importance to sight, and in this way dividing reality. Arguedas's music transcends such division, taking apart the repressive codification of existence. It frees one's being from the power that had colonized it. The matter "of which all of us are made," in coming in contact with that music, we are told, "is stirred by piercing joy, with totality." Against capitalist alienation and reification, being and the world unite. The musical celebration has a penetrating, a saturating effect; personal boundaries are broken once again, but now this no longer takes on a tragic dimension; from the perspective of the newly freed social forces articulated by the text, a joyful transformation of all reality is effected.

Translated by Alita Kelley

Note

1. This chapter is a translation of the speech given by William Rowe on being granted an honorary professorship by the National University of San Marcos, Lima. The original Spanish version appears in *Revista de crítica literaria latinoamericana* (Lima) 13, no. 25 (1st semester 1987): 97–107.

Works Cited

Arguedas, José María. 1961. "La soledad cósmica en la poesía quechua" (Cosmic loneliness in Quechua poetry). *Idea* 12, no. 48–49: 2.

———. 1968. Letter to Dr. Marcelo Viñar, January 11, 1968. Sybila Arredondo Archives.

———. 1971. *El zorro de arriba y el zorro de abajo* (The fox from above and the fox from below). Buenos Aires: Editorial Losada.

———. 1976. *Señores e indios* (Lords and Indians). Montevideo: Arca.

———. 1978. *Deep Rivers.* Trans. Frances Barraclough. Austin: University of Texas Press.

———. 1983. *Obras completas* (Complete works). Ed. Sybila Arredondo de Arguedas et al. 5 vols. Lima: Editorial Horizonte.

———. 1985. *Indios, mestizos, y señores* (Indians, mestizos and lords). Lima: Editorial Horizonte.

Cornejo Polar, Antonio. 1973. *Los universos narrativos de José María Arguedas* (The narrative universes of José María Arguedas). Buenos Aires: Editorial Losada.

Needham, Joseph. 1983. "Science, Technology, Progress, and the Breakthrough: China as a Case Study in Human History." Paper presented at the Nobel Symposium "Progress in Science and its Social Conditions," Royal Swedish Academy (August), pp. 14–15.

Ortiz, Juan L. 1970. *En el aura del sauce* (In the aura of the willow). Rosario, Argentina: Editorial Biblioteca.

Vargas Llosa, Mario. 1978. "Ensoñación y mágica en José María Arguedas" (Dream and magic in José María Arguedas). Afterword to *Deep Rivers* by José María Arguedas, Austin: University of Texas Press (1978), 239; prologue to *Los ríos profundos*, Santiago: Editorial Universitaria, (1967), 9.

Voloshinov, V. N. 1973. *Marxism and the Philosophy of Language*. New York: Seminar Press.

The Neo-Postcolonial Condition of the Work of Art in Latin America

Evidence from Peruvian Ethnoliterature

Rita De Grandis

First World cultural studies on Latin America have been dominated by approaches that are for the most part, ideologically self-serving and functionally supportive of the economic and political interests of the developed world. The indiscriminate use of current First World categories of analysis, such as postmodernism, postcolonialism, and postindustrialism in Latin America seems to trigger a placebo effect in the exchange of theories between the two worlds.[1] On the one hand, it soothes the conscience of the theory makers, and on the other, it gratifies the colonized intellectuals, who, in adopting foreign models of representation as their own, hinder their ability to construct categories of analysis that will address the deepest constitutive relationships between politics, fiction, and power.

Postcolonialism and postmodernism in contemporary literary criticism are, in some aspects, converging notions. In fact, according to Ian Adam, these concepts appear in postcolonial cultures as "prominent literary practices" that are equally dedicated to "a subversion of authoritative and monocultural forms of genre, history and discourse" (Adam 1991, 81). Although Adam notes that postcolonialism, like postmodernism, stems from the developments of structur-alist and poststructuralist literary theories, his proposal of an "indigenized" base for postcolonial theory that particularly includes "counter-discursive practices" supports indications of current departures from the aforementioned programmatic formalizations.[2]

On consideration of such a proposal, it becomes evident that an "indigenized" theory and "counter-discursive practices" result from an attempt to reinstitute within the realm of cultural theory, the political and power relations between the center and the periphery, among different gender and ethnic groups, both in First and non-First World societies.

In many recent studies of the phenomenon of postmodernism, Latin American literature has proved to be useful not only as an example of but also as a paradigm of postmodernism. In *A Poetics of Postmodernism* (1988), Linda Hutcheon draws on examples from Alejo Carpentier, Julio Cortázar, Carlos Fuentes, Gabriel García Márquez, and Manuel Puig; and in *Uncommon Cultures: Popular Culture and Postmodernism* (1988), Jim Collins employs the following works as models: Cortázar's *Hopscotch*, Puig's *Kiss of the Spider Woman*, and Solanas's film *Tangos, el exilio de Gardel* (Tangos, the exile of Gardel).[3] At first glance Latin American literature seems to provide the raw material for postulating models of postmodernism in the First World. The works of writers such as Cortázar, Fuentes, and García Márquez illustrate textual strategies characteristic of this phenomenon. The problem, however, lies in the fact that all the aforementioned examples pertain to the hegemonic Latin American narrative of the sixties, known generically as the boom narrative; thus, when heralded into world recognition, the boom constituted *the* model for Latin American literature.

Such selective analyses deal solely with a small cross-section of Latin American narrative, as is the case with "historiographical metafiction" in Linda Hutcheon's study. The overall tendency is to choose the textual experimentation of modernism to the detriment of a broader sample that would include other contemporary manifestations such as testimonial or ethnoliterature. This fragmentation of Latin American literature reduces the question of postmodernism to an overlapping of textual strategies between First World and non-First World literatures, independent of a consideration of the literary systems that produce them, seeking to redefine a pluralistic conflicting system in politically *safe* or *neutral* terms.

Reference to the conflicts between the boom narrative and other regional or local literary systems competing for hegemony are omitted. Latin American testimonial and ethnoliteratures, for example, require a specific engagement with the relationship between center and periphery, uneven development and cultural conflict. Such is the case of the Andean ethnoliterary system best illustrated by the works of José María Arguedas, who has not been cited by the critics mentioned, and whose literary proposition in turn was in conflict with those proposed by the boom writers. Consequently, the generalization that the First-World theorists make paradoxically undermines the dialogism that postmodern theories strive for, because these analyses fall into some sort of monologism.

Other critics have engaged in the ongoing debate about postmodernism and Latin America (particularly Frederic Jameson, George Yúdice, and Jorge Ruffinelli), and in indicating the limitations outlined above, have claimed that a more viable interpretation of the rise of postmodernism should include a study of the nature of modernization.[4] In this manner, it is relevant to query the possibility of a relationship between postmodernism and Latin American literature, as this literature is the product of underdeveloped societies within colonial and neocolonial economic systems. Moreover, many Latin American literatures are involved in a process of questioning their own entrance into modernity. Jorge Ruffinelli considers the possibility of a parallel being drawn between those theoretical discourses originating in postindustrialized societies of the First World and semifeudal or neocolonial societies whose industrialization process is barely beginning to appear or remains undeveloped or without function (or both). He wonders if it is possible to establish the same correlation for postcolonialism as for the present stage of modernization in "post-industrial" or even "post-capitalist" societies (Ruffinelli 1990, 31–43).

To discuss the epistemological validity of postcolonialism as a category of analysis poses its own problems and is beyond the scope of this study; instead, I wish to question Latin American cultural practices within postcolonialism as a field of research. In so doing, we must explore—along the lines of the above-mentioned critics—Latin America's entrance into modernity since the clarification of its fundamental geopolitical variable is essential when dealing with the genesis of the term *postmodern*, which has been applied to non-First World literatures by First World scholars. As their studies neither address the passage from modernity to postmodernity in relation to dependent capitalism nor employ Latin American cultural and literary theories, in order to address such shortcomings, I incorporate Angel Rama's "transculturation model" and José María Arguedas's ethnoliterary proposition in order to demonstrate their attempt to theorize from what I consider to be a neocolonial subject position.

Primarily, if it is assumed that postcolonial, like postmodern cultures, merge in postindustrialized societies, when appraising the cultures of Latin America as postcolonial, one must take into account the characteristics of Latin American modernism. Jorge Ruffinelli, on consideration of Habermas's conception of modernism as an incomplete project, draws a parallel between it and Angel Rama's definition of Latin America as an "unfinished avant-garde project."[5] Ruffinelli also points to the impossibility of interpreting the Latin American philosophical, literary, and political expressions as postmodern, when modernization has not yet been fully realized.

Undertaking the general assumptions of the dependency theory, a distinct intellectual group from the sixties and early seventies (among which Angel Rama is the most renowned) proposed models to explain the cultural practices of Latin America. They adopted the concept of neocolonialism, which had previously been limited to the social sciences to describe the modern capitalist relationship between the United States and Latin America. Let us remember that the dependency theory arose as a neo-Marxist critique of modernization and development theories.[6] Specifically, in order to explain the literary phenomenon of neoregionalism (which would include ethnoliterature) Angel Rama follows the findings of the Cuban anthropologist Fernando Ortiz in order to conceptualize local Latin American cultures as the result of a process of "transculturation" or "neoculturation" of metropolitan models.[7]

According to Rama, José María Arguedas's proposition best illustrates a new regional subculture that takes from realist aesthetics and the modernist avant-garde, striving for the construction of a Latin American subject that will ultimately break from the Eurocentric logos. In order to manifest this act, Arguedas's proposition demands the restoration of the indigenous past, its myths, traditions, and languages—Quechua and Aymará—as an alternative to the hegemonic models conveyed by the boom narrative. Thus, unlike the works of Alejo Carpentier and Julio Cortázar, which are deeply rooted in the surrealist tradition—pointing to the weighty European avant-garde influence within the boom narrative—Arguedas's works, based on ethnological investigations, are a model for an *indigenista*-based theory.

Specifically, I have chosen to examine Arguedas's short story "La agonía de Rasu-Ñiti" (Rasu-Ñiti's agony, 1962) and his transcription of an oral Quechua narrative entitled "El sueño del pongo" (The Indian servant's dream, 1965) in order to demonstrate just how this *indigenista*-based theory operates. I aim to make particular reference to the indigenous cultural practice of *Taqui-Oncoy*, to the Inkarrí myth, and finally, to the act of translation, that is, of an *indigenista*-based language that is intimately linked to the challenges that Arguedas's proposition has had to confront.

The *Taqui-Oncoy* is a "ritual of the sick" dance that resembles a trance or a dance ritual of the possessed.[8] As Steve J. Stern affirms, *Taqui-Oncoy* literally signified a "dancing sickness," which was centered primarily on the almost uncontrollable singing and dancing by "those possessed" (Stern 1982, 52). This "dancing sickness" came into existence during the conflictive decade of the 1560s, as a response to a vigorous campaign by the church and the state to "extirpate idolatries."[9] As Sara Castro-Klarén notes, at the time of the Spanish conquest and the colonization period, Andean society did not merely collapse and accept Spanish colonial rule but rather resisted, accommodated, and even cooperated with the colonial powers. In fact, in Tahuantinsuyo after 1532, a complex social structure incorporating elements of the conflicting Andean and Spanish societies emerged, making *Taqui-Oncoy* a central practice of resistance (Castro-Klarén 1989).[10] The "sect's" leaders acknowledged the end of Spanish domination, noting the presence of the *wak'as* (local deities), and their quest to eliminate the Christian God—*Dios*. Under the threat of being turned into animals, people were persuaded by the leaders that the *wak'as* did not want them to participate in the practices of the Spanish lifestyle. In this capacity, the leaders espoused a form of preaching, admonishing their people to not attend church, listen to evangelists, eat Spanish food, or even to wear Spanish clothing.

Yet, the *Taqui-Oncoy* ceremony does combine elements of both indigenous and Spanish colonial religious practices, interacting in a subversive manner. That is to say, the Spanish colonial practices are insidiously and ironically undermined and resisted, rendering *Taqui-Oncoy* a counterdiscursive practice. Notwithstanding, contrary to the belief propagated in the sixteenth century during those campaigns against idolatries that claimed that such practices had been eliminated, the *Taqui-Oncoy* remains in the memory of the ancestors of its practitioners and believers. Even today, its presence may be traced not only through Andean folk festivals but also has surfaced from within liberation movements such as the Shining Path (Sendero Luminoso) (Castro-Klarén 1989, 71).[11]

The power of this counterdiscursive practice as a vital means for the preservation of cultural identity reached Arguedas's creative repertoire. In "La agonía de Rasu-Ñiti," he evokes elements of the *Taqui-Oncoy*, tracing the events leading up to a ritualistic death dance. The main character, an old *danzak*, Rasu-Ñiti, rises from his sick bed to prepare for his last performance. His glorious *danzak* outfit echoes the typical European garb of the colonial period; the material is composed of precious Andean "cintas labradas" (embroidered ribbons) and luxurious European silks and velvets, while his pants, jacket, and hat are tailored like those of a bullfighter's "traje de luces" (sequined suit). People from surrounding villages have gathered to wait for him with great anticipation, considering this *danzak* to be the "luz en las fiestas de centenares de pueblos" (the "light" in the festivities of hundreds of towns). Rasu-Ñiti occupies a place of great importance for his people. He embodies the spirit of *Taqui-Oncoy* in the sense that he will splendidly perform the traditional *Taqui-Oncoy* dance, where the elements of music and ecstasy still pervade, as they did in the past. Interestingly, Sara Castro-Klarén identifies a "four-fold combination" for the *Taqui-Oncoy* (dance, preaching, music, and ecstasy) and, as the narrative progresses, we come to realize that Arguedas omits the second component—preaching.[12] What could the possible explanation for this exclusion be?

Seemingly, the power of the word has yielded to the power of dance, music, and ecstasy. If the deity that inspires Rasu-Ñiti to dance is the *Wamani* ("mountain god that materializes in the figure of the condor")[13] this *Wamani* does not speak, but listens to all and communicates through dance; therefore, "discourse is not the privilege of this deity" (Castro-Klarén 1989, 181). A transformation has taken place through which the religious content of the ritual dance has become implicit knowledge shared by the dancer and his people; an internalized belief and practice that assures not solely the survival of the community, but its strength, its unbreakable bond. Thus, when one of Rasu-Ñiti's daughters is unable to see the *Wamani*, Rasu-Ñiti tells her, "No tienes fuerza aún para verlo" (you do not yet have the strength to see it). Finally, we might call Rasu-Ñiti's dance a performing of the power of the *Wamani*, bringing us to an understanding of the new locus of enunciation that the journey of the *Taqui-Oncoy* has transformed itself into. In so doing, Arguedas manifests the interrelations of the *Taqui-Oncoy*'s colonial semiosis (to use Walter Mignolo's term), implying "a plurality of conflictive and coexisting worlds" (Mignolo 1993, 128).

Furthermore, there is another implicit knowledge among the people who have congregated to see Rasu-Ñiti, this time about the social reality they secretly share: that of the oppression of "El Patrón" (the Master). When Rasu-Ñiti responds to his daughter's whispered query as to whether or not he hears the gallop of the master's horse, he replies yes, adding:

> Also that which that horse's hooves have killed. The crap that has spattered over you. I also hear the growth of our god that will swallow those horse's eyes. Those of the master, no. Without the horse, he is merely lamb's excrement! [Rasu-Ñiti, 135]

It is this shared knowledge of a double reality and its "secret" language of expression that has allowed for the conservation of their collective identity, confirming what Castro-Klarén purports to be the *Taqui-Oncoy*'s still active nodal elements surviving in a "kind of secret and non-discursive inscription" (Castro-Klarén 1989, 176).

In "The *Pongo*'s Dream" elements of the *Taqui-Oncoy* resurface, this time incorporated with references to the post-Hispanic myth of Inkarrí, discovered only a decade before publication of this story. "The *Pongo*'s Dream" appeared for the first time in a bilingual version (Quechua-Spanish) in 1965, as a reproduction of an oral Quechua narrative compiled and edited by Arguedas, under the title *Pongoq mosqoynin*.[14] Arguedas's choice of "The *Pongo*'s Dream" as the title of this story demonstrates his recognition of the significance of dreams as a means of unveiling reality in the Andean world.

In this story, a dream sequence is used to bestow the Inkarrí myth upon a *pongo* (an Indian servant). In the Inkarrí myth, Inkarrí (a hybrid Andean deity) obtains the powers of both the Christian God that judges life and death and the Incan deity—the son of the Sun. In this dream sequence, the *pongo* is transformed into the judge of his master under the Christian name of Saint Francis, allowing him to conceive of indigenous liberation, reversing the oppressor-oppressed roles typical of conquest encounters. As Julio Noriega suggests, this dream sequence could be interpreted as an "inverted" reenactment of the colonial encounter between Francisco Pizarro and the Inca Atahualpa (Noriega 1989, 91–103).

As in "Rasu-Ñiti's Agony," "The *Pongo*'s Dream" also reproduces elements related to the historic movement of *Taqui-Oncoy*. The *pongo* as the protagonist of an inverted order becomes a figure that undoubtedly projects the image of Chocne, the leader of the *Taqui* movement. Likewise, in appealing to the same rituals and doctrine of Catholicism, the *pongo* is capable of concealing subversion. Similar to the manner in which Mary and Mary Magdalene allow Chocne to feign acceptance of Spanish religious beliefs to disguise the objective of the *Taqui* movement, the Ave María facilitates both the *pongo*'s submission and insurrection in "The *Pongo*'s Dream." As we can see, religion acts not solely as a means of catechism and domination, but also, ironically, as a vehicle of Indian liberation. Moreover, "The *Pongo*'s Dream" retains the most striking feature of the *Taqui-Oncoy* ritual—the ceremony of smearing the body, in this case, with excrement (as opposed to the traditional smearing of the body with dyes and paints).

Finally, the mechanisms of liberation through the *Taqui-Oncoy* ceremony and the Inkarrí myth in "Rasu-Ñiti's Agony" and "The *Pongo*'s Dream" lead to the fulfillment of Pachacuti's prophecy. As Noriega notes, in this prophecy, the *wak'as* were more powerful than

Christ since they simultaneously supported the Spanish and the Indian doctrines. In resurrecting, the *wak'as* emerge as symbols of justice, giving the conquerors a taste of their own medicine (Noriega 1989, 100). According to Pachacuti, the renewal of the universe is cyclical and governed by supernatural laws, hence, the perpetuation of the biological trends of the pre-Columbian ethnic groups is assured. Not coincidentally, Arguedas employs this prophecy in his proposition of a new indigenism, since in the 1960s, the ethnic communities were challenged by yet another wave of colonial penetration; the U.S. economic infiltration that targeted the fishing industry not only forced the Indians to migrate from the highlands to the coast, but also challenged their cultural heritage and their biological foundation.

Consequently, it is possible to conceive the *Taqui-Oncoy* and the Inkarrí myth as counterdiscursive practices. The reuse of these cultural manifestations serve as an ethnoliterary proposition arising implicitly from these narratives in particular, and I would add, from all of Arguedas's works, pointing to the creation of a new aesthetic model that corresponds to colonial dualism.

Furthermore, the use of indigenous counterdiscursive practices implies a "counter-mediational" conception of art, that is, an expression in which the neocolonial cultural penetration is mediated by inversion. In this sense, Rama's "transculturation" model and Arguedas's ethnoliterary proposition merge. In the words of Neil Larsen, the mediating agent that covertly permeates, and consequently interposes the impact of the Western agenda, is at first "barbarism" and not "reason" (Larsen 1990).[15] Hence, the work of art, in conjunction with subaltern cultural practices, becomes the imaginary equivalent of barbarism projecting the inversion of barbarism and reason to its structural level.

Finally, an indigenized based theory has to face the inevitable challenges that arise from the reality of translation. Let us remember that during the years of the boom narrative, one of the main difficulties for international readership of Arguedas's texts would have to have been confronting translation, since the concept of translation and the problems that it provokes also dominates most of Arguedas's work, particularly his Spanish translation of *Dioses y hombres de Huarochirí* (Gods and men of Huarochirí) and his last novel—*El zorro de arriba y el zorro de abajo* (The fox from above and the fox from below, 1971) (see De Grandis 1989, 1990, 1994). As in the aforementioned works, "The *Pongo*'s Dream" considers the recuperation of an oral narrative as part of a national cultural project that envisioned a construction of a cultural and literary identity from the indigenous languages and not from the Castilian. Therefore, it is fitting to consider what place the translation of an ancestral language—in this case, Quechua—occupies in the Peruvian culture of the seventies, in what context it occurs, and what importance the act of translation acquires in an ethnoliterary practice.

"The *Pongo*'s Dream" was born from a Quechua story: first passed down through oral tradition, later transcribed in the Latin alphabet, and finally translated into Spanish. As Antoine Berman points out, an idealistic conception of translation presupposes a distinction between pure language and empirical language; a pure language deals with the platonic, metaphysical intention of an ideal and abstract language more than the empirical reality of a natural one (Berman 1986). Arguedas is faced with a desire to restore the pure language of Quechua, naively believing (or struggling to affirm) that it is possible to return to a state of purity in the translation of the narrative. However, what he has to work with is an impure language mixed with words that do not pertain to it and an invented spelling that in turn corresponds to a discursive hybridization that affects the process of conceptualization, which is also impure.

Upon examining the transcribed Quechua portion of "The *Pongo*'s Dream" that has been juxtaposed to the left of the Spanish, it is evident that there are definite incrustations of Spanish into the Quechua text. [16] All italicized words include a mestizo concoction of both Quechua and Spanish blended together. Moreover, clear examples of pure Spanish can be found among the Quechua. For example, while on the Spanish side when the *patrón* says to the *pongo* "¡A ver! ... por lo menos sabrá lavar ollas..." (Hey! ... at least you will know how to wash pots...), the Quechua equivalent mimics his interjection: "¡A ver! Mankallatapas maylliyta yachanchá..." (182–83). Other clear examples dispersed throughout the Quechua text include the word *tristesa* (sadness) and any words remotely related to Christianity such as *Ave María, Dios,* and *ángel* (Hail Mary, God, angel) Likewise, in "Rasu-Ñiti's Agony," a narrative that appears to be written in Spanish, Quechua words are dispersed throughout. For example, "el hakakllo, el chusek o el San Jorge... tocó el *jaykuy* (entrada) y cambió en seguida al *sisi nina* (fuego hormiga) [played the entry and quickly changed to the fire ant] . . . empezó el *yawar mayu* (río de sangre) [the blood river began]," to name a few. The translator juxtaposes a Quechua with a Spanish word or phrase that conveys the sense of the Indian world. Hence, Arguedas's use of Quechua transcriptions is a response to the institutional marginalization of Quechua as a language and his desire to elevate it to a literary status.

In sum, the literary inscription of counterdiscursive practices in Arguedas's narratives illustrates the countermediatory operation that Rama inadvertently refers to in his "transculturation" model. According to Larsen, Rama's theory describes this operation in which the Latin American work of art actively transforms, and reformulates the modernism of the metropolis. This process combines features of "pre-rationalization" or "pre-modern rationalization" with "anti-rationalization" practices, incorporating both indigenous tribal cultural elements and the proposition of the avant-garde movements (Larsen 1990). I would add that this countermediatory approach to the work of art is crucial and inevitable when analyzing Latin American literatures; their relationship with hegemonic models is inextricably subverted, and this phenomenon creates cultural models of hybridity.

Notes

1. Cristina Santaella suggested the word *placebo* to describe this phenomenon.

2. In defining counterdiscourse, Adam draws upon Terdiman, and incorporates concepts proposed by Althusser and Foucault, introducing a notion of generalized agency. In turn indigenization represents an example of a counterdiscursive mode necessarily inscribed in postcolonial writing. By assuming such modality, the artist becomes increasingly conscious of and chooses to work within modalities particular to his or her culture which have little in common with their European counterparts. Adam, 79–94.

3. Likewise, in *The Postmodern Turn* (1987), Ihab Hassan quotes Borges, and to a lesser extent, Cortázar and García Márquez. See also, *Nuevo texto crítico* 7 (1991).

4. Frederic Jameson, following Ernest Mandel's stages of capitalism, correlates the phenomenon of postmodernism with late capitalism, or third-stage capitalism (Jameson 1984, 53–92).

5. For Rama, modern Latin American literature is the result of the European avant-garde movement of the twenties.

6. The dependency theory argued that contemporary manifestations of development and underdevelopment were not different stages in the evolution of mankind, but were, in fact, two aspects of the same historical process. Emerging in the sixteenth century in Western Europe, capitalism spread, first through mercantile expansion, and then through direct colonial rule, over the entire globe. As this process was characterized by international relations of dominance and subjugation, in which the Western countries reorganized the structure of society and the economy of the overseas lands to suit their own needs, its benefits were not evenly spread. A. G. Frank's *Capitalism and Underdevelopment in Latin America* (1967) expanded and formalized the theory of dependency and underdevelopment, postulating the concept of "metropolis satellite" to characterize the nature of imperialist

worldwide economic relations. He became the best-known dependency theorist.

7. Angel Rama's *Transculturación narrativa en América Latina* (Narrative transculturation in Latin America, 1982) is probably the most systematic and critical elaboration of modern Latin American literary studies.

8. The most current meaning for *taqui* is "song," although other meanings have appeared in the chronicles of the conquest and colonization period. I refer the reader to Luis Millones, "Un movimiento nativista del siglo XVI: El Taki Ongoy," in *Ideología mesiánica del mundo andino* (*The messianic ideology of the Andean world*), ed. Juan M. Ossio A., Lima: I. Prado Pastor, 1973, pp. 85–101.

9. Although Huamanga served as the center for the movement, *Taqui-Oncoy* "converts" were noted in Cuzco, Arequipa, Lima, and even La Paz. During this time, Spaniards accused a rebel Inca in Vilcabamba, Titu Cusi, of promoting this "apostasy."

10. Sara Castro-Klarén and others note that the Andean people during the crisis of 1532 were confronted with the difficulty of how to deal with Spanish rule. They could choose "to live under the Church's rule of the Spanish colony," or "try to struggle to overthrow or resist Spanish domination and the works of 'Dios.'" Castro-Klarén points out that the choice to fight back carried with it the "expectation of a restoration, during their lifetime, of the autochthonous gods and the reinstatement of themselves" as masters of Andean material and social life. Finally, she maintains that by the time the *Taqui-Oncoy* was detected by Cristóbal de Albornoz, there had been several responses and forms of resistance to colonial rule, mentioning four modes of resistance that combined acts and discourse, allowing the possibility of maintaining continuity with the Andean. There might be others but these four have been documented (Castro-Klarén 1989, 172).

11. Castro-Klarén reminds us that Luis Millones believes there is a link between the *Taqui-Oncoy* and present-day festivities. Manuel Burga's study of the fiestas and in particular his work dealing with the *comparsas* (masquerades) as ritual reenactments of the people's sense of history provides evidence for the Andean perpetuation of the symbology and ritual of the sacramental *taquis* (ritual dances).

12. Castro-Klarén reveals that "of the four-fold combination of the *Taqui-Oncoy* (dance-preaching-music-ecstasy), three elements have survived, and

one, the preaching has been lost" (Castro-Klarén 1989, 181). The reader may find it interesting to note that dancing is not restricted to "Rasu-Ñiti's Agony" in Arguedas's texts, as dancers, music and musicians repeatedly appear in Arguedas's fiction and would suggest that the power and survival of the *Taqui-Oncoy* ritual is crucial for Arguedas. Other characters include: Cámac in *El Sexto* (The Sexto prison, 1961), Ernesto in *Los ríos profundos* (Deep rivers, 1958), Tankayllu in *Yawar Fiesta* (1941), and Don Diego in *El zorro de arriba y el zorro de abajo* (The fox from above and the fox from below, 1971).

13. This and all subsequent translations are mine.

14. This story hasn't been studied much since its authorship is questionable; Arguedas was simply a compiler.

15. Larsen's approach to Latin American cultural and literary theories is unique (at least among his North American contemporaries) in that he uses the previously mentioned Latin American critics and writers taking into consideration the different literary traditions (i.e., boom, ethnoliterature).

16. Interestingly, Arguedas dedicated the story to the memory of Don Santos Ccoyoccossi Ccataccamara, who was the "comisario escolar" (superintendent of schools) of the Umutu community from Cuzco. According to Arguedas, Don Santos went to Lima for the first time at the age of sixty and he was considered by Arguedas to be a monolingual Quechua. Any attempt for this community to create literature implies a "deterritorialized" language: invaded, in its use, by elements of other languages, as "The *Pongo*'s Dream" illustrates. Arguedas's acknowledgment of Don Santos seems to divulge in the spirit of his dedication, the fact that Don Santos is protecting the culture of his marginalized collectivity in the afterlife. In accord with this collective sense of guardianship that Arguedas attributes to Don Santos, the writer himself assumes a collective role, and represents this community.

Works Cited

Adam, Ian. 1991. "Breaking the Chain: Anti-Saussurean Resistance in Birney, Carey, and C. S. Pierce." In *Past the Last Post: Theorizing*

Post-Colonialism and Post-Modernism, ed. Ian Adam and Helen Tiffin. New York: Harvester Wheatsheaf.

Arguedas, José María. 1988. "La agonía de Rasu-Ñiti" (Rasu-Ñiti's agony). In *Relatos completos* (Complete stories), 132–42. Madrid: Alianza Editorial.

———. 1988. "El sueño del pongo" (The Indian servant's dream). In *Relatos completos* (Complete stories), 181–92. Madrid: Alianza Editorial.

Berman, Antoine. 1986. "La traduction et ses discours" (Translation and its discourses). *Cahiers, confrontations* 16 (Autumn): 83–95.

Burga, Manuel. 1988. *Nacimiento de una utopía: Muerte y resurrección de los Incas* (Birth of a utopia: Death and resurrection of the Incas). Lima: Instituto de Apoyo Agrario.

Castro-Klarén, Sara. 1989. "Dancing and the Sacred in the Andes: From the Taqui-Oncoy to Rasu-Ñiti." *Dispositio* 14:169–86.

De Grandis, Rita. 1989. "Los zorros de Arguedas: Una traducción mestiza" (Arguedas's Foxes: A mestizo translation) in *Lenguas, literaturas, sociedades* 2 (1st semester): 149–58.

———. 1990. "*El zorro de arriba y el zorro de abajo* de José María Arguedas: Une traduction métisse" (José María Arguedas's *The fox from above and the fox from below*: A mestizo translation). In *Parole exclusive, parole exclue, parole trangressive* (Exclusive speech, excluded speech, transgressive speech), ed. Antonio Gómez-Moriana and Catherine Poupeney Hart, 481–502. Longueuil, Quebec: Le Préambule.

———. 1994. "La segunda versión de una crónica mestiza en los zorros de Arguedas" (The second version of a mestizo chronicle in Arguedas's foxes). In *Conquista y Contraconquista: La escritura del Nuevo Mundo* (Conquest and counterconquest: The writing of the New World), ed. Julio Ortega and José Amor y Vázquez, 575–85. Mexico City: El Colegio de México–Brown University.

Jameson, Fredric. 1984. "Postmodernism or the Cultural Logic of Late Capitalism." *New Left Review* 46:53–92.

Larsen, Neil. 1990. *Modernism and Hegemony: A Materialist Critique of Aesthetic Agencies*. Minneapolis: University of Minnesota Press.

Mignolo, Walter. 1993. "Colonial and Post-Colonial Discourse: Cultural Critique or Academic Colonialism?" *Latin American Research Review* 28, no. 3: 120–31.

Millones, Luis. 1973. "Un movimiento nativista del siglo XVI: El Taki Ongoy" (A nativist movement of the sixteenth century: The Taki Ongoy). In *Ideología mesiánica del mundo andino* (The messianic ideology of the Andean world), ed. Juan M. Ossio. Lima: I. Prado Pastor.

Noriega, Julio. 1989. "El sueño del pongo: Una forma de liberación utópica" (The Indian servant's dream: A form of utopic liberation). *Imprévue* 2:91–103.

Rama, Angel. 1982. *Transculturación narrativa en América Latina* (Narrative transculturation in Latin America). Mexico City: Siglo XXI editores.

Ruffinelli, Jorge. 1990. "Los 80s: ¿Ingreso a la posmodernidad?" (The '80s: Entry into postmodernity?). *Nuevo texto crítico* 6:31–43.

Stern, Steve J. 1982. *Peru's Indian Peoples and the Challenge of Spanish Conquest: Huamanga to 1640.* Madison: University of Wisconsin Press.

The Persistence of Center

José María Arguedas and the
Challenge to the Postmodern Outlook

Alita Kelley

José María Arguedas (1911–1969), the Peruvian writer and anthropologist, based his novels and stories on the life and outlook of the Quechua-speaking Indians living in a world forced upon them, and saw as his literary mission the expression of what another writer, speaking of current literature in the language of another oppressed people, the Irish, recently called a "unique and unrepeatable way of looking at the world" (Ní Dhomhnaill 1995, 28).

In recent years the terms *posmodernismo* and *posmodernidad* have begun figuring with increasing frequency in critical texts in Spanish, with little or no clarification as to usage. Subsequent to such clarification, Arguedas's work will be considered within the context of modernity and postmodernity, with his final novel *El zorro de arriba y el zorro de abajo* (The fox from above and the fox from below, 1971) viewed as his ultimate rejection of the latter. Arguedas's rejection of postmodernity, however, is no mere defense of modernity in the face of a later development, but is expressed in such a way as to leave in no doubt his innovative position in an emerging world literature, one outlined by Nuala Ní Dhomhnaill, and in which the voices of the dominant Western culture are no longer the only ones, nor even those that prevail.

Awareness of postmodernity in Latin American fiction appeared in an essay by the Chilean José Promis Ojeda, "En torno a la nueva novela hispanoamericana: Reubicación de un concepto" (The new Hispano-American novel: Rethinking a concept, 1977). In it Promis Ojeda berates critics of the sixties and seventies for claiming that a "new" Latin American novel, one that incorporates thematic and textual innovations, such as auto-referentiality, a nonchronological story line, stream of consciousness passages, levels of reality other than the everyday empirical, and change of narrative viewpoint, came into being during the boom years. The critics were dating this so-called new novel from the 1950s or, perhaps, the forties (Brushwood 1975, 333–34) and virtually ignoring fiction written from the 1920s on by Latin Americans such as Macedonio Fernández, Jorge Luis Borges, María Luisa Bombal, Teresa de la Parra, and Martín Adán, alongside Proust, Joyce, Mann, Woolf, Hemingway, Faulkner, and others. The "new" novel was almost half a century old at the time of the boom but had been ignored or misread by positivist critics enamored of Zola's naturalist *roman experimental* (Promis Ojeda 1977, 17–18), which had purported to produce a scientistic social document based on detached observation of empirical reality and to eschew aesthetic creation and lyrical language (Promis Ojeda 1993, 17–23; Braun 1965, 308–11).

In 1976 in *Modernism: 1890–1930*, the British critics Malcolm Bradbury and James McFarlane coined the term "cultural seismology" to define "the shifts and displacements of sensibility in art, literature, and thought," and to bring attention to upheavals within those shifts (1976, 19). A German neologism, *Modernismus*, was taken over by most Western languages as an umbrella term to denote the spirit behind a cataclysm that appeared to shake the arts before and after the first World War. In Catalan and Spanish, the term *modernismo*, however, had been preempted by the nineteenth-century art-for-art's-sake tremor that produced Art Nouveau, symbolism, and Decadence immediately preceding modernity, which is categorized in Spanish as *vanguardismo* in poetry or *neo-realismo* in prose. Incongruously, no umbrella term in Spanish defined "modernity" until the recent appearance of *modernidad* to cover the spirit that informed the plastic arts, music, and literature vis-á-vis the terms *posmodernidad* and *posmodernismo*, already in use as a translation of French and English usage, possibly disseminated through a 1971 essay of that name by Ihab Hassan (Bradbury and McFarlane 1976, 35; Calinescu 1987, 141–43).

Bradbury and McFarlane incorporate the nineteenth-century tremors, including Hispanic *modernismo*, within the literature of modernity as they point out the plethora of conflicting concepts the term denotes. There is no particular theme or style unique to modernity, though "modernism/modernity" has "a recognizable general meaning" that clearly serves as "a broad stylistic description" (23). Pio Baroja's laconic tone, from which Hemingway took much of his "pared down style," might appear to be poles apart from Thomas Mann's baroque sentences, yet the three are modernists inasmuch as their writing reveals a will to produce an original voice. The works of modernity are informed by a common creative attitude of mind, and the period of modernity can be seen as the culmination of a romantic mind-set that extends from the late eighteenth century through the first half of the twentieth, during which time the artist, musician, or writer is "perpetually engaged in a profound and ceaseless journey through the means and integrity of art" (29), with redemption and transcendence often ascribed to the creative act itself. During the time of modernity proper such belief combines with a search for new transcendent codes to replace the eroded underpinnings of Western culture (Promis Ojeda 1977, 19) and which is found in the Latin American novel of the early boom years (23). In several Latin American writers of modernity, Eliot's search for "the Tradition," Hemingway's longing for "the Code," or Yeats's quest for a private mythology (Olsen 1990, 27) find an equivalent in the favoring of an indigenous concept of reality—for example, in Miguel Angel Asturias in *El señor presidente* (Mr. President, 1948), Alejo Carpentier in *Los pasos perdidos* (The lost steps, 1952), and Augusto Roa Bastos in *Hijo del hombre* (Son of man, 1960), while José María Arguedas is consistent in advocating the outlook of the Quechua Indians from his first publication in the thirties to his death in 1969, but particularly in the autobiographical *Los ríos profundos* (Deep rivers, 1958) and in his final, posthumous novel, *El zorro de arriba y el zorro de abajo* (1971).

In *Los ríos profundos* Arguedas depicts moments of oneness with nature and with the people with whom Ernesto, the young protagonist, identifies (64, 65, 71–80, etc.). Ernesto, raised by the Quechua, learned his views on life from them; he speaks of his pride in the discovery of his own literary voice possessed of a lyricism born of the Quechua tradition, and not the high-flown, romantic Spanish style he affected until that time; his new voice was "neither a wail of sorrow nor one of despair. I left the classroom proud and erect, as sure of myself as when I swam across rushing rivers swollen by January floods" (79).[1] In his last work, *El zorro de arriba* (1971), Arguedas writes again of such a worldview learned through an upbringing among Indians and states a literary credo: "I live to write and I believe one must live unconditionally if one is to interpret the chaos and order of things" (26).

In the boom years of the Latin American novel, writers and critics familiar with world literature and the latest literary theories flourished; Arguedas felt incapable of rebutting their sophistries and affected ignorance of literary techniques (1971, 15; Narradores peruanos 1969, 71, 174), but in doing so, contradicted earlier statements in "La novela y el problema de la expresión literaria en el Perú" (The novel and the problem of literary expression in Peru, 1950), in which he outlines the problems confronting the writer who wishes to depict the reality and outlook of the Quechua in literary Spanish (69). According to Margot Beyersdorff, from as early as 1931 Arguedas's "overriding concern" was to find a means of transposing Quechua speech characteristics (1986, 28). She also notes that several critics have been fascinated by this genesis of his literary voice (28–30), including William Rowe, who shows how Arguedas's attempts to find a convincing way to express Quechua speech forces his prose through complex experimental stages from text to text. A given usage might be tried, abandoned, modified, and taken up again (1979, 41–66), and this awareness of language and will to experiment gives Arguedas his unique literary voice. It also separates him from writers of the indigenist school of Andean social realism, born of Zolan naturalism. While the dichotomy between the writing of modernity and that of the scientist naturalists, who supposedly produced reports based on empiric observation, is less total than critics and practitioners believed (Knapp 1975, 41; Promis Ojeda 1993, 9–31), Arguedas's will to original literary expression and need to represent moments of transcendence clearly place him in the modernist camp from the start of his literary career.

As published, *El zorro de arriba* begins and ends with, and the story line includes, sections classified by the writer as "diaries," written "in the hope of emerging from the unexpected well into which I have fallen . . . half consumed by a recurrence of my old illness" (207). The diaries contain comments on a wide variety of topics and include reflections on the natural world and the writer's sense of union with it (24, 27, 96, 206–7), memories of earlier times (28–31), and discussion of the author's acute physical pain (21) and state of clinical depression, which finally led to his suicide (11, 18, 95–99). He offers views on the writer's vocation and refers to other writers with whom he can or cannot empathize (15–30, 209–11).

In the 1960s an unfortunate, widely disseminated dispute had taken place in print between Arguedas and the Argentinean postmodernist Julio Cortázar; Arguedas refers to it specifically in his last novel (204). Each debated the nature of the writer and the literary act as he conceived it. Once again, reference to José Promis Ojeda's 1977 essay sheds light on this occurrence. Promis Ojeda believes that, as critics earlier had not recognized in the literature of Latin America the modernity that had started in the 1920s, they now were overlooking the change in outlook that was taking place in the novel of the sixties.

Textual and thematic experimental techniques did not originate with the boom novels nor with the French *nouveau roman*. They can, in fact, all be found as in a sampler in Joyce's *Finnegans Wake* of 1940, but a different spirit does begin to inform the Latin American works of the sixties, as it also informs the *nouveau roman* and an increasing number of works of Western fiction from many countries (Barth, Gass, Olsen, O'Neill). Promis Ojeda refers to this as a "fall, or loss of center," which strangely echoes Yeats's earlier auguries of impending chaos: "Things fall apart; the centre cannot hold" (1973, 210–11). The Chilean considers the whirlwind that carries away the written word at the end of Gabriel García Márquez's *Cien años de soledad* (One hundred years of solitude, 1967) emblematic of a new Weltanschauung (Promis Ojeda 1977, 26) that has now been identified with the postmodern. It had already manifested itself in the earlier part of the boom in Cortázar's *Rayuela* (Hopscotch, 1963), a tragic story told facetiously by a narrator who searches frantically but fruitlessly for transcendence. The postmodernist can find no redemptive forces, nothing in which to place hope of transcendence: all metanarratives have failed, God is dead, belief in historicism is not justified, reason has let us down, science dooms us to chaos. The modernist's only option appears to be laughter in the face of reality, and the absurdist playwright Eugène Ionesco, echoing Nietzsche, does in fact assert that "to become conscious of what is horrifying and to laugh . . . is to become master" (Esslin 1969, 158). This lends credence to Kristeva's assertion that, while the literature of modernity deals with the tragedy of existence, postmodern literature deals with the tragedy that is the human comedy (1987, 151).

Arguedas's last novel chronicles an appreciation of the new fiction of the sixties but ends by revealing his knowledge that he will never be able to come to terms with the postmodern viewpoint. He cannot, he says, consider writing as a "profession," since, for him, to write is to live and is allied to his will to depict the moments of union with the natural world that he describes for an uncomprehending adversary (204, 210–11). However, Arguedas sees the "new" literary techniques of the sixties as necessary for depicting the new, man-made reality so different from the natural world with which he identifies. He says, "I should have learned something, at least; perhaps I should have learned a lot from the Cortázars," but that would have meant being a very different person and leading a very different life (210).

Postmodernism is usually viewed nowadays as a literary Zeitgeist that starts around mid-century, but it can also be viewed as a constant in literature (Hillis Miller 1975, 31) that reflects a writer's individual temperament as much as the spirit of a given time (Kronik 1994). Kafka, Nabokov, and Borges were postmodernists during the heyday of the modernist outlook. A postmodern spirit might be said to inform *Don Quixote* and *Tristram Shandy*, and a character in Arthur Koestler's novel *The Call-Girls* (1972) insists that a similar spirit informs the words of Ecclesiastes, who "dates from the Bronze Age and God was still supposed to be alive then" (67).

Nothing could be further from postmodern mockery than the simple wonder expressed in Arguedas's lyrical prose in *Los ríos profundos,* or when the writer describes his experiences of redemption in the diary sections of his last novel. Arguedas spent his life attempting to communicate the "love, hate, and tenderness" (Narradores peruanos 1969, 36) that he learned, along with a sense of oneness with nature, as a child, as he says in his last novel "raised among don Felipe Maywa's folk, placed in the very *oqllo* [breast] of the Indians" (20). Just as Koestler finds that Ecclesiastes shows cynicism in the Bronze Age, it can be argued that efforts to convey the sense of such unity with all that is natural form a literary constant in religious expression from the Bronze Age and even earlier.

The difference between Arguedas and many modernist writers

lies in the simple fervor with which he insists on the validity of his be-liefs. In the "First Diary" of his last novel, he tells once again how and where he came upon his view of reality, stressing that such a view is based on his earliest perceptions of love (22–23) that have comforted him throughout his life. He is aware, however, that similar attitudes regarding the views of native peoples have become fashionable among some sophisticated writers, and he mentions one by name (17). His own commitment to artistic creation is typical of the spirit of modernism, but he is adamant in his abhorrence of literary postur-ing. Arguedas advocates the order he perceives as natural, and to de-scribe it he prefers metaphors taken from the natural world (206, 207, 209, etc.), so that when the narrator of his last novel affirms his friendship with a tree: "two yards from its powerful, blackened trunk one hears a sound, the typical sound that flows forth at the foot of those who stand alone" (206), the reader senses his insistence that this is something he truly feels, as well as his fear that his sentences might be construed as fine writing.

In spite of the resentment that Arguedas feels for the new "profes-sional" novelists and his insistence in his last novel that he is "a provincial" (25), he is remarkably successful in producing a totalizing text that incorporates the techniques he takes to be boom innova-tions. The story line of *El zorro de arriba* is set in the port of Chim-bote, a once quiet backwater that in the 1960s became Peru's boom town due to the international fishmeal industry. As European and North American modernists looked to the Greek myths, so the An-dean incorporates elements from Inca mythology. The novel covers all strata of Chimbote society, including some actual living persons, and its protagonists range from the displaced Indians of the shanty towns who, working at jobs created by the fish meal boom—not the least important occupation being prostitution—to Peruvian and for-eign capitalists who have turned the town into an inferno. Yet, in spite of the chaos, there are those beings who survive and even transcend the reality around them.

Arguedas was a very slow and careful writer who made many

revisions. The jerky, impressionistic passages, which combine many styles, even elements of different genres, more than comply with the techniques considered mandatory for a novel written during the boom years, yet only a first, uncorrected draft of the novel exists, and no edition wholly complies with the writer's stipulations. The unfinished novel is in fragmentary form, with a stylized résumé near the end that proposes a denouement: Arguedas wanted the "chapters" of story line classified as "ebullitions" (212), as if to imply that they were being emitted by some uncontainable force.

The foxes of the title derive from the tricksters of a colonial Quechua document on myths of Huarochirí, a locality in the highlands, inland from Lima. In Arguedas's novel, the fox from the coast and the fox from the highlands first appear in order to discuss, critically, the writer's efforts to generate a new form of narrative (31–32). Diego, the fox from the coast, an "Inca hippie," later performs an act of magic realism by powering the machinery in a fishmeal factory by dancing the traditional scissors-dance (130–34, 153), and he is also present as a stutterer magically cured of his affliction (151–53). The fox appears to symbolize Arguedas's faith in the indigenous population's ability to master the niceties of Western technology and custom without sacrificing its own culture and magic. Over the centuries, the Quechua have proven their capacity to prevail, and to take what they wish from the environment that was forced upon them, without relinquishing the qualities essential to their own particular vision. This also forms the subject of the Quechua poetry written by Arguedas in his later years (Murra 1978, xiii–xv; Rowe and Schelling 1991, 61).

There are factors in Arguedas's last novel that have proven troublesome to critics. William Rowe compares unfavorably the intellectualizing language of the "diaries" and their greater use of adverbs and adjectives with the gentle, onomatopoeic lyricism of *Los ríos profundos* dealing with identical material (1979, 197–99). There is a pervasive sexuality about the final novel. The action appears to take off from a description by the narrator in the "First Diary" of an enigmatic, infantile sexual experience (28–31), and Rowe ventures that the sexual element might mean to evoke the connotations possessed by the coast in the serrano mind (1979, 200–202); it is an element that figures prominently in Latin American boom literature but that appeared only mutedly in Arguedas's previous work. Arguedas incorporates into his last novel and his late poetry an unusual technique of deliberately comparing the natural to the man-made. A *huayronqo* (horsefly) is likened to a helicopter (27). While this brings to mind Dr. Johnson's famous observation that comparison of the man-made to the natural ennobles the man-made, and comparison of the natural to the man-made denigrates nature, denigration of nature is obviously not Arguedas's intent, yet the comparisons are so deliberate and insistent as to invite speculation. The text, unfinished as it is, shows that Arguedas "was an old dog with the adaptability to learn new tricks" (Higgins 1987, 211), but, as throughout the diaries, the narrator speaks repeatedly of beliefs that are firm and above changes of literary fashion.

Arguedas's repeated thesis was that in Peru the Quechua language has exercised more than substratum influence, and Rowe has pointed out in this context that the culture has produced two Quechua speakers, Guamán Poma de Ayala and José María Arguedas, who undertake to strengthen and extend the scope of the native tradition in time of crisis by depicting the Quechua outlook for the reader of Spanish. Rowe classifies the two as "translators" who attempt to present the Quechua world view to readers whose language is constituted quite differently from Quechua (1979, 53); according to culturally oriented translation theory, such translation ennobles and bestows authority on the source language (Lefevere 1992, 123).

Arguedas's writing in Spanish appears to possess such clarity of intent that its lyricism is evident, even in translation into other languages. The following is my translation of a passage from *Los ríos profundos*:

> The rivers were always mine and the bushes growing on the slopes of the mountains, even the little villages and the houses with their red

roofs streaked with lime, the blue fields of alfalfa, and my beloved cornfields. But whenever I was returning from the courtyard as night fell, the motherly glow of the world would melt before my eyes, and as soon as it was dark, my loneliness and isolation would grow. [64]

In recent years Arguedas's popularity with readers of different languages and cultures appears to substantiate the success of his literary endeavor, but I do not believe that his fervor in presenting the Quechua vision should be construed as proselytizing to those who might or might not understand. He was aware from the start that the nuances of spoken language cannot be seen in print and that some Quechua concepts will not translate (1950), yet he does not hesitate to use them. Rosaleen Howard-Malverde in discussing Bruce Mannheim's writing on the Quechua principle of reciprocity, *ayni,* remarks that the concept is embedded in the language with suffixes indicating grammatically a sense of interpersonal obligation in Quechua speakers that functions below the level of consciousness (1994, 120). Arguedas told John V. Murra that he was persuaded to write in Spanish, though he had intended to write only in Quechua. Late in life he returned to writing in his first language (Murra 1978, x–xi). Arguedas's true intended reader must surely sense the niceties of that language and testify to the authenticity of the Quechua vision; Arguedas is addressing someone who reads Spanish but is familiar with the Quechua tradition. Such Peruvians, the first or second generation in their families to go to school, make up a considerable part of the population of Peru. For them, Arguedas's work has the appeal of writings by a close personal friend; his literary voice gives voice to their beliefs and outlook.

Ní Dhomhnaill, on speaking of her own poetry in the Irish language, voices the sentiment that appears to have inspired Arguedas's work. Ní Dhomhnaill stresses that she speaks not only for her own "defeated" language but for others throughout the world, and states that she believes such voices offer the only viable current alternative to the "originally Anglo-American, but now genuinely global, pop monoculture that reduces everything to the level of the most stupendous boredom" (1995, 28).

Arguedas's modernity consists in showing that, in spite of the fundamental viability of Ní Dhomhnaill's argument, her choice of wording is very wrong; the culture of the Quechua in Peru is anything but "defeated." We are seeing that the staying power of a culture is not to be measured only in terms of economic and political hegemony or lack of same, as Rowe and Schelling (1991, 51–64) and others have shown. Anyone who visits Peru today, after a hiatus of several years, cannot but be astonished by the way in which the Andean culture is not merely surviving in the sierra but flourishing in the cities, where its presence has become ubiquitous; meanwhile, admiration for José María Arguedas, the "translator" of this culture—the man, his literary creativity and its message—has increased so greatly in the quarter century since his death that at times it almost reaches adulation.

That the sector of society whose culture Arguedas wrote of has been oppressed for over four hundred years and continues to be so to this day is certainly true, but we are coming to realize that the Quechua culture was never defeated, and that this might also be said of Ní Dhomhnaill's Celtic inheritance, and of that of many other peoples. Indeed, even in the face of total physical annihilation, a culture can prevail and influence its oppressors in ways never imagined. In directing his modernistic aesthetic toward the depiction of the Quechua and what he sees as the redemptive qualities of their culture, Arguedas, unlike most modernists, was expressing faith in what he knew from within. This lends to his work an unusual verisimilitude that flies in the face of the postmodern despair of the contemporaries with whom Arguedas debated in his final years. That he could master the purely technical aspects of so-called avant-garde prose writing he showed in his final novel, even as he insisted, to the very end of his life, through his depiction of the society he knew, that there is more to the human being and human culture than the society that has produced postmodernism could know or was willing to explore. In the case of the Quechua, as Julio Ortega has affirmed, Arguedas's writings show not only Peru's awareness of misfortune, but also its dream of what might be (1984, 89).

Note

1. All quotations from Spanish originals have been translated into English by the author.

Works Cited

Arguedas, José María. 1950. "La novela y el problema de la expresión literaria en el Perú" (The novel and the problem of literary expression in Peru). *Mar del Sur* (Lima) 3, no. 9 (January–February): 66–72.

———. 1964. *Los ríos profundos* (Deep rivers). Lima: Nuevo Mundo; 1978 *Deep Rivers*. Trans. Frances Horning Barraclough. Austin: University of Texas Press.

———. 1971. *El zorro de arriba y el zorro de abajo* (The fox from above and the fox from below). 2d ed. Buenos Aires: Editorial Losada.

Barth, John. 1967. "The Literature of Exhaustion." *Atlantic* 220 (August): 29–34.

———. 1980. "The Literature of Replenishment: Postmodernist Fiction." *Atlantic* 245 (January): 65–71.

Beyersdorff, Margot. 1986. "Voice of the Runa: Quechua Substratum in the Narrative of José María Arguedas." *Latin American Indian Literatures Journal* 2, no. 1 (Spring): 28–48.

Bradbury, Malcolm, and James McFarlane. 1976. "The Name and Nature of Modernism." In *Modernism: 1890–1930*, ed. Malcolm Bradbury and James McFarlane, 19–55. London: Penguin.

Braun, Sidney D., ed. 1965. *Dictionary of French Literature*. New York: Fawcett.

Brushwood, John S. 1975. *The Spanish American Novel: A Twentieth-Century Survey*. Austin: University of Texas Press.

Calinescu, Matei. 1987. *Five Faces of Modernity: Modernism, Avant-Garde, Decadence, Kitsch, and Postmodernism.* Durham, N.C.: Duke University Press.

Esslin, Martin. 1969. *The Theatre of the Absurd.* Rev. ed. Garden City, N.Y.: Anchor-Doubleday.

Gass, William. 1987. "The First Seven Pages of the Boom." *Latin American Literary Review* 15 (January–June): 33–56.

Higgins, James. 1987. *A History of Peruvian Literature.* London: Francis Cairns.

Hillis Miller, J. 1975. "Textual Strategies: Deconstructing the Deconstructers." *Diacritics* 5, no. 2 (Summer): 24–31.

Howard-Malverde, Rosaleen. 1994. Review of *The Language of the Inka since the European Invasion,* by Bruce Mannheim. *Bulletin of Latin American Research* 13, no. 1 (January): 120–21.

Knapp, Bettina. 1975. *Maurice Maeterlinck.* Boston: Twayne.

Koestler, Arthur. 1976. *The Call-Girls.* London: Pan.

Kristeva, Julia. 1987. "The Pain and Sorrow of the Modern World: The Works of Marguerite Duras." *PMLA* 102, no. 2: 138–52.

Kronik, John. 1994. "Strains of Postmodernism in Modern Narrative." Taft Speaker, paper read at 14th Cincinnati Conference on Romance Languages and Literature, 14 May, at the University of Cincinnati, Cincinnati, Ohio.

Lefevere, André. 1992. *Translating Literature: Practice and Theory in a Comparative Literature Context.* New York: Modern Language Association of America.

Murra, John V. 1978. Introduction to *Deep Rivers,* by José María Arguedas. Trans. Frances Horning Barraclough. Austin: University of Texas Press.

Narradores peruanos (Peruvian writers). 1969. *Primer encuentro de narradores peruanos* (First meeting of Peruvian writers). Lima: Casa de la Cultura del Perú.

Ní Dhomhnaill, Nuala. 1995. "Why I Choose to Write in Irish, The Corpse That Sits Up and Talks Back." *New York Times Book Review* (January 8): 3, 27–28.

Olsen, Lance. 1990. *Circus of the Mind in Motion: Postmodernism and the Comic Vision.* Detroit: Wayne State University Press.

O'Neill, Patrick. 1990. *The Comedy of Entropy: Humour, Narrative, Reading*. Toronto: University of Toronto Press.

Ortega, Julio. 1984. *Poetics of Change: The New Spanish-American Narrative*. Trans. Galen D. Greaser, with the author. Austin: University of Texas Press.

Promis Ojeda, José. 1977. "En torno a la nueva novela hispanoamericana: Reubicación de un concepto" (The new Hispano-American novel: Rethinking a concept). *Chasqui* 7, no. 1: 16–27.

———. 1993. *La novela chilena del último siglo* (The Chilean novel in the last century). Santiago: Editorial La Noria.

Rowe, William. 1979. *Mito e ideología en la obra de José María Arguedas* (Myth and ideology in the work of José María Arguedas). Lima: Instituto Nacional de Cultura.

Rowe, William, and Vivian Schelling. 1991. *Memory and Modernity: Popular Culture in Latin America*. London: Verso.

Part Two

Transliterary Reconsiderations

Mindful of the political, if not polemical, cast of contemporary literary perspectives, the following essays take as their place of meeting Arguedas's holographic transliterary production, as it flows from and within both autobiographical, individual, as well as collective, Andean experiences. Not unlike the previous section, which undertook analysis through the horizon of "nomadic migration," John Landreau confronts us with Arguedas as the "outsider" or *forastero*, who employs his autobiographical persona as a living bridge between the Quechua- and Spanish-speaking worlds. As Arguedas "translates between languages and cultures" he comes "to embody the struggle of Andeans 'to defend themselves' in a rapidly modernizing, increasingly national society." Contrary to previous critics' mistaken depictions, Landreau lucidly demonstrates that Arguedas uses autobiography to legitimate "an appropriation and translation of the Quechua oral tradition . . . for the purposes of an intellectually sophisticated, and unequivocally modern literary practice."

While Arguedas is best known as a writer of prose narratives, and more recently of ethnographic and socioanthropological works, he has yet to be accorded significant recognition as a Quechua poet.

Martin Lienhard continues this latest effort (begun by Antonio Cornejo Polar) in his diligent analysis of Arguedas's form of poetic exposition in the context of both past and recent Quechua poetry, as well as "historical emergence." While recognizing the significance of cosmic and aesthetic codes of oral Quechua culture, Lienhard also emphasizes the importance of the "urban cultural space" and complex literary system (both oral and written) to which all the poems importantly belong.

Arguedas's "metatestimonial" work, *El Sexto* (The Sexto prison), has, even among Spanish-speaking audiences, received not only scant, but misguided attention[1]—this despite recent calls to reassess this work as predictive of Arguedas's intellectual foresight,[2] and in light of recent postmodern cultural criticism. Ciro Sandoval and Sandra Boschetto-Sandoval attempt to reconsider this text from within an "analectic" (as opposed to "dialectic") framework: from and within a paradigm of cultural and philosophical liberation or revindication that opposes the fixation of value-neutral political rationalizations, in favor of a paradigm of utopic nuance that does not ignore the relations of other representational forms and other social and metaphysical practices. Claudette Kemper Columbus discusses the symbolic and decentering significance of the trickster figures in Arguedas's experimental, posthumous novel, *El zorro de arriba y el zorro de abajo* (The fox from above and the fox from below) within the context of the problematic dialogue between two foxes in the Quechua Huarochirí myth, and that serves as novelistic "pre-text." As "masters of information and of discourse," the tricksters are unable to bring about liberating transformation because in the age of mechanical reproduction and loss of memory of the past, they have lost both the power to listen and the ability to sing and dance "divinely." As the author notes, "the racket of technology in the fishmeal factory extinguishes any but its own, blunted universe of noise."

Notes

1. See, for example, Mario Vargas Llosa's prologue to the Editorial Laia (Barcelona, 1973) edition of *El Sexto*, "'El Sexto' de José María Arguedas: La condición marginal" (José María Arguedas's *El Sexto*: The marginal condition) in which Vargas Llosa notes that, along with *Yawar Fiesta* and *El zorro de arriba y el zorro de abajo*, *El Sexto* is the "most imperfect" of Arguedas's novels, a mere parable on the condition of the writer, that "solipsistic Narcissist" who was only capable of inventing worlds and speaking about others from the standpoint of his own and by speaking of himself (20).

2. At the 1995 International JALLA Conference (Jornadas Andinas de Literatura Latinoamericana) in Tucumán, Argentina, William Rowe, among others, called for a much-needed reevaluation of *El Sexto* in order to better contextualize Arguedas's ideological and cultural enterprise.

Translation, Autobiography, and Quechua Knowledge

John C. Landreau

A central figure in many of the stories and novels written by the bilingual Andean novelist and anthropologist José María Arguedas is that of the outsider or *forastero*. Typically this character, a modern figure marked by alienation and by longing, appears as a first-person narrator. I am referring to characters like Ernesto in *Deep Rivers* and Gabriel in *El Sexto* (The Sexto prison), who, like Arguedas himself in his autobiographical representations, must confront a world "of monsters and of fire" in which Quechua and Spanish cultures collide. Torn between languages and social worlds, the experience and point of view of the Arguedean *forastero* are crossed with tensions and contradictions. He is a pivotal figure, a participant, and at the same time an outsider, an observer. In this context his role is often to translate, to mediate, and to interpret.[1]

Like these first-person characters who play such an important role in his fiction, it is as a translator and as a mediator that Arguedas conceives of, and represents, his own intellectual and literary project:

Forever impassioned by songs and myths, carried by fortune all the way to the University of San Marcos, speaking Quechua all my life but thoroughly integrated as well into the world of the tormentors, joyous visitor to the immense cities of other nations, I ventured to change into written language what I was as an individual: a living link, strong and capable of becoming universal, of the imprisoned Quechua people and the generous, human side of their oppressors . . . . [Arguedas 1983, 5:13][2]

In this famous quotation from his acceptance speech upon receiving the prestigious Inca Garcilaso Prize in 1968, Arguedas employs his autobiographical persona in order to legitimate and explain his self-assigned role as literary mediator between the Quechua- and Spanish-speaking worlds that constitute Peru. The importance and validity of his life story, as this quotation clearly indicates, is that it seems to be emblematic of a collective experience: the author who translates between languages and cultures comes to embody the struggle of Andeans to "defend themselves" in a rapidly modernizing, increasingly national society. From this perspective, the diglossic, hybrid character of Arguedas's style is legitimized as reflective of a collective, Andean experience.

The purpose of this essay is to contribute to an understanding of the complex relationship in Arguedas's writing between autobiography and translation. I begin by reviewing the concept and practice of translation that motivates Arguedas's entire literary and intellectual project. Subsequently, I will examine the autobiographical space within which Arguedas inscribes his work, in order to better understand the value and effects of his life story on his ambitious endeavor of cultural translation. Finally, I will argue against simplifying interpretations of Arguedas's life story (such as Vargas Llosa's) because they ignore the complexities of Arguedas's appropriation of Quechua knowledge and orality in his literary practice.

What is Translation?

Until the 1960s Arguedas wrote almost exclusively in Spanish for a non-Andean reading public. Accordingly, given the Andean referent of most of his writing, he conceives of his literary, as well as his ethnographic labors as forms of translation. This concept underlines what Arguedas sees as the constitutive dynamic of his writing: the gulf of misunderstanding, racism, and difference separating the oral, Quechua-speaking world of his childhood and the predominantly literate, Spanish-speaking world of Lima, which he inhabits as an adult writer. Thus, as Arguedas describes in his most famous literary statement, his goal as a writer is one of cultural translation:

> To realize oneself, to translate oneself, to transform a seemingly alien language into a legitimate and diaphanous torrent, to communicate to the almost foreign language the stuff of which our spirit is made: that is the hard, the difficult question.[Arguedas 1985b, 18]

In this context, he explains, conventional, "literary" Spanish is incapable of adequately representing a universe in which Quechua is the legitimate language.

> Many of the essences I felt to be best and most legitimate could not be diluted into Spanish terms of familiar construction. It was necessary to discover subtle ways to disarrange the Spanish in order to make it into the fitting mold, the adequate instrument of expression. [ibid., 20]

Ideally, for Arguedas, *translation* designates a place where the languages and cosmovisions of these conflicting social worlds converge and animate one another. Concretely, *translation* refers to the active incorporation of aspects of Quechua orality into the form and language of written texts in Spanish.[3]

Arguedas advances the notion of translation not only to explain and legitimate his own writing but also, more ambitiously, to invest it with a collective value as the authentic mode of Andean literature in general. In his ethnographic writing, Arguedas emphasizes the related idea of *transculturation*. Using this concept, borrowed from the Cuban anthropologist Fernando Ortiz,[4] Arguedas stresses the resistance of Quechua culture to Spanish domination in the central and southern Andes by showing the strategies of adaptation it adopts in response to changing historical circumstances. The vitality of Andean culture, according to Arguedas, is due to a complicated process of cultural change in which many elements of Spanish culture have been absorbed and Quechuized. If the process of transculturation can be safeguarded in the future by creating the possibility for Quechua speakers to participate in the social, political, and economic life of a rapidly modernizing Peru then, Arguedas believes, Quechua cultural traditions not only can survive but can become the foundation of an original (and inclusive) national culture. As Angel Rama has argued, Arguedas's literary project of *translation*, in which Quechua orality becomes an active element in the structure of Spanish genres, serves as a model in miniature of the *transcultural*, Andeanized Peru he envisions.[5]

The Language of Translation in Deep Rivers

Translation, Arguedas argues, is the necessary mode of writing of the bicultural, bilingual Andean writer working in Spanish. This is beautifully exemplified by Ernesto in *Deep Rivers*, as he approaches the task of writing a love letter for his friend Markask'a to an Abancay "señorita" named Silvinia. Markarsk'a asks Ernesto to write to Silvinia, with whom he has fallen in love, because he has heard that Ernesto writes like a poet. Later, as Ernesto is contemplating the ambitious task of writing the love letter, to feign Markask'a's voice in order to move Silvinia to love him, he begins by imagining his reader: who is Silvinia and what does she look like? He knows the neighborhood she lives in but, he indicates, "I wasn't familiar with the señoritas of the town. . . . I always considered them as foreign beings . . ." (Arguedas 1983, 3:69–70).[6] The distance between Ernesto and the world of the "señoritas," which he does not understand, and to which he does not belong, looms large as he faces the challenge of writing to Silvinia on Markask'a's behalf. Nonetheless, he says,

> In spite of everything I knew that I could cross that distance, like an arrow, like a burning coal rising through the air. The letter that I was committed to writing for Markask'a's sweetheart would reach the doors of that world. "Now choose your best words—I told myself—and write them!" It didn't matter that the letter was for another, perhaps it was better that way in the beginning. "Black sparrow hawk, wandering sparrow hawk, raise your wings and fly," I cried out. [ibid.]

Ernesto is inspired by the difficult literary challenge. Even though the letter is not his own, but rather Markask'a's, he still feels confident that he can do the job. In fact, he wonders if it isn't better to begin with another's letter as he makes his first attempts at reaching Silvinia's world with his words. Just before he begins to write, Ernesto remembers a verse from a song and recites it *aloud*, thus bolstering himself for his writer's task with the feeling and sound of words from the oral tradition of the *huayno*.

Ernesto begins to write the letter but suddenly stops, arrested by an uncertainty.

> But a sudden uneasiness, a kind of stinging embarrassment, made me interrupt the letter. I rested my arms and head on the desk; with my face hidden I paused to listen to these new feelings. "What are you doing, where are you going? Why don't you go on? What are you frightened of? Who has broken off your flight?" After these questions, I listened feverishly again to my feelings.

> And if those girls knew how to read? And if I could write to them?

> And those girls were Justina or Jacinta, Malicacha or Felisa; they didn't have bangs or loose, flowing hair, nor did they wear veils over

their eyes. No, they wore black braids, and wildflowers in their hatbands. . . . "If I could write to them, my love would surge like a clear river; my letter would be like a song that soars through the sky toward its destination." To write! To write to them was futile, useless. "Go, wait for them on the mountain paths, and sing! And if it were possible, if I could begin to do it?" And I wrote:

"Uyariy chay k'atik'niki siwar k'entita. . . ." [ibid., 71]

The uncertainty arises because he is writing for a girl he doesn't know on someone else's behalf. His confidence is disturbed by the presence of his own desires, and consequently by the presence of other implied "readers" of the love letter he is composing.

Ernesto writes a line in Quechua, in the fashion of a verse from a *huayno*, imagining that he is speaking for himself to his own love. Writing in Spanish would be useless and absurd to reach Indian girls like Justina and Jacinta that Ernesto so fondly remembers. Instead, one might wait on the mountain paths and sing *huaynos* to them in Quechua. With these thoughts, Ernesto resumes the letter to Silvinia.

Listen to the emerald hummingbird who follows you; listen to him, do not be cruel; he will speak to you of me. His little wings are exhausted, he can fly no more; stay now and listen. Nearby is the white rock where wanderers pause to rest; wait there and listen to him; hear his sobs; he is the messenger of my young heart, he will speak to you of me. Listen, pretty one, with your eyes like great stars, beautiful flower, flee no more, stay now and listen. I bring you a command from the heavens: they bid you to be my sweetheart . . . ! [ibid.: 71]

He resumes the letter by translating the Quechua line he has written into Spanish. Thus bolstered, he goes on to finish the letter to Silvinia on Markask'a's behalf. The image of the nightingale as the messenger of the lover, and the final dramatic statement or declaration of love at the end, give the letter the unmistakable shape and tone of a Quechua *huayno*.

The complex intersection of languages (Quechua and Spanish), of oral and written forms of expression (the love letter and the *huayno*), of distinct and incompatible readers-listeners (Silvinia and the Indian girls) and of distinct purposes and desires (those of Markask'a and those of Ernesto) converge and animate one another in the letter Ernesto writes. Writing *translates* these heterogeneous presences into a text whose strength and beauty gives Ernesto a feeling of pride and accomplishment.

> I left the classroom with my head high, feeling a confident pride, like when I used to swim across the rivers in January burdened with the heaviest and most turbulent waters. [ibid., 71]

Translation, like the anthropological notion of *transculturation,* which is ubiquitous in Arguedas's anthropological writings, is a form of creative remembering in which cultural identity is reaffirmed and recreated in new contexts. Ernesto, depending on Quechua sources, and reminded of his own desires, writes a love letter in Spanish for a friend. In the process, he reaffirms his own Andean identity and memory: the beauty of the words in Spanish make him feel as proud as when he swam the deep rivers.

This complex scene of writing described by Ernesto is one which is crossed by multiple tensions: by Quechua and Spanish, and by the exigencies of incompatible readers. It also aptly describes many of the dilemmas and problems that are negotiated in Arguedas's writings in general. For Arguedas, to adequately tell an Andean story requires the hybrid language of translation in which multiple voices and languages are brought into contact.

Autobiographical Space

But who has the authority and knowledge to tell such a story? Arguedas clearly seeks to establish the legitimacy and truth value of his texts autobiographically. Much of his fiction, and a good number of his essays in folklore and anthropology, are narrated in the first person. In addition, Arguedas commonly defends and explains his work in specifically autobiographical terms. This *autobiographical space* legitimates his texts in several ways.[7] In the first place, the authorial standpoint is that of a privileged observer of the Andean world. In the second place, as I previously indicated, Arguedas uses his life story to defend and explain his style, which he conceives of as tense encounter between Quechua and Spanish. In this sense, Arguedas's autobiography takes on a collective value: the narrating "I" who translates between conflicting languages and cosmovisions comes to embody the struggle of Peruvian culture to define itself between these worlds. This emblematic sense of the meaning of Arguedas's life and work was lucidly articulated by José Rouillón:

> Arguedas has taught us to see and to experience Peru. Perhaps no one has been able to unite his life's destiny with that of his country like Arguedas. His intimate story has been turned into the meaning of our history. [Rouillón 1979, 379]

Unfortunately, the autobiographical dimension of Arguedas's writing has often been interpreted as a sign of simplicity, and even of innocence, rather than as an important element in a complex literary endeavor. In fact, the bulk of Arguedean criticism has been reluctant to regard Arguedas's life story critically, as a "literary fact."[8] While the story of Arguedas's life, and in particular his childhood, has been, and continues to be, an immensely productive and valid source of critical insight, in my view it has also been a source of misunderstanding, and in certain cases (most notably that of Mario Vargas Llosa), it has been used to belittle his literary achievement. For that reason a critical evaluation of (which I hope can be distinguished from an attack on the "truth" of) Arguedas's life story is in order. The emotional, ethical, and artistic allegiance of José María Arguedas to the Quechua world of his childhood is beyond doubt. I propose, simply, to analyze the relationship between his life story and his work as a "literary fact."

Life Story

José María Arguedas was born in 1911 in Andahuaylas, the small mountain capital of the province of Lucanas, near Ayacucho. His mother, Victoria Altamirano Navarro de Arguedas, was from a "distinguished family" in San Pedro de Andahuaylas, and his father, Víctor Manuel Arguedas Arellano, a Cuzcueño, was a lawyer and judge. When his mother died in 1914, Arguedas was sent to live with his paternal grandmother in Andahuaylas for almost four years. In 1917 Víctor Manuel remarried to a rich landowning woman of San Juan de Lucanas, and Arguedas went to live with them in Puquio (which lies on the most direct overland route from Lima to Cuzco). In 1918 he moved to San Juan de Lucanas with his stepmother, thereafter seeing his father only sporadically. The six years Arguedas spent in San Juan de Lucanas (and in the nearby hacienda, Viseca), when he was between the ages of seven and thirteen, are the period of his intimate contact with monolingual Quechua speakers.[9] It is this period that Arguedas narrates repeatedly in his autobiographical texts and fragments. Also, these places are the setting of his first books: the stories in *Agua* (1935) take place in San Juan de Lucanas, and in the nearby hacienda of Viseca; *Yawar Fiesta* (1941) takes place in Puquio; *Los ríos profundos* (1958) takes place in Abancay.

Arguedas's various autobiographical statements emphasize, as I mentioned, the years spent with his stepmother in San Juan de Lucanas. The narrative of Arguedas's childhood, which is repeated in numerous autobiographical texts and fragments, is a story of abandonment and cruelty on the part of his natural family, and of tenderness and rescue on the part of Quechua-speaking servants and *comuneros* (peasants). When Arguedas is three, his mother dies, and his father, like Ernesto's in *Los ríos profundos*, leaves Arguedas in the care of others while he travels for prolonged periods of time. The surrogate parents in whose care he is left (particularly his stepmother and stepbrother) are despotic and cruel.[10] Consequently, Arguedas passes his childhood largely among the Indian servants at his stepmother's hacienda, and among the *comuneros* of the nearby free *comunidades* (communities), who care for him with great tenderness. Quechua, he claims, is his native language,[11] and as a child he sees the world as a *runakuna* (the Quechua word for Quechua- speakers).

> Due to very unusual circumstances my childhood took place in two Andean towns where the predominant language was Quechua. Due to the same circumstances, as a child I fell into the protection of monolingual Quechua Indians. My mother died when I was three. Among the Indians I found adequate compensation for my orphanhood. They were my family. . . . I understood and experienced the world as they did . . . the rivers, the trees, the canyons, many insects, certain rocks and caves had a special meaning and life. Happiness or evil could be caused by them. . . . [Arguedas 1966, 2][12]

There is nothing unusual about the fact that Arguedas spoke Quechua since even today most inhabitants of the southern Peruvian Andes speak the language. However, by the 1950s Arguedas increasingly emphasizes that he had been originally monolingual in the language ("La narrativa en el Perú contemporáneo," 412), and that as a child he had viewed the world entirely with the magico-religious cosmovision of a Quechua speaker. This extraordinary childhood sets him apart, and lends special status and legitimacy to his role as author-translator.

During the fifties and sixties Arguedas applies his autobiographical "legend" retrospectively to his early narratives from the thirties and forties.[13] Thus, the autobiographical sensibility of Arguedas's now-famous "The Novel and the Problem of Literary Expression in Peru" (1950) comes to characterize the entire corpus of his writings. The year 1950 is not a threshold dividing a before and an after— autobiographical space is created in Arguedas's writings gradually— but it does mark a moment in which the autobiographical aspect of Arguedas's work coalesces. The legitimizing power of Arguedas's childhood story plays a fundamental role in his rise to literary prominence especially during the fifties and after.

After the mid-sixties, when the first critical essays are written about Arguedas's fiction,[14] the autobiographical space in which his work is inscribed becomes the common frame of reference for Arguedean criticism. The image of Arguedas as an "Indian of the heart" (Muñoz 1982) dominates critical reception of his writings: the author's perspective is commonly seen as that of a witness whose privileged testimony represents and illuminates the world he describes.[15] Juan Larco in his preface to the first major collection of essays on Arguedas writes,

> Still an adolescent Arguedas, son of a white lawyer in the provinces, spent the decisive years of his childhood among the Indians. . . . adopted by them, Arguedas adopted their language, Quechua.. . . Arguedas was "torn" from the maternal care of the Indians. . . . When he arrived in Lima in 1928, at seventeen years of age, he spoke Spanish with difficulty. . . . [Larco 1976, 8]

The notion that Arguedas could barely speak Spanish at seventeen years of age is, as Roland Forgues has shown, an exaggeration (Forgues 1991). Nonetheless, this image lends tremendous authenticity to his voice, and legitimacy to his point of view. First-person protagonists like Ernesto in *Deep Rivers* seem to embody both a collective and an individual experience: their marginality, homelessness, and suffering are plotted both as autobiography and as social testimony. In this context, Arguedean autobiographical space serves as the touchstone for an analysis of his texts as "intuitive" or transparent representations of an "experience" or social reality.

While this perspective has been used mostly to laud Arguedas's intellectual and literary accomplishments, as I indicated earlier, in several cases, most notably that of Mario Vargas Llosa, it has been used to diminish them. The case of Vargas Llosa is significant because his essays on Arguedas's literary texts are by far the most widely disseminated since they appear as introductions to so many editions of his novels. A binary opposition between "modern" (logical) culture and "primitive" (illogical) culture is fundamental to Vargas Llosa's interpretation of Arguedas. It leads him to portray Arguedas as a nostalgic, Arcadian writer who dreams of the return to an archaic world, thus rejecting modernity and "progress."[16] Nonetheless, for Vargas Llosa, the most authentic Arguedas, the one he praises, is the one who clings to this "utopia" of a world he describes as

> uncontaminated by modernity, far removed from the coast and everything that is foreign. It is a world that Arguedas called "Peruvian." But his idea of what constituted "Peruvian" is inseparable from the sierra and from antiquity. It is a world seen as uncorrupted, virginal, pure, magical, ritual, a world that sinks its roots in the Peruvian past. A world that has survived almost miraculously.... [Vargas Llosa 1981, xi]

This quaint, intuitive Arguedas is, according to Vargas Llosa's verdict, a generally mediocre writer. He has flashes of brilliance, and one good novel to his name *(Deep Rivers)*, but overall he is a primitive:

> His subject matter is rich, original, and alive because, in the domain of language, on the basis of intuition and hard work, Arguedas achieved a personal creation. The great limitation of his narrative is of a technical character. With the exception of *Deep Rivers*, Arguedas's novels exhibit a fairly shoddy construction. They are primitive and clumsy: Arguedas lacked something that—in his era—only the European and North American novelists that he hadn't read could have given him. [Vargas Llosa 1974, 8]

It is not clear, at least to me, that Arguedas is as "unread" and innocent as he often portrays himself in his autobiographical representations—a myth Vargas Llosa repeats here.[17] Moreover, Vargas Llosa cannot imagine that any serious intellectual would consider the Quechua oral tradition as a primary source for the construction of a modern Peruvian literature. Arguedas writes intuitively, he believes, without the benefit of modern technologies of writing, and without a sophisticated literary knowledge. In essence, Vargas Llosa takes Arguedas's autobiographical representations at face value, thus enabling him to minimize, in the guise of paternalistic approval, Arguedas's achievement. From this view Arguedas is a primitive writer whose accomplishment is due to his personal experience and "intuition."

In contrast, I believe that it is crucial to make a distinction, as Alberto Escobar has done, between the sociolinguistic dynamics of Peruvian heteroglossia and Arguedas's intrepid experiment at writing across languages. In addition, Arguedas's life story must be viewed critically in terms of its place and function within what is in fact a fascinating, and tremendously complex, literary endeavor. In my view translation, in texts like *Deep Rivers* and *Yawar Fiesta*, is an intricate, textual mediation not an intuitive or transparent form of representation.

Quechua Knowledge

One of the most important aspects of Arguedas's endeavor is that he takes the Quechua oral tradition quite seriously as literary source material. Several critics have underscored Arguedas's intellectual indebtedness to that tradition, especially in terms of the language, and organizational logic, of his narrative fiction.[18] Arguedas himself clearly articulates his intellectual indebtedness to Quechua sources in his polemic with Julio Cortázar in the diaries of *El zorro de arriba y el zorro de abajo*.[19] What distinguishes his "provincialism" from Cortazar's "cosmopolitanism" is not modern versus antiquated technologies of writing—although Arguedas has some anxiety that he should know even more than he does of "modern" techniques—but a difference in perspective. In the first place, he denies absolutely the superiority of what we might call the anthropological viewpoint, that of the observer overlooking the other's experience:

> . . . this Cortázar, so annoyingly good-natured, with his solemn conviction that the essence of national reality can be best understood

from the elevated realm of the supernatural. As if I, raised among Felipe Maywa's people, placed in the very *oqllo* [breast] of the Indians during part of my childhood, and later returned to the realm of the "super-Indian" from which I had "descended" to live among the Quechua, were to say that I understood better, that I interpreted more essentially Don Felipe's spirit and his yearnings than Don Felipe himself. A complete lack of respect, an illegitimate lack of consideration! It cannot be justified. . . . [Arguedas 1983, 5:22]

Here Arguedas clearly distinguishes his own viewpoint from that of don Felipe Mawya. At the same time he fiercely defends the "provincial" character of his intellectual trajectory, whose heterogeneous sources make it distinct from, but not inferior to, the knowledge of urban, cosmopolitan writers.

> Are we so different, those of us who have served as food for the lice in San Juan de Lucanas or in El Sexto, are we so different than Lezama Lima or Vargas Llosa? We're not different in terms of what I was thinking when I spoke of "provincials." We are all provincials, Sir Julio (Cortázar). Provincials of a nation or of the supernatural, which is also a realm, a constricted domain. . . . [ibid., 28]

Later, in the "tercer Diario" of *El zorro* he clarifies his point of view further.

> Sir Julio has tried to reprimand and to ridicule me, he's so pissed off because I say in the first diary of this book, and I will say it again now, that I am a provincial, that I have learned less from books than I have from the differences I have felt and seen between a cricket and a Quechua dignitary, between an ocean fisherman and a fisherman from Titicaca. . . . *And this knowledge has, of course, just as much as book knowledge, its realms and its depths.* [ibid., 144; emphasis mine]

What is striking about this passage, as well as the ones I quoted earlier, is Arguedas's strident defense of the presence of a legitimate and significant "knowledge" in the heart of his intellectual endeavor, whose origins lie in rural, Quechua oral culture. What he rejects most vehemently is the notion that this knowledge is inferior to, or less valuable than the knowledge associated with writing and the city.

"Huk doctorkunaman qayay"

In a 1966 poem, "Huk doctorkunaman qayay" (Address to certain intellectuals), written for an implied Quechua reader, Arguedas stridently defends Quechua knowledge against that of the "doctors" (see Arguedas 1983, 5:252–56). This text provides additional testimony which confirms Arguedas's intellectual commitment to Quechua sources and knowledge.

> Manas imatapas yachaniñachu, atrasus kayku; huk
> umawansi umaykuta kutichinqaku.
> Manas sonqoykupas allinchu; ancha mancharisqas, nisiu
> weqeyuqsi, waqaq tuyapa hina, nakasqa turupa
> hinas; chaysi mana allinchu.
> Huk ducturkunas chayta nin; kikin allpanchikpi miraq,
> wirayaq, qilluyaq ducturkuna.
> Nichkachunku ya, hinata nichkallachunku.

> [They say that I know nothing, that I am backward, that
> they must replace my head with another.
> They say too that my heart is weak, that I am too
> afraid, that I am full of tears like a suffering
> dove, they disapprove of me, saying I am as unruly
> as a decapitated bull.
> This is what some doctors are saying, doctors who are
> advancing themselves upon our earth, fattening
> themselves, turning yellow.
> Let them talk, let them say what they want.] [ibid., 5:252][20]

The narrator, addressing a Quechua reader, raises his voice against the imperial knowledge of the "doctors" who imagine Quechua-speakers as ignorant, backward, and chaos-producing. This construction of the Quechua "other" is based on fear.

¡Ama ayqewaychikchu, ducturkuna, asuykamuychik!
Qawaykuway, wayqechay; maykamataq suyasqayki.
Asuykamuy, oqariway helicopteruykipa oqllunkama.
   Noqañataq waranqa clase qorakunapa kallpachasqa
   suminwan kallpachasqayki.
Ancha ritimanta ukumari wayqokunakama waranqa waranqa
   watapi mirachisqay kausaykunawan.
Titi saykuynikita hanpisaq, pachak kinua waytapa
   kanchariyninwan, sumaq kuyakuq tusuchayninwan;
   tuyapa lirpu sunqunwan; qapariq mayupa, manchachiq
   yana qaqapa sunqunmanta chuya takikuq yaku urqusqaywan.

[Do not flee, doctors, do not be frightened!
Look at me, little brother; how much longer must I wait
   for you.
Come closer, lift me into the embrace of your
   helicopter. I will restore you with the sap of a
   thousand herbs whose lives I have watched for
   thousands of years, from the high snows to the
   warm valleys of the bear.
I will heal your leaden weariness with the light from a
   thousand flowering quinua, dancing on the air,
   stroking my hidden valleys; with the heart of the
   contented doves; with the perfect water that I
   bring singing from the river's heart, crashing its
   way down the canyons that frighten all creatures
   with their darkness. . . .] [ibid., 254]

The narrator addresses the "doctors," who are outside the discursive loop of the text, indicating that it is "fear" that has prevented them from understanding Quechua speakers, or sharing with them their modern technology. The request to be lifted into the helicopter is not a desire to be assimilated. With a proud sense of identity the narrator, speaking from "thousands of years" of accumulated knowledge, offers in exchange to "heal" the doctors, who in their greed, their ignorance and their fear have become destroyers. He suggests the possible complementarity of the technical knowledge of the "doctors" and the human and ecological knowledge of Quechua speakers.

The function of autobiography in Arguedas's work is to legitimize (to a Spanish reader) his access to, and use or translation of, Quechua knowledge and Quechua forms within his texts. In contrast, in "Huk doctorkunaman qayay" the narrator addresses a Quechua interlocutor with whom he shares understandings and perceptions that are belittled and persecuted by the "doctors." The poem translates *for a Quechua reader* the knowledge of the "doctors" by underscoring its limitations and its misunderstandings and thereby demythologizing its terrible power.

"Carnaval en Tambobamba"

How are we to understand the function and place of autobiography in Arguedas's writings if we question the legitimating image he creates of himself—and which many critics have reiterated—as a writer who writes or "translates" directly from his experience? An article Arguedas wrote in 1942 for *La Prensa* in Buenos Aires, entitled "Carnaval de Tambobamba," may provide the beginnings of an answer. To my mind this article is one of the finest pieces of prose Arguedas ever wrote. The essay moves musically, like the carnival song that is translated within it, orchestrating the visual and aural elements of the place, the people and, finally, the carnival celebration itself. The narrator begins by describing the Tambobamba valley and the Apurimac River, which runs through it. From the pueblo

> one cannot see the river, but its deep and eternal song covers everything. It is in the heart of the people who live in the valley, in their minds, their memories, their loves and their tears; it is beneath the

breasts of the songbirds who populate the cornfields, the forests, and the underbrush, beside the streams that flow from the great river; it is in tree branches that also sing in the dawn breezes; the river's voice is what is essential, the poetry and the mystery, the sky and the earth, in these valleys so deep, so untamed, and so beautiful. [Arguedas 1985a, 152]

The narrator moves on to summarize the valley's history, and then hones in on his central theme: the yearly carnival which is celebrated in the town of Tambobamba. He reviews the history of the carnival, describes its current celebration, and translates the carnival song. The impact of the song on the participants-listeners (among whom the narrator includes himself) is reminiscent of Ernesto's response, in *Los ríos profundos*, to the *huaynos* he hears in the *chicherías* of Abancay.

This song inspires a boundless desperation, a sadness that is born with all the force of the soul. It is like an overwhelming desire to brawl and to lose oneself, as if night's darkness, impelled by the river's deep voice, had taken possession of *our* consciousness, singing without stopping, each time with more dread and more anguish. It is an unleashing of sadness and courage. All the essence of human life shaken with an impassioned violence within our sensitive inner world. Those who do not speak Quechua listen to the song with great seriousness and they can guess the tragedy and cruelty of its content. [ibid., 154; emphasis mine]

The narrator's authority comes from two sources. He speaks from experience as a witness and participant whose voice articulates the perspective of a "nosotros" (we). At the same time he translates that experience for "those who do not speak Quechua." In fact the reader's access to the carnival, and to the emotion of the song, is literally through the narrator's translation, both in the Spanish version of the song *and* in the interpretation that follows. The implied reader, like the non-Quechua listener, hears the music and guesses "todo lo trágico y cruel que es su contenido" (all that is tragic and cruel in its content) because the translator's language has so moved him. Astonishingly, the last paragraph of the article reads:

> I hope to reach Tambobamba, to arrive in the town, and to sing [the carnival song] in the plaza, in chorus with the people from the valley, with fifty guitars and drums, listening to the voice of the great river mixed together with the song, which is its truest fruit, its insides, its living image, its human voice, charged with pain and fury, better and more powerful than its own river-voice, enormous river that has cut a thousand leagues of channel through solid stone. [ibid., 155]

In fact, the translator has not been to Tambobamba. He has never seen the valley. He has never participated in the carnival. His represented status as participant is part desire, part imagination. What does he translate? His authority to speak is not grounded, as it appeared to be, in the "experience" of an insider. On the contrary, the ultimate legitimacy and truth of his description-translation seems to reside, magically, in the lyrical power of his voice. Like the reverberating river Apurímac, whose voice animates all life in the valley, the narrator's voice gives life to the world he names. His ability to mediate the incommensurable distance that separates the world of Tambobamba and the world of the reader is founded on the magical power of language not on his status as insider.

The lesson we learn from "Carnaval de Tambobamba" is that in Arguedas's work autobiography legitimates a story, told lyrically, but it is does not make the story a form of unmediated testimony. The situation is much more complex, and much more interesting, than that. Arguedas is not, as Vargas Llosa sees him, a nostalgic, intuitive writer who writes directly from his own "experience" as a Quechua-speaking Andean. Instead, autobiography legitimates an appropriation and translation of the Quechua oral tradition—of Quechua knowledge—for the purposes of an intellectually sophisticated, and unequivocally modern literary practice.

Notes

1. Georg Simmel describes the modern "stranger," like the Arguedean *forastero* who serves as mediator-translator, as possessed of a heterogeneous consciousness that is the product of simultaneous "nearness and remoteness." While his experience is fragmented, at the same time, as a "character of mobility," his position affords him a privileged perspective (Simmel 1950, 402–8).

2. All English translations of Spanish and Quechua texts quoted in this article are my own unless otherwise noted.

3. This involves more than simply integrating Quechua lexicon into Spanish. Over the course of his life Arguedas conducts an extraordinary experiment with form that involves *translating*, in the literal sense of moving from one place to another, oral genres such as songs, tales, and myths, as well as mythical uses of language, into the structure of *literary* genres such as the novel, the short story, and the essay. The active, and to varying degrees subversive, presence of these elements within the structure of Arguedas's texts, with several exceptions, has not received the critical attention it deserves. The question of style in Arguedas is complex specifically because of the tense, dialogic relationship in his texts with an implied reader who may regard the presence of Quechua orality within his writing as strange and even unintelligible. Arguedas's poetry in Quechua, as well as the radical subversion of the form of the novel in his posthumous *The Fox from Above and the Fox from Below (El zorro de arriba y el zorro de abajo)* must be seen in part as the response to the at least incipient possibility of a literate Andean reading public as a result of bulging urban populations of Andeans and the consequent Andeanization of the coast. See Martin Lienhard 1981 for an enlightening analysis of the presence of Andean forms and Andean readers in *El zorro*.

4. Ortiz questioned the term *acculturation* because, according to him, it failed to account for the complexity of the process of cultural change in Cuba (and in all of Latin America). In these contexts culture was not only being "acquired" (acculturation) but also lost. Moreover, most important, new cultural phenomena were being created. Thus he proposed the alternative term *transculturation* in order to try to account for the complexity of

these three phases of cultural change. Ortiz's accent on the hybridity of Cuban culture, its original character as a product of the mix of African and European elements, was certainly an influential model in the context of nascent Peruvian anthropology during the late 1940s and 1950s for anthropologists like Luis E. Valcárcel, José Matos Mar, and Arguedas who were studying and writing about similar issues. Moreover, the active dimension of selection and transformation that characterizes "transculturation" gave Arguedas a conceptual tool with which to explain, defend, and promote the hybrid character of his style. Indeed, it is as an anthropologist that he describes, in his famous 1950 "La novela y el problema de la expresión literaria en el Perú" (1950), the mestizo writer's search for an adequate literary form not as a superficial question of "style" but rather as a problem of culture. See Fernando Ortiz 1978.

5. "Literature operated . . . like *a model in miniature of transculturation,* where one would be able to show and to prove the eventuality of its realization in the sense that if it were possible in literature it could also be possible in the rest of culture" (Rama 1982, 202; emphasis mine).

6. In the following section I have preferred to supply my own translations of the quotations from *Deep Rivers* because the published English language version of the novel is, in my view, inadequate. Interested readers can refer to Arguedas 1978, 71–75.

7. The term "autobiographical space" comes from Phillip Lejeune who uses it to refer to the way some writers extend the "autobiographical pact" to the whole of what they have written, especially their fiction. In these cases it is neither the specific autobiography nor the works of fiction that compose the autobiographical space, but rather the relationship between them. "What becomes revealing is the space in which the two categories of texts [autobiography and fiction] are inscribed, and which is reducible to neither of the two. The effect of contrast obtained by this procedure is the creation, for the reader, of an "autobiographical space" (Lejeune 1989, 27).

8. Boris Tomasevskij comments, "There are writers with biographies and writers without biographies . . . for a writer with a biography, the facts of the author's life must be taken into consideration. Indeed, in the works themselves the juxtaposition of the texts and the author's biography plays a structural role. The literary work plays on the potential reality of the author's subjective outpourings and confessions. Thus the biography that is useful to the literary historian is not the author's curriculum vitae or the in-

vestigator's account of his life. What the literary historian really needs is the biographical legend created by the author himself. Only such a legend is a literary fact" (Tomasevskij 1978, 55).

9. For biographical details see Merino de Zela 1970.

10. For the most complete description of the stepmother and stepbrother see Narradores Peruanos 1986, 36–38. Also, the character of the brutal, and sexually perverse, *gamonal* (cacique) in "El horno viejo" is modeled after the stepbrother. See Arguedas 1983, 1:221–27.

11. "I was a monolingual Quechua speaker; I lived during my infancy and childhood in many towns within the immense area in which what Alfredo Torero calls Quechua II is spoken" (Arguedas 1968, 84). In the prologue to the 1954 version of *Agua*, Arguedas writes that the book contains "two works written by a man who learned to speak in Quechua. *Agua* was published nineteen years ago, when the author had entered the university and was still, substantially, a Quechua" (Arguedas 1983, 1:76).

12. In an interview in 1966, Arguedas declares similarly, "I felt an immense love for the Indians, because they protected me like a father, like a mother; I learned their songs, their games. I lived in their world. I believed that everything was divine, that the river was a god, that the mountains were gods. In that way until I was ten years old my childhood was that of an indigenous boy. Today I believe I still retain that indigenous vision of the world" (Christian 1983, 222).

13. The second edition of *Agua*, published along with *Diamantes y pedernales* in 1954, was accompanied by a prologue entitled "Algunos datos acerca de estas novelas" (A few facts about the novels), which is essentially a version of "La novela y el problema de la expresión literaria en el Perú." Likewise, Arguedas uses a revised version of "La novela y el problema" as the prologue for the 1968 republication of *Yawar Fiesta*. See the notes in José María Arguedas 1983, vols. 1 and 2, for details on these editions.

14. Before the 1960s critical reception of Arguedas consists of newspaper reviews in Peru of his various publications. It isn't until the 1960s that Arguedas begins to be included in anthologies of Latin American literature; at the same time Sebastián Salazar Bondy, Julio Ortega, Alberto Escobar, and others write the first literary essays about Arguedas. Although a history of the critical reception of Arguedas is outside the scope of this essay, it seems to me that two factors are crucial for understanding his rise to prominence during this period: the Argentine publication of his work by Alejandro

Losada, and his positive reception (and dissemination) in postrevolutionary Cuba.

15. The specific autobiographical statements that critics and scholars most often cite can be found in: Arguedas 1950; Narradores Peruanos 1986, 36–43; and Castro-Klarén 1975.

16. ". . . in Arguedas's work one finds a rejection (visceral, irrational, but obvious) of progress, of the very idea of progress" (Vargas Llosa 1981, xiii).

17. Alberto Flores Galindo has emphasized the complexity of Arguedas's intellectual endeavor in contrast to the primitivist image promoted by Vargas Llosa and others. In a 1988 talk he commented, ". . . I am not going to speak about Arguedas as the little Indian man; on the contrary, I am going to speak. . . about an author who has left us a complex work, who is not an elemental or primitive writer, but rather, despite the fact that he represents himself as completely spontaneous, has reflected a lot more than he suggests or supposes about his problems, and moreover who has read much more than he admits . . ." (Flores Galindo 1990, 18).

18. See, for example, Rama 1982 and Lienhard 1981.

19. Arguedas, in his "primer diario," which he published separately in *Amaru*, no. 6 (1968): 42–49, criticized statements by Cortázar to the effect that a "supernational" perspective sometimes sharpened a writer's sense of the essence of the "national." Subsequently, Cortázar, in an interview with *Life en español*, defended his position, somewhat angrily, and criticized Arguedas's self-declared "provincialism." See Cortázar 1969.

20. Elsewhere, this poem has been partially translated into English by Regina Harrison and John Murra. See Harrison 1989, 189 and Murra 1978, xiii–xv.

Works Cited

Arguedas, José María. 1950. "La novela y el problema de la expresión literaria en el Perú" (The novel and the problem of literary expression in Peru). *Mar del Sur* 3, no. 9: 66–72.

———. 1966. "La literatura como testimonio y como contribución" (Literature as testimony and as contribution). In *José María Arguedas*. Lima: Editorial Juan Mejía Baca.

———. 1968. "Acerca de una valiosísima colección de cuentos quechuas"

(Concerning a most valuable collection of Quechua stories). *Amaru*, no. 8: 84.

———. 1976. "La narrativa en el Perú contemporáneo" (Narrative in contemporary Peru). In *Recopilación de textos sobre José María Arguedas* (Compilation of texts about José María Arguedas), ed. Juan Larco, 407–20. Havana: Casa de las Américas.

———. 1978. *Deep Rivers*. Trans. Frances Horning Barraclough. Austin: University of Texas Press.

———. 1983. *Obras completas* (Complete works). 5 vols. Lima: Editorial Horizonte.

———. 1985a. "Carnaval en Tambobamba" (Carnival in Tambobamba). In *Indios, mestizos y señores* (Indians, mestizos, and lords), 151–55. Lima: Editorial Horizonte.

———. 1985b. *Yawar Fiesta*. Trans. Frances Horning Barraclough. Austin: University of Texas Press.

Castro-Klarén, Sara. 1975. "José María Arguedas, sobre preguntas de Sara Castro Klarén" (José María Arguedas, on questions from Sara Castro Klarén). *Hispania* 10:45–54.

Christian, Chester. 1983. "Alrededor de este nudo de la vida: Entrevista con José María Arguedas" (Concerning this problem called life: An interview with José María Arguedas). *Revista iberoamericana*, no. 122: 221–34.

Cortázar, Julio. 1969. "Un gran escritor y su soledad" (A great writer in his solitude). *Life en español* 33, no. 7: 44–55.

Flores Galindo, Alberto. 1990. "Los últimos años de Arguedas (intelectuales, sociedad e identidad en el Perú)" (Arguedas's final years: Intellectuals, society, and identity in Peru). *Literaturas andinas* 2, no. 3–4: 17–35.

Forgues, Roland. 1991. "El mito del monolingüismo quechua de Arguedas" (The myth of Arguedas's Quechua monolingualism). In *José María Arguedas: Vida y obra* (José María Arguedas: Life and work), ed. Hildebrando Pérez and Carlos Garayar, 47–58. Lima: Amaru Editores.

Harrison, Regina. 1989. *Signs, Songs, and Memory in the Andes: Translating Quechua Language and Culture*. Austin: University of Texas Press.

Larco, Juan. 1976. Prologue to *Recopilación de textos sobre José María Arguedas*, ed. Juan Larco, 7–20. Havana: Casa de las Américas.

Lejeune, Phillip. 1989. *On Autobiography*. Translated by Katherine Leary. Minneapolis: University of Minnesota Press.

Lienhard, Martin. 1981. *Cultura andina y forma novelesca: Zorros y danzantes en la última novela de Arguedas* (Andean culture and novelistic form: Foxes and minstrels in Arguedas's last novel). Lima: Editorial Horizonte.

Merino de Zela, E. Mildred. 1970. "Vida y obra de José María Arguedas" (Life and work of José María Arguedas). *Revista peruana de cultura*, no. 13–14: 127–78.

Muñoz, Braulio. 1982. "Indian of the Heart." *Américas* 32, no. 3: 25–29.

Murra, John. 1978. Introduction to *Deep Rivers* by José María Arguedas. Austin: University of Texas Press.

Narradores peruanos (Peruvian writers). 1983. "*Los ríos profundos*, ópera de pobres" (*Deep Rivers*, opera of the people). *Revista iberoamericana* 44, no. 122: 11–41.

———. 1986. "Primer encuentro de narradores peruanos" (First Meeting of Peruvian writers). Proceedings of a conference sponsored by the Casa de la Cultura de Arequipa, 1965. Lima: Latinoamericana Editores.

Ortiz, Fernando. 1978. *Contrapunteo cubano del tabaco y el azúcar* (Cuban counterpoint, tobacco and sugar). Caracas: Bibilioteca Ayacucho.

Rama, Angel. 1982. *Transculturación narrativa en América Latina* (Narrative transculturation in Latin America). Mexico City: Siglo XXI Editores.

Rouillón, José. 1979. "Arguedas y la idea del Perú" (Arguedas and the idea of Peru). In *Perú: Identidad nacional* (Peru: National identity), ed. César Arróspide de la Flor, 379–402. Lima: Centro de Estudios para el Desarrollo y la Participación.

Simmel, Georg. 1950. *The Sociology of Georg Simmel*. Trans. and ed. Kurt H. Wolff. Glencoe, Ill.: Free Press.

Tomasevskij, Boris. 1978. "Literature and Biography." In *Readings in Russian Poetics: Formalist and Structuralist Views*, ed. Ladislav Matejka and Krystyna Pomorska, 47–55. Ann Arbor: Michigan Slavic Publications.

Vargas Llosa, Mario. 1974. "Consideraciones sobre narrativa" (Considerations on narrative). *Insula*, no. 332–333: 8–10.

———. 1981. "Arguedas, entre la ideología y la arcadia" (Arguedas, between ideology and utopia). *Revista iberoamericana*, no. 116–17: 33–46.

Arguedas, the Quechua Poet, and Recent Quechua Poetry[1]

Martin Lienhard

Introduction

It is well known that José María Arguedas's fame stems from his prose narratives, and especially from *Los ríos profundos* (Deep rivers, 1958).His ethnographic and socioanthropological work was "discovered" much later. His poetry, however, has yet to receive adequate critical attention. With very few exceptions (Cornejo Polar 1976), no one has publicly considered its value, and the most common critical attitude to his poetry has been silence. To what can we attribute the long period that this part of Arguedas's work spent in limbo? There are two principal reasons: on the one hand, the non-European language in which the poems are written, and on the other, perhaps even more important, the difficulties of situating such work within the panorama of Peruvian and Latin American written poetry.

As well as in other fields of literature and social science in Peru, José María Arguedas was a pioneer in modern Quechua poetry. It is true that there had been *mistis* (the former Andean upper classes) such as Alencaster or Meneses who wrote in Quechua before and at the same time as Arguedas, but their influence has proved insignificant on the trend inaugurated by Arguedas in 1962 with "Túpac Amaru kamaq taytanchisman: - Haylli taki" (To our father-creator Túpac Amaru: A song of triumph) ["Katatay," 1983, 223–233], a trend currently represented by the work of authors such as Eduardo Nina-mango Mallqui (*Pukutay*, 1982), Dida Aguirre ("Poemas quechuas," 1983), and Isaac Huamán Manrique ("Nanay," "Taytachallay," "Qamuy," "Llaqtaysi," n.d.). Most of these poems may presently be found in the first existing anthology of Peruvian written Quechua poetry (Noriega Bernuy 1993). It is to this latest poetic trend that the current essay is addressed .

Written Quechua poetry has, in fact, existed since the beginning of the colonial period. The *qarawi* (celebratory musical composition), somewhat "disturbed" by foreign elements, and to which Felipe Guamán Poma de Ayala refers in his sixteenth-century chronicle (1980, 317–19), may be said to constitute an isolated example of an inaugural practice still close to the traditional oral poetry of the Incas. More systematic, however, was the production of Catholic hymns in Quechua by generally anonymous colonial churchmen (Arguedas 1955); in these texts numerous formal elements of Inca origin are integrated into poetic Christian discourse. In the eighteenth and early nineteenth centuries the *qarawis* contained in the anonymous dramatic work *Ollantay* (1958) and in the notably Hispanicized poems of Wallparrimachi (1979) bear witness to the existence of "polished" Quechua poetry written by certain members of aristocratic sectors of Andean society. In more recent times, *mistis*, especially in Cuzco, have enthusiastically endeavored to keep alive this written tradition of "polished" Quechua verse. Their literary aesthetic, however, even in the work of their best representative, Andrés Alencastre Gutiérrez (1955), demonstrates a notable lack of connection with the living foci of Quechua culture: the discursive cosmos of Andean peasants and their descendants, and poor mestizos. Edmundo Bendezú has said of Alencastre's work that it is in a high-flown literary language, at times difficult, if not impossible, to reach from the lowly ground of spoken

Quechua (1986). The *misti* tradition of writing Quechua poetry can be categorized as the "low" norm—not much more than a "pastime"—within the diglossic cultural system of this former aristocratic group now in full decadence. It is only when an intense dialogue with contemporary foci of Quechua culture is reached, as in the poems of Porfirio Meneses (1988), that such verse can be said to be anything but a petrified cultural inheritance.

The development of a new Quechua poetry coincides with what Jesús Barquero has called "the great torrent of mobilization taking place in the countryside" (1980) and with the profound modifications of the relationships between the Quechua communities and global society in general. The Quechua peasant communities in the Andes are invaded by the mercantile capitalist economy and by formal education, while at the same time Quechua speakers from the Andes are inundating the cities, especially the capital, even turning urban metropolitan space into quasi-agglomerations of Andean villages.

It is within this modern urban context, and not in the earlier Quechua tradition of the *mistis* that, little by little, a written Quechua poetry is emerging that has little or nothing in common with contemporary Peruvian poetry in the Spanish language. Neither does it follow the tradition of sung poems. This poetry, while still marginal and seeking its public outside the zones dominated by orality, could, according to political and cultural options now coming into force, become one of the significant expressions of those urban social groups that are of Andean origin. Until now, however, the obstacles impeding wider development of this practice appear to have formed a vicious circle: few authors and few editors will take the risk of producing or editing a poetry that, they assume, will have few readers. The readers are few because, among other reasons, publications of these works lack continuity. The fundamental obstacle, however, is the ostracism of the Quechua language within the Peruvian educational system; as long as it forms no part of the literacy program and remains apart from the linguistic and literary education of young people, neither a consistently creative group of writers nor a mass reading public can be expected to exist for Quechua.

I shall now attempt, starting with the analysis of certain privileged aspects, to outline the fundamental characteristics of this new type of Peruvian poetry, for which the poem "Túpac Amaru kamaq taytanchisman" by Arguedas (1983, 223–33), in every respect a "manifesto poem," will be used as a paradigm of analysis.

The Poetic Speaker

In Arguedas's poem, mentioned above, a poetic speaker of collective characteristics addresses a divine or deified being: Túpac Amaru. Now, if Túpac Amaru is the syntactic addressee of the poem, the "message" of the poem is directed toward the persons making up the collective "we." Quite unlike the subjective "I" typical of modern Western poetry, the pronoun used is the Quechua "exclusive" first person plural, *ñoqayku*, or "we alone." Although it is somewhat indistinct at first, the exact "personality" of this "exclusive we" becomes clearer as the poem progresses: it refers to the vast number of Quechua-speaking migrants who have settled on the coast, the most active portion of a "we" that includes all oppressed groups of the Quechua-speaking population, and especially the Andean peasants. Thus, the poetic speaker coincides "sociologically" with the most likely possible public, the one most familiar with reading. That sector is revealed as the one with the best qualities to represent all Quechua speakers, for those who have stayed behind in their Andean communities and for those who moved to the cities. Their sector's memory, in fact, encompasses the entire historical Andean experience: that of living in the Quechua-speaking communities in the rural areas and also that of living in the modern megalopolis.

In the poems by the three contemporary writers mentioned, the poetic speaker's voice assumes various grammatical forms, all of them different from the exclusive first person plural of Arguedas. Dida Aguirre opts for *ñoqanchik*, "all of us," the "inclusive" first person plural, grammatically addressed to itself. Semantically speaking, however, the very active "we" speaks to a more passive addressee, "us." Defined without sociological precision, the collective entity encompassed by both first person plural forms is that of the poor or marginal *(waqchakuna)*: those who are exploited, those who wish to reinforce or return to that intimate relationship with mother-earth *(mama pacha allpachallanchik)*, with the plants and the stones—a relationship that is threatened by the *mistis*. In *Pukutay* (1982) by Ninamango Mallqui, "we" is also inclusive, *ñoqanchik*, a combination of an "I" and a second person singular ("you" in a collective sense). Here "I" and "you" represent, respectively, the active and passive poles of "we": "... listen, brother, it is not the time for weeping" *(. . .wauqey uyariy, manañas wakay punchauñachu)* says the first speaker to his interlocuter. Both are characterized by their connection with the earth *(allpa)*, although this relationship is not as intense as in Aguirre's work. Finally, Huamán Manrique always employs an "I" that is totally impersonal and, in semantic terms, a collective entity—only here the collectivity is more abstract and not characterized by its relationship to the earth: it is "Quechua" or "Andean" in a generic sense. To sum up: the solutions chosen by the three young poets in the construction of the poetic voice are grammatically different, one from another and from that of Arguedas, but converge in their semantic purpose: the sender and addressee of the message are a collective entity that, like any collective entity, is subdivided into segments that are unequally "active" or "aware." It is remarkable, however, that none of these poems, however, unlike Arguedas's, pinpoints the poetic speaker with sociological precision. It is as if sufficient complicity now existed between the poetic speaker and his addressee for such characterization to become superfluous.

Forms of Poetic Exposition

As indicated by its subtitle *(Haylli taki)*, Arguedas's poem explicitly revindicates the tradition of the *qaylli,* a triumphal song in honor of a victorious Inca, or a harvest song, as it still survives today. The repercussion of scornful sentences that are usually directed to adversaries in ritual Andean battle is particularly manifest in the discoursive violence. This entire "triumphalist" tradition competes in the poem with the tradition of Incan hymns to the divinity Wiraqocha. Thus, in the poem, two types of discourse alternate: the more lyrical voice of invocation and the other affirming triumph in violent terms. Regarding metrics, the poem does not fit that of Quechua song. A tape made by Arguedas himself confirms that it is in relatively free verse and its effect lies in rhythmic repetition of certain syntactic constructions or combinations of suffixes. Far from imitating the oral form of Quechua song, and equally removed from the traditions of creole poetry, it attempts, in its poetics, to explore a virtually new terrain, although it walks a path traced by avant-garde poetry in European languages.

The Quechua employed by Arguedas in his poems is also a type previously unheard-of. Basically oral and contemporary, far removed from the "Incaic" purism of Cuzco *misti* poetry, it combines traits from the Quechua dialects of both the Cuzco and the Chanka (Huancavelica-Ayacucho) regions. The morphology is mainly from the Cuzco region; phonetically, it is fundamentally Chanka, while the lexicon moves about freely in both dialectal areas. Arguedas has invented, so to speak, a literary Quechua language that is both "artificial" and deeply rooted in oral language. His poem, in this regard, is a serious candidate for a future Quechua literary language, as distant from the "imperial Quechua" norm as it is from any dialectical norm.

The three young poets, for their part, explore different forms, but all are related to those used by Arguedas. Dida Aguirre comes closest, in both her poetic grammar and use of images, to the forms of oral

Quechua song. Each one of her poems begins with the traditional invocation of the cosmic element: the fire flower, the *waranway* bush, the hawk. The dominant traits are those of traditional song: synonymic repetition, as in *ripukullasunña / pasakullasunña* (we shall go / we shall leave); syntactic parallelism as in *purun rumipi / pata pukrupi* (in the wild stone / on the terrace in the hole); repetition by syntagmatic inversion, as in *ripukullasunña–pasakullasunña / pasasunña–ripukullasunña* (we shall go–we shall leave / we shall leave–we shall go). Also typical of the oral songs is the brevity of rhythmic units, which, for the main part, are pentasyllabic. If many of these elements can be seen as "traditional," the form of the poems as a whole, far from imitating that of the oral songs, must be considered new.

Ninamango Mallqui's poetic style (poetics) is "freer" with regard to oral tradition and difficult to place within any codified tradition, although it doubtless bears the mark of the creole poetic avant-garde. Although syntactic parallelisms are not absent, they are often swallowed up in a type of discourse that, if we departed from the graphic presentation of verse, it would lean toward a "Western" use of hyperbaton (inversion of idiomatic word order). Like Arguedas's poem, Mallqui's work might be seen as an example of poetic prose, in free rhythm but with marked cadence; however, Mallqui's prose poems, unlike the example by Arguedas, do not tend to be narrative in nature.

At least two of the poems by Huamán Manrique, "Taytachallay" and "Qamuy," can be broadly considered as falling within the notoriously syncretic Hispano-Quechua tradition of Catholic Quechua hymns. His message, however, is not one of supposed insertion within a tradition, but is, rather, a "subversion" of tradition: in these poems, in fact, an Andean perspective recuperates control of the text in its entirety. The other two poems that we have mentioned by this poet are "Nanay" and "Llaqtaysi," the latter being of a narrative nature, while the former has poetic recourse to paradigmatic associations. In all the poems, Huamán Manrique works within a more regular meter than Ninamango, though his poetic grammar does not approximate that of Quechua song. The literary language used by the three poets is based on the present-day Chanka variety of Quechua.

The World Evoked

The worlds evoked by these variants of poetic discourse all stress a situation of historical emergence; the collective "we," aided by a "superior force," launches the decisive offensive against its "main enemy."

HISTORICAL EMERGENCE

A growing revolution, both social and cosmic, forms the narrative axis of Arguedas's poem,that does not document this great event so much as form part of it. "We," that is to say, the Quechua people, reconquer, in the form of an avalanche *(lloqlla),* their lands *(allpa),* their towns *(llaqta),* and all four parts of their world *(lliu tawantin suyo)*; the country of the Quechua viewed as instrument of production, social organization, and political entity. Victory over their oppressors is no longer a dream, but a fact as inevitable as day following night, and *pacha-wara,* the morrow of the world, is, along with *pacha-tikray,* cosmic revolution, one of the concepts that name the event evoked in the poem. Such concepts are related to that of *pacha-kutiy*—translatable as "sociocosmic revolution" that, according to the traditional Andean viewpoint, will right the world that is now turned upside down. *Revolution*, then, to some extent implies a return to a better past. In the case of Arguedas's poem, it is clearly indicated at the end that no tabula rasa is intended, but rather the reorganizing, thanks to guidelines taken from the past, of the world as it now exists. The choice of Túpac Amaru as the entity evoked has similar implications. The figure assimilates that of *Pacha-kamaq,* the supposed Andean creator god, whose function was not to create the world ex nihilo, but to set it in order. The very mass of the dispossessed will now be the agent that fulfills this function. Contrary to the worlds evoked in the more recent poems, Arguedas's is markedly "historical." The decisive stages of modern Andean history appear within it, if not exactly in chronological order: the conquest; the colonial period; Túpac Amaru's insurrection; the offensive launched by the landowners during the nineteenth and early twentieth centuries, known as the second conquest; and the radical transformation that is taking place in the contemporary period, namely, the exodus from the rural areas and the "andeanization" of the capital, and so on.

As in Arguedas's poem, the "event" evoked by Ninamango Mallqui, Huamán Manrique, and Aguirre takes the form of a social cataclysm of cosmic dimensions that is either already underway or imminent. Its historical characterization, however, is far more diffuse.

In the "Quechua Poems" by Dida Aguirre, the one who unleashes the cataclysm is no other than the very same collective "we," a particularly active "we," perfectly identifiable with the natural cosmos. This provoked cataclysm of sociocosmic dimensions is a response to a situation of oppression and unbearable exploitation. Its program will be to reestablish the union with mother-earth that existed at the time of the "gentiles," when Andean autonomy reigned. Its resources are collective force, guaranteed by the intensity of its links with sierra space.

The very title of Ninamango's collection, *Pukutay* (Storm), announces the tone of the poems. Indeed, "the heart of the earth trembles" *(pachapa sonqonsi kununununchkan)* and the *wamani* (contemporary mountain gods) in the Chanka area (Huancavelica-Ayacucho) are making the earth, trees, and stones dance *(pachatapas sachakunatapas rumikunatas tusuchichkanku)*. Within this generalized cataclysm, the voices of the "ancestors" of the mighty past are heard, and, as in Arguedas's poem, it is announced that the land *(allpa)* will once again belong to "us"—to the Andean peasants.

In Huamán Manrique's hardly denotative poems, the "event" as well as the "enemy" are not named directly. The current cosmic havoc will bring about, or is bringing about, an equally cosmic response: in "Llaqtaysi," "the mountain of the sun is opening its heart" *(ñas intipa orqonnin / sunqunta kichachkan)*, while in "Taytachallay," the aid of a superior force is invoked to make the world tremble *(kuyuchiy kay pachata)*. But the "cosmic" response, given Andean cosmic conceptions, is also that of the people. The collective, "cosmic" poetic speaker in "Nanay" will bring about a powerful brilliance, and, in "Llaqtaysi," the joy of the children is also the joy of the mountains *(kusirikuchkankul orqokunawan kuska)*. As with the previous poems, the "event" evoked in these continues to be the socio-cosmic cataclysm.

THE ENEMY

In Arguedas's poem, the "enemy" appears as a collective character who, during the time of Túpac Amaru, or of both Túpac Amarus, was known as "Spaniards" but is now given the name *kita wiraqochakuna* (despicable *wiraqocha*s). In former times, *wiraqocha*s meant the gods, but, in an inversion of values, now denotes a bloodthirsty band of thieves who steal farms and lands (sequences 10–11).

In the first poem by Dida Aguirre, the enemy is referred to directly as "the black hearted *mistis*" *(yana sonqo mistikuna)*, and their behavior is described with poetic precision: like eagles they hover and ambush *(ankallaña qaway qawamuchkan pawaykamuqllaña)* and ultimately steal the fruits of the toil *(apaq aparqunampaq)* of the collective first person plural, "we." The enemy is not only a conquistador and robber of land, but an omnipresent oppressor and exploiter. In *Pukutay* by Ninamango Mallqui, on the other hand, the enemy is never directly called by name. The first poem ("Nanay") evokes the pain felt by the speaker: the hunger, the bellyless misery *(mana wiksayoq muchuy)*, and the drought *(usia)*. "The people suffer" *(runakuna ñakarin)*, adds the second. The third, finally, exposes the wound: "the land is no longer ours" *(allpas . . . manaña ñoqanchik-*

paqchu). The unnamed enemy, the one who stole the commonly owned land of the people, has caused this situation.

In the poems by Huamán Manrique the enemy is depicted in a darker form than in those of Ninamango. The pain *(nanay)* evoked in the homonymous poem recalls apparently cosmic phenomena, such as rivers running red *(mayukunapas pukayanmi)* and a sun that comes up without its customary golden hair. Another poem ("Qamuy") alludes to ash as scattered *(uchpa chamqasqa)* on the group represented by the poetic speaker. The "enemy" whose presence causes such cosmic havoc can only be an entity so insidiously infiltrated in the poetic universe that the speaker cannot take sufficient distance as to call it by name.

THE SUPERIOR POWER

In Arguedas's poem the presence of "superior power" is called by name: Túpac Amaru. But, in actual fact, what elements constitute that entity? The reader immediately thinks of the historic personage José Gabriel Condorcanqui, also known as Túpac Amaru, who was the leader of a great eighteenth-century Andean insurrection and whom the peasant masses saw as an Inca reincarnation. This historical figure, through his name and historical deeds, recalls another protagonist of Peruvian history: Túpac Amaru, the last Inca of the Vilcabamba region.

More than invoking a historical figure, Arguedas's poem addresses a Túpac Amaru who has been turned into a mythic hero, a divinity. He appears as an Andean reincarnation of Jesus Christ; a Christ who died not for the whole of humanity, but for his people, for "us," the exclusive first person plural of the "Quechuas." The presence of Jesus Christ in a Quechua song should not surprise us, since in the pantheon of the southern Andes, Christ exists a god of intermediate status *(apu)* who specializes in hearing complaints when injustice has been suffered. Mythification of Túpac Amaru is also based on the "calling forth" of the very name or title *amaru*. The addressee of the poem already knows (although the text does not specify) that the mythological serpent of this name always appears in "moments of cosmic crisis" *(pachakutiy)*. Túpac Amaru, *amaru* or son of *amaru*, has close ties with a series of natural elements that form part of the cosmos. As the "waterfall that sheds light on the path" *(ñan kanchariq . . . paqcha)*, he was born of the snows of Mount Sallqantay, where the people of Apurímac and Cuzco believe the Quechua supreme divinity is to be found. Moreover, Túpac Amaru, under the ancient title of He Who Orders the World *(kamaqkamaq)*, is precisely that supreme divinity.

The poetic speaker invokes the divinity that is, at one and the same time, "new" (created by the poet) and "familiar" (made up of traditional Andean components), addressing him as "my father" *(papay)* and "my brother" *(wauqey)*; the new Quechua creator-god, a mythified historical figure, is much closer to "men" than the distant Wiraqocha invoked by the Incas in their hymns.

All in all, *Túpac Amaru kamaq taytanchis* (literally, "our father Túpac Amaru who orders the world") is simply the name for the historical memory, culture, and limitless collective force of the Andean people, in consubstantiation with its mountain landscape, rivers, trees, and stones. The speaker, a member of this Andean collective, dialogues with a divinity who stands for values preserved by a society colonized during the last 450 years

In the poems of Dida Aguirre, the identification of the collective "we" with the natural cosmos appears with maximum intensity. There is no "superior force" similar to a "divine entity." The human collectivity itself consubstantiated with the natural world assumes this role. The "we" has its foundation in a "wild stone" *(purun rumi)* whose qualifier, *purun,* alludes to a powerful earlier age of humanity: the first one, according to Guaman Poma de Ayala's evolutionary schema (around 1615). Supported by this stone, the collective "we," like a burning rock *(qaqa ruparichaq hina)*, "speaking like the rain, the wind and the lightning" *(para wayra wakrillaña rimarispa)*, becomes an unbeatable force. In *Pukutay* (by Ninamango Mallqui), the poetic speaker invokes "our ancestors" *(machu taytanchikuna)* and "those who cry from the very heart of the mountains" *(orqokunapa kikin sonqonmantas qaparimuchkanku)*, begging for the blood of the "old gods" *(ñawpa apunchik)* or of the very "god of the earth" *(pachapa apun)*. The collective awareness speaking as "I," and corresponding to Arguedas's "we," begs the aid of the forebears and the god-mountains *(apu)*. In this poem, the "superior force" resides, thus, in the most meaningful elements of the natural cosmos (the mountains) and in the representatives of a more powerful, more ancient humanity. By appealing to this force that is their own, the people, strengthened by their suffering, give life to an "unknown god" *(mana reqsipaq apu)*.

This call to some stronger entity, whatever this might be, doubtless expresses, in a broad sense, a "religious" conception of the world. In Huamán Manrique's poems, this "stronger" being (a function, not a person), appears in a whole range of variations. In "Nanay," the powerful partner in the dialog is *sinchillay*, "my powerful beloved," the epithet by which the Andean warriors were addressed; the "I" in the same poem seems to share some of his force when he says: "I shall bring forth a great splendor" *(lluksichisaq sinchi kanchariyta)*. Between the speaker and this superior force, the relationship (as in the poem by Arguedas) is between equals, literary echo of reciprocity found in the Andean universe between the different beings of the natural and the social cosmos. In "Taytachallay" the "I" reproaches a god resembling the one depicted in the Christian tradition for his uncaring attitude towards humanity and for abandoning it. Finally, it urges him:

Kuyuchiy kay pachata	Make the earth tremble
qechipraykiwan, tatay;	with your eyelash, my Father;
ñoqam inkari nisayki	I shall call you Inkarrí
taytachay.	my great Father.

The delay in the return of the Inkarrí, the beheaded god or mythic hero, is becoming unbearable. In "Qamuy," finally, the interlocutor is a "brother" *(wauqey)*, but an older one with a voice of thunder *(sullallalla rimayniykiwan)* who will raise the speaker with his "mountain-hands" *(auki makiykiwan)*—no doubt alluding to a god-mountain. All these powerful interlocutors appear as variants, avatars of a multiple Andean divinity whose relations with humanity are reciprocal.

Conclusions

I realize that the present analysis and interpretation are far from conclusive. My primary objective has been to examine the relationships between Arguedas's poetry and a small number of more recent poems written in that language. As far as the poetic speaker and fundamental traits of the world evoked are concerned, such relationships most certainly exist and suggest a definite similarity of attitude vis-á-vis a Quechua cosmovision. The major differences between the poems are found at the formal level of poetic exposition. These are primarily explainable given the lack of a recognized tradition of written Quechua poetry. The poems discussed constitute, in this sense, a kind of laboratory where the efficacy of diverse formulas currently imaginable is tested out: the partial updating of pre-Hispanic and colonial poetic forms, written reinterpretation of songs or oral poetic discourse, and the creative reception (adaptation) of some worldwide modernistic impulses of avant-garde origin, especially as regards freedom of verse form. It must be stressed that such poetry cannot be interpreted by reference to the cosmic and aesthetic codes of oral Quechua culture alone, but that for the poetry to have been engendered, international avant-garde poetry appears to have been an equally indispensable factor. Here, precisely, lies the importance of the urban cultural space to which all these poems belong. This is not "rural" poetry, created in the countryside in order to circulate therein, but rather poetry of a fully modern nature, whose main public audience can only be Quechua speakers in the urban centers, and therefore familiar with both the Andean and the creole cultures.

This written Quechua poetry does not stand in opposition to the Quechua poetry that is sung, nor does it pretend to or cancel its right to existence or to replace it in any way. Both kinds of poetry tend to form a complex literary system with two faces: oral and written. This is analogous, to a certain extent, to the system composed by the assembly of Andean communities and the colonies of migrant *comuneros* (peasant workers) in large cities within a socioeconomic system: a system of mutual exchange between sierra (mountains) and coast that perhaps prefigures, within social and cultural spheres, what the nation itself might become were discrimination and oppression to cease.

Appendix: Texts

JOSÉ MARÍA ARGUEDAS

"Túpac Amaru kamaq taytanchisman: Haylli taki" (To our father-creator Túpac Amaru: A song of triumph) (selection)

> Taytay: mayukunata uyariykuy, sutilla; hatun yunkapipas
> manchay sachakunata uyariykuy; la mar qochapa supay,
> yuraq takinta, waqayninta uyariykuy, papay, Amaruy.
> Kausasianikun! Chay rumi, sacha, mayu kuyusqan-
> mantan; mayu muyurisqanmantan, wayra tususqan-
> mantan, astawan hatunta, astawan yawar kallpata
> hapisiayku. Hatarisianikun, qan rayku, apu sutiyki, apu
> wañuyniyki rayku!
> > Llaqtakunapi, wawakuna, imay mana sonqonchanwaw
> > waqasianku.
> > Punakunapi, mana pachayoq, mana loqoyoq, mana ima
> > qoñiqniyoq, ñausa,

wakcha runakuna waqasianku, khuyayta; astawan
wawa weqenmantapas khuyayta (. . .)
Chay hatunkaray kiriykimanta, mana pipas taniy atiq
ñakarisqaykimanta hatarin ñoqaykupaq, sirkaykipi timpuq
rabia. Hatarisaqkuñan, papay wayqechay, Amaruy.
Manañan manchanikunichu millay weraqochakunapa
pólvora illapanta, balanta, metrallantapas; manañan
anchata manchanikunichu. ¡Kachkaniraqkun! Sutiykita
qaqarispa, lloqllariq mayu hina, puriq nina hina, mana
usiaq sisi hina lloqllasaqku, ñoqanchispa llapan
allpanchista hapinaykukama; llaqtanchispas llaqtanchis-
puni kannankama.

[My father: pay attention to the voice of our rivers, hear the fearsome
trees of the great forests, the white demon-song of the sea; hear them,
my Father, Serpent God! We are still alive! From the movement of the
rivers and the stones, from the dance of the trees and the mountains,
from all their movement, we drink a powerful blood, stronger all the
time. We rise up for your sake, we remember your name and your
death!

In the towns the children weep with their tender hearts. On the high
desert, uncovered, hatless, unprotected, almost blind, men are weeping, more sadly, more sadly than the children (. . .)

From your pain, your deep wound that none could close, an anger is
rising for us as it boils in your veins. We must rise, Father, Brother, my
Serpent God. We no longer fear the fire of the great men's powder,
nor their bullets nor their munitions, we no longer fear them so
much. We are still alive! Calling your name, like the surging rivers and
the fire that devours the ripe straw, like the infinite multitudes of for-
est ants, we must go forth, until our land is truly our land and our
towns our towns.]

DIDA AGUIRRE

"Poemas Quechuas I" (Quechua poems I)

Nina waytachalla
purun rumipi
pata pukrupi
wiñay
wiñariyña
waylluy waylluylla

chay yana sonqo mistikunam
ankallaña qaway qawamuchkan
pawaykamuqllaña

chaynataña
weqenchik
chaynataña tuta punchau
llamkay llamkallanchik
kallpallanchikta pampaykullaspa
ankallaña
apaq aparqonampaq
ankallaña

qaway qawaykachanampaq
nina paras paranqa
chaymi
purun rumipi
pata pukrupi
qaqa ruparichaq hina
juñurikuykusun nina wayta
    sisarichinapaq
lliu llapallanchipa
allpalla kanampaq
wiñray pacha jintilpi jinapas.

[Little fire flower
in the wild stone
on the terrace in the hole
    grow!
loving it wanting it

those men of evil heart
predatory as eagles
he is spying on us circling
over us
like that
night and day
already we cry
working
and hiding our strengths
like eagles
so that he might spy on us
like eagles
so that he might rob us

they say a rain of fire
    will fall
for that reason
in the wild stone
on the terrace in the hole
like burning rock
    we will reunite
the fire flower to make it
    bloom
and may this land be ours
as in the first age
of our ancestors.]

DIDA AGUIRRE

"Poemas quechuas II" (Quechua Poems II)

Sapan waranwaychallay

sapachallaykis
waqakullanki
chamana taya waqtakunapi
amaya
ama chaynaqa waqakusunchu
waqcha lliki llikanchikta
manchay mayu hinam
weqenchik timpu timpukunqa!
qaparikuspa!
qayarikuspa!
ripukullasunña
pasakullasunña
lliu llaki wauqenchik
waqchakunata
aysarikuykuspa
chipay chipaymi
ripukullasun
pasakullasun
kay mama pacha allpachallanchik
ñoqallanchikwan
kausarinampaq
pasasunña ripukullasunña
kuchpallaña ankallaña
timpukullaspa

[Little tree with yellow blossom
they say you weep all alone
amid the bushes from hillock
    to hillock
we shall not weep
    no

over our threadbare rags
like fearsome rivers
our tears shall boil!
shouting!
calling!
we shall go
we shall leave
taking sadness
taking fraternal poverty by the hand
we shall go as a throng
    as a crowd
we are going already
we are leaving now
so this dear mother earth
may live again
    with us
let's run like falling stones
like eagles boiling!]

EDUARDO NINAMANGO MALLQUI

"Pukutay III" (Storm III)

Allpas manañas mosoqñachu
chaynas manaña ñoqanchikpachu
pillpintukunapa waqasqan pukiupis
urpikuna llakinta saqechkan.
Wauqey uyariy
        manañas waqay punchauñachu
machu taytanchikunapa rimariyninta uyariy
orqukunapa kikin sonqunmantas qaqarimuchkanku
amaña anchata waqaychu
sonqoysi nanan
ritipi qapariq kundurpa qinas
sonqoy nanan

maynas pampa kuyaq turu
wañuyta munan chay pampan saqenantaqa
chaynas sonqoy nanan
qam hinas pachapa apun
yarqaymanta, yakumanta wañuq wikuñapa
qaqte yawarnin manaña upiay munaq.
Wauqey uyariy
        manañas waqay punchauñachu
allpan ñoqanchikpa uqtawan kanqa
paranchiksi qamuchkanña,
chaynas llakinchikpas qamuchkan
qori kausay challwata apamuspa
machu taytanchikuna
qanay pachapi uqtawan tusunampaq.

[Because the land is no longer virgin,
no longer ours,
the doves are leaving their lament
in the spring where the butterflies weep.
Listen brother,
    it is not the time for weeping,
hear the voice of your ancestors
calling from the heart of the mountains
because our rainstorm is about to break;
do not weep so, since my heart aches,
like the condor that cries in the snows,
like the bull that defends its grazing land,
like you,
god of the earth
who no longer wants to drink the blood
of vicuñas that die of hunger and thirst.
Listen brother,
    it is not the time for weeping;
the land will once again be ours
because the rainstorm is about to break,

the rainstorm is coming
to our people,
bringing golden fishes, blue
as the sky where our ancestors dance.]

ISAAC HUAMÁN MANRIQUE

"Nanay" (Pain)

Nanaychu astawan kutichiwanqa
llapan ritinwan,
sichi llakinwan
ñanniyta ripuspa ripuspa.
Nanaymi ñausayniyta tukuchinqa
rapapapaspa llullunmanta.
Imapaqmi, kay intiqa,
lluksirqa mana qori chukchanwan,
mayukunapas pukayanmi
astawan kay tukuymantam.
Nanaychu, icha sonqollaykichu
sachamanta ruasqa
apamuwanqa kausayta?
Ama, ama sonqoykita tukuchiychu
astawan poqochiy ancha
mayukunawan, sinchillay.
ñan hina maskaway
kuska poqonapaq
kuska qaparinapaq
maykamañapas makikunawan.
ñoqam lluksichisaq sinchi kanchariyta,
tutapipas pawasaqmi
quñunakuspa ancha qoyllurkunawan
nanayta samachinapaq
nanayta tukuchinapaq
ama qamunanpaq

Must the pain make me return
with its great snow,
with its great pang of sorrow?
Along my way, walking, walking:
will it be the pain, will it end my blindness
shining from the tenderest part?
Why is it the sun
has risen without its golden halo?
And even the rivers run red
for all that befalls us.
Will it be the pain, or perhaps your heart
made of trees
that brings me life?
NO, do not make your heart end;
nourish it still, nourish it more,
with all the rivers, my mighty one.
Seek me like the way
to reach fullness together,
to cry out together for all this
to where our hands can reach.
I shall bring forth great splendor
and by night I shall leap
to join all the stars
and lessen this pain,
end this pain, so it never returns:
   my PAIN.

Translated from the Spanish by Alita Kelley with the author and editors

Note

1. An earlier version of this essay was published in Spanish and included in the collection *Rencontre de renards,* ed. Roland Forgues, 281–305. Proceedings of the International Conference on José María Arguedas. Grenoble, France: Centre d'Etudes et de Recherches Péruviennes et Andines, Université Stendhal, 1989.

Works Cited

Aguirre, Dida. 1983. "Poemas quechuas" (Quechua poems). *Mundo andino* (Huancayo) 2 (March): 7.

Alencastre Gutiérrez, Andrés. 1955. *Taki parwa Kilku Warakía*. Cuzco.

Arguedas, José María. 1955. "Los himnos quechuas católicos cuzqueños: Colección del padre Jorge A. Lira y de J. M. B. Farfán" (Catholic Quechua hymns from Cuzco: A compilation by Father Jorge A. Lira and J. M. B. Farfán). *Folklore americano* (Lima) 3:121ñ232.

———. 1983. "Katatay." In *Obras completas* (Complete works). Vol. 5. Lima: Editorial Horizonte, pp. 221–70.

Barquero, Jesús. 1980. "La poesía quechua actual en el Perú" (Quechua poetry in present-day Peru). *Tarea* (Lima) 3 (December): 39–40.

Bendezú, Edmundo. 1986. *La otra literatura peruana* (The other Peruvian literature). Mexico City: Fondo de Cultura Económica.

Cornejo Polar, Antonio. 1976. "Arguedas, poeta indígena" (Arguedas, indigenous poet). In *Recopilación de textos sobre José María Arguedas* (Compilation of texts about José María Arguedas), ed. Juan Larco, 169–76. Havana: Casa de las Americas.

Guaman Poma de Ayala, Felipe. 1980. *El primer nueva corónica y buen gobierno* (The first new chronicle and good government), ed. J. Murra and R. Adorno. Mexico City: Siglo XXI Editores.

Huamán Manrique, Isaac. n.d. "Nanay," "Taytachallay," "Qamuy," "Llaqtaysi." Lima: University of San Marcos.

Lara, Jesús. 1979. "Cuatro poemas de Wallparrimachi [Juan Maita]." In *La poesía quechua* (Quechua poetry), 182–86. Mexico City: Fondo de Cultura Económica.

Meneses, Porfirio. 1988. *Suyaypa llaqtan/País de la esperanza* (Country of hope). Lima: Mosca Azul Editores. [Bilingual edition: Quechua/Spanish.]

Ninamango Mallqui, Eduardo. 1982. *Pukutay/Tormenta* (Storm). Lima: Tarea. [Bilingual edition: Quechua/Spanish.]

Noriega Bernuy, Julio. 1993. *Poesía quechua escrita en el Perú: Antología* (Quechua poetry written in Peru: An anthology). Lima: Centro de Estudios y Publicaciones. [Bilingual edition: Quechua/Spanish.]

Ollantay. 1958. *Ollantay: Comedia trágica de Ollantay en titulo Los rigores de un padre y generosidad de un rey* (Ollantay: A tragicomedy about Ollantay entitled The trials of a father and the generosity of a king). Copy of the Santo Domingo Manuscript by Bertha D. de Nieto and Luis Nieto. Trans. Julio G. Gutiérrez. Cuzco: Festival del Libro Cuzqueño.

José María Arguedas's El Sexto

The Gestation of an Andean Paradigm of
Cultural Revindication

Ciro A. Sandoval and Sandra M. Boschetto-Sandoval

> We desire technical know-how, the development of science,
> the dominion of the universe, but at the service of human be-
> ings, not to cause them to mortally confront each other nor to
> make their bodies and souls so uniform that they are born
> and raised worse than dogs and vermin, because even the ver-
> min and the dogs have their individual differences, their
> voice, their buzzing, their color, and their distinct size....
> —Gabriel in *El Sexto*

In a recent chapter on the postmodernist debate in Latin America, Martin Hopenhayn cites "technologist triumphalism," and the grow-ing predominance of instrumental reason over the values and utopias characteristic of humanism, as causes for critical unease with moder-nity (102).[1] Latin American critics concur that this general "exasper-ation"[2] peaked in the 1960s, a period Fernando Calderón calls "years of tragic and lucid schizophrenia."[3] These are, coincidentally, the years that comprise not only the composition and publication of José María Arguedas's most important literary contributions—*Los ríos profundos* (Deep rivers, 1958), *El Sexto* (The Sexto prison, 1961), *Todas las sangres* (All bloods, 1964), and *El zorro de arriba y el zorro de abajo* (The fox from above and the fox from below, 1971; posthumous)—but also his untimely death.

Several critics have pointed to Arguedas's aesthetic and ideological contemporaneity; among them, Alberto Flores Galindo in the "precursory, futuristic" quality of his work (6), and Juan Larco in its problematic cultural, economic, and anti-imperialistic stance (20).[4] If the postmodern narrative borrows from multiple disciplinary sources, and if John Beverley and José Oviedo are correct in their assessment that in Latin America the social sciences "have assumed the problematic of postmodernism," (6) then José María Arguedas, as ethnographer, anthropologist, and folklorist, as well as literary writer, is legitimately positioned to question the interrelation between the respective spheres of modernity—whether cultural, ethical, or political. First and foremost, by the way his work is bound up with the dynamics of interaction between local, indigenous culture and omnipresent global culture, Arguedas's aesthetic and ideological project is necessarily implicated in a countercolonizing, counterassimilating scheme. Secondly, Arguedas was himself strategically positioned "in the in-between" of tension-filled nodes of encounter, and overlapping communities: Fourth World (indigenous), Third World, and First World; archaic and modern; proletarian and intellectual; private and public; rural and urban; subaltern and official. The difficulties as well as the privileges of moving between these very distinct yet interconnected worlds—weaving between accommodation and resistance—afforded him a unique multifaceted perspective, from whence to glimpse a new cultural tapestry.

Given the limitations of our present endeavor, the intent here is to probe "the initial bubbling up" or "boiling over" ("hervores" [ebullitions] as inserted in *El zorro de arriba y el zorro de abajo* [Fell 1990, 180]) of Arguedas's synthesizing project, starting from his testimonial novel *El Sexto*, a work to which critics and scholars surprisingly have paid scant attention. We shall consider this text as socioethnographic "corpus," focusing attention on its ethnopoetic texture.[5] *El Sexto* can thus invite reflection on alternative paradigms of individual and cultural liberation from oppression.[6]

Our ultimate endeavor is to revisit *El Sexto* as prefiguration of Arguedas's aesthetic, ethical, and ideological efforts to move beyond an inherited postivistic and now postmodern "centrism" and fragmentation. This vision corresponds to what Enrique Dussel calls a project of "trans-modernity": the search for a utopian paradigm of historical continuity and revindication hewn with elements from traditional Marxism, Christian eschatology, and popular and indigenous cultural (autochthonous) memory. To focus this perspective, Arguedas positions himself "metatestimonially" within the text, in a manner that allows him to speak both as witness and as cultural critic. Thus, Arguedas uses this form of narrative articulation both to denounce (to testify against) and to reflect (to analyze) the social entropy that underlies the modernist and postmodernist avalanche, and whose pressures on the Andean world were of constant concern to him. Arguedas's desired Andean paradigm also comprises, in the words of Beverley and Oviedo, "an entirely different theoretical and historical register," one that might make possible the constitution of "another/an Other way of thinking and feeling" (10).[7]

Metatestimonio: Between Auto-ethnography and Literature

> Today I have spoken about myself with myself.
> —César Vallejo from Paris

> [You say] this is not a testimony. Fine, hell! If it is not a testimony, then I have just existed; I have lived in vain, or I have not lived.
> —José María Arguedas, *¿He vivido en vano?*
> (Have I lived in vain?)

The first epigraph above could well replicate José María Arguedas's own self-reflection: in speaking both to and with himself, Arguedas speaks for and about the community in which he is also reflected. Arguedas's testimonial discourse speaks of the cancellation, within a (post)modernist project, of an "archaic" Andean utopia at the hands of the industrializing penetration of culture. His words in April of 1966, after a first attempt on his own life, are symptomatic of the situation in which Arguedas sees himself as "pitiful [individual and collective] witness to events" in a world in which "[he] cannot bear to live without fighting, without doing something to give to others what [he] learned to do and to do something to debilitate the perverse and the selfish who have converted millions [of people][8] to the condition of work animals" (Primer Diario [10 May 1968], *El zorro de arriba y el zorro de abajo,* 9-10). Paraphrasing René Jara, Arguedas's narrative is an "urgent" one that "needs to be told" (Vidal and Jara 1986, 3), because implicated in its telling is the simple yet tragic struggle for both individual and collective survival. The following excerpt, taken from his essay, "La narrativa en el Perú contemporáneo" (Narrative in contemporary Peru) is eloquent in itself:

> . . . I decided to write, not with the express intent of publishing, but rather to vent my state of bitterness, of discontent, of quasi-exasperation against this totally false description that was being given of the indigenous population. [*Recopilación,* 413]

Arguedas's "urgent narrative" witnesses to a writing of social and individual commitment, commitment cultivated in the convergences of autobiographical, literary, and nonliterary terrains. We use the term *metatestimonio* in speaking of *El Sexto* to characterize this narrative intertextuality mediated by an academic "learned" discourse, a *testimonio* woven in the praxis of writer and translator of ethnocultural visions and ideologies, as opposed to the traditional concept of *testimonio* as essentially oral, "unlearned" discourse. Based on a survival experience—significantly that of incarceration in one of Lima's most infamous prisons, and from whence he takes the title of his novel—Arguedas's text attempts an ideological reevaluation-revindication of a most significant personal and collective experience. As such, it functions as both an imaginative re-creation[9] and rhetorical device[10] that seeks to persuade toward an unfamiliar way of thinking, by modern or postmodern standards.

We note that at the beginning of the opening chapter of this metatestimonial novel, Arguedas signals the lengthy gestation period of his text: "I began to draft this novel in 1957; I decided to write it in 1939."[11] Arguedas never provides his readers an explicit reason as to why Gabriel, the author's voice in the novel, was incarcerated in El Sexto,[12] but whatever the reasons for his own imprisonment the experience was a traumatic one for Arguedas, as evidenced in the nineteen-year hiatus between the lived experience and its translation and transcription to the literary text (Flores Galindo, 18). Thus, more than a slice of life, *El Sexto* uncovers a gradual ideological awakening.[13] As Don Policarpo, one of the prisoners and a provincial "piurano" (a native of Piura, on Peru's northwest coast), tells Gabriel in the novel: "One, it seems . . . encounters one's destiny not [free] on the street, but rather while a prisoner" (149).

In conversation with Tomás G. Escajadillo, Ariel Dorfman, and Alfonso Calderón, (published in the Chilean magazine *Portal* and later included in Juan Larco's *Recopilación*), Arguedas recalls the impact his prison experience would bear on his political, social, and religious frame of mind:

> There I found what sociologists would call a complete "model" of Peru. Among the 500 prisoners were those most perverted by the city as well as the purest political and militant leaders, the most clear-minded, serene, and the most fanatical. They were distributed on floors freely interconnected by stairs. I saw there, as well, what I would continue to call infernal scenes and sexual conflicts. One of the books I most admire is *The Sepulchre of the Living* by Dostoyevsky. It was in El Sexto that I came to understand why Dostoyevsky was able to overcome these conflicts. I thought I was extremely prepared, given my initial Catholic upbringing and the subsequent influence of

socialism that cured me of the religious fear of these atrocious sins, which I could perhaps describe with pity rather than horror. Without exaggerating, I continued meditating on that so complicated theme (political, social, moral), a little over fifteen years. [28-29]

The prolonged meditation spawned in the penal institution emerges as a complicated ideological hybridity that leads Arguedas to reflect on alternative visions capable of counterbalancing a hegemonic rationality, advancing on the wings of a modernizing and transformative ideology of progress.

Within Arguedas's testimonial perspective, *atestiguar* (to testify) acquires special significance. We best capture this in the various ethnographic expeditions, between mountain and coast, through the geographical, social, and cultural Peruvian panorama, accomplished by Arguedas from early childhood. These travels allow him to speak in a manner parallel to that which Clifford Geertz terms "ventriloquism," which is to say a strategy that allows Arguedas (as ethnographer and traveler) "to speak not just about another form of life but to speak from within it" (1988, 145). In this vein, Alberto Escobar's comment concerning Arguedas that "he expresses a most individual tendency and nevertheless a plurality" (1984, 92) is tellingly reflected in *El Sexto*.

By means of this "ventriloquism" we evidence Arguedas's struggle to capture and represent a reality in a more totalizing, multifaceted way, which also borders on the limits of the utopic.[14] This is in line with Antonio Cornejo Polar's astute observation that realism imposes itself as a primary and essential necessity for Arguedas. The Cartesian hypothesis that purports to objectively separate the observer from that which is observed is, in Arguedas's portrayal, underscored as mere illusion. As Cornejo Polar well emphasizes, Arguedas's observer, "upon observing reality, upon revealing it, describes and reveals [him]self [simultaneously]; this is to say that [he] mixes and fuses, in one whole universe . . . vision and introspection . . . which assumes, then, the internal and the external, the subjective and the objective, physical matter and psychic energy, reason and magic, the individual and society, humanity and the world" (n.d., 54–55). Arguedas's aspiration to capture reality in an all-inclusive, globalizing way is reflected in a strategy Alberto Escobar calls "speaking realism." It is in this sense, too, that Arguedas's discourse is characteristically metatestimonial. As both Escobar and Arguedas suggest, the writer's intention is more than "the production of an artistic literary text." His intention is primarily that of converting this text into a speaking reality, or a speech act. Within this perspective, the reality of the speaker "does not necessarily coincide, nor has reason to coincide, with that of the author or writer of literary texts" (Escobar 1984, 66). This strategy is also in line with the concept of *ars poetica* as social act.

Within this same perspective, Arguedas's desire for synthesis also transcends literary, ideological, and intercultural borders. This is glimpsed in *El Sexto*, for example, in the creation of a participant narrative voice, both real and fictional, that weaves between a personal, autobiographical "I" and an ethnographic "I" as social voyeur (Clifford and Marcus 1986). This "I" sees and speaks from diverse positions. The opening paragraphs of the text, for example, focus a plural collective representation of experience. This is overtly captured in the first person plural verb forms: "we moved," "we spent," "we would go," "we would start," "we would carry," as opposed to a singular disguised representation. There appears to emerge, therefore, a mobile autobiographical and metatestimonial presence capable of dispersal (or erasure, or both), and by means of which the authoritative presence of the hero (Gabriel), is, at times, displaced or replaced by a most problematic collective presence (that of the prison inmates of El Sexto prison).

The use of this "imagined" metatestimonial narrative voice is significant because it points to a subaltern-subversive form of social analysis, as well as to the projection of a possible (new) emergent subject who speaks as first person plural collective, that is to say as "we."

It is not so much that Arguedas chooses to conceal himself behind a discursive plural subject; but rather that he prefers to play the role of (synecdochean) bridge in order to speak from other mythological narrative positions. Rather than an authorial presence, Gabriel assumes the position of collective "companion." In this way, he joins with other voices in the denunciation of both moral and social degradation, perceived in El Sexto and from there in society at large. This act of "solidarity with" suffering once again positions the text as urgent testimonial act.[15]

As one of Arguedas's first novels to insinuate the recurrent theme of urbanization and displacement of the agricultural migrant to the polis (Lévano 1962, 315), of the traditional to the modern, *El Sexto* represents a locus of convergence for geographical (mountain village and coastal city), social, and cultural spaces; for indigenous, white, and black races; for diverse classes; and for ideological formations. As Arguedas himself clarifies, "in the prisons was to be found the worst and the best of Peru" ("La narrativa en el Perú contemporáneo," 420). In *El Sexto* Arguedas extols the sociocultural insights of the native peoples of the Andes, while at the same time recognizing that Andean identity is a tapestry of complex weave, and that, in reality, all Latin Americans share coexisting identities; that is, they have lived, as Fernando Calderón observes, simultaneously "in incomplete and mixed times of premodernity, modernity, and postmodernity" (55), since, as Arguedas adds, their natural development has remained incomplete or truncated ("La literatura como testimonio y como una contribución"). From within this perspective, Arguedas realized that he could not truly describe the indigenous population he so dearly loved, and of which he felt himself a part, to a particular audience (indigenous, mestizo, or "transculturated") without also incorporating those other ethnic and social groups with which the native destiny is interwoven.[16] Arguedas's desired intent is to portray a "total human world," "a complete social context," which must include both the Indian and the mestizo (*Primer encuentro* 172; quoted by Cornejo Polar n.d., 58). *El Sexto*, as metatestimonial discourse, mirrors this complexity most uniquely in its multilogical texture.

A Postmodern Disenchantment with 'Rational' Politics

In the face of a hegemonically imposed system over cultural and linguistic Andean tradition, *El Sexto* suggests complex social and individual asphyxia. Within this perspective, Arguedas's *metatestimonio* can be read as the attempt to create a textual aperture toward the external world, a world whose dystopic contours become progressively more visible in later works such as *Todas las sangres* and the posthumous *El zorro de arriba y el zorro de abajo*.

Ariel Dorfman contextualizes Arguedas's work prior to *Todas las sangres* as essentially introspective and mystical: "the struggle for the human being to overcome the evil encountered in the world, by routing temptations, vile deeds, the evil menace intuited within oneself." From within this "Christian, Dostoyevskian" existential perspective, one questions the salvation of the world, taking as starting point one's own personal salvation (Dorfman 1969, 327). As Dorfman tells us, in the post-*Sangres* phase, Arguedas, after many years of struggle, succeeds in transcending that internal vision of perversion of the presence of evil in the world, and fear of contamination by the same, that underlies the human psyche. That reflection leads him toward the external world, which, in turn, results in an epiphany: the introspective experience of his indigenous roots, which allows him to embrace a vision of collective struggle (with the masses) or, as Dorfman notes, "a collective struggle of the people in rebellion" (328). In *El Sexto*, therefore, Arguedas prefigures an existential posture, seeking, through the novel, to transcend the interior world of personal demons by moving toward a sociopolitically rationalized external ambiance. From this perspective there emerges a sociopolitical metatext constructed on a mystical, mythological world. As a transitional text from the inner to the outer world, Arguedas's *metatestimonio* attempts to unravel a vision of individual, collective, and cultural redemption that bridges seemingly discontinuous discourses (spheres) of faith, individual morality, and politics. To better contextualize the space in which this vision takes place, a summary description of the Sexto prison is necessary.

Lodged in the prison are three distinguishable socioeconomic cultural groups, each on separate floors, but permanently and freely interconnected by means of bridges and stairs. The third and top floor is occupied by political prisoners; these include Apristas as well as their rival communists. Gabriel occupies a cell on this same floor, despite the fact that he is considered "apolitical" but with definite Marxist sympathies, as evidenced in his conversations with leaders of other political affiliations. Luis, the Aprista leader, informs the reader of the opinion that the majority of the prisoners have of Gabriel: essentially a bourgeois intellectual "dreamer," an opinion that Luis himself reconfirms when he interjects rhetorically: "—What do you know about politics? I see that you're [nothing more than] a poor student, a pseudocommunist" (74).

In descending order, the second floor is occupied by the hardened criminals, the most sanctioned from a social, cultural, and moral point of view. This group is that of the transvestites, murderers, and homosexual pimps, who profit from human and institutional degradation.

Finally, the first and lowest floor is occupied by the *vagos*, lowly members of both the prison social hierarchy and of modern Peru. These "vagrants" contribute most visibly to the ambiance of social, moral, and institutional nausea in the Sexto prison. The vagrants epitomize the refuse of society and are the target of the most perverse and degrading carnivalesque pranks of the groups who wield power over them. To aggravate their situation even further, this group is forced to perpetuate their own destitution by serving as messengers, runners, or *paqueteros* (package carriers) (25, 98) for the other groups. In summary, this floor is tantamount to the excremental cross-section of society. The words of Cámac, Gabriel's cellmate and most lucid communist idealist, provide us with an eloquent vision of this social dissection: "We're living on top of crime, my student friend; it's below us and we're on top; in Morococha and Cerro it's the opposite; the bloodsuckers are on top, and below are the workers; they're either below the earth—in the mine—or in the tin shanties. . ." (12). These prophetic sentences are also captured in the comparisons made between the perverse and degrading practices of the second-floor criminals and those carried out in the world outside. From there, Cámac's ironic query: "What's the difference between those on the outside and these here inside?" (29). Beyond the allegorical metaphors of the prison as monstrous and hellish entity,[17] wherein the narrator, engulfed by a kind of social entropy, feels the world "like a nausea that was trying to drown me" (29), *El Sexto* stands as a clear indictment of socioeconomic and political structures that maintain class divisions and human exploitation.

Aside from the lack of freedom, what most undermines existence in the prison is the ubiquitous lack of communication and community at every level, a lack made present precisely in its Derridean absence. Ironically, *El Sexto* opens with the prisoners singing in a "competing [counterpoint] fashion" (5) both Aprista and communist anthems. Both political groups intone their "hosannas" by way of announcing their offensive postures, thus loading the atmosphere with hatred, collective censorship, mutual suspicion, and enmity.[18] Gabriel is witness to this from the first day of his incarceration (5–6). Pedro, another communist inmate, also acknowledges it: "Gentlemen . . . we ought not to squabble like delinquents" (45).

As to be expected, most in evidence about the so-called *políticos* is their ideological rigidity, an attitude regulated by rationalizing principles and formal procedures. According to Pedro, this regulation is required to maintain a necessary order. The three floors of the Sexto must remain separated so that order may exist in the prison, an order without which, as he tells us "we cannot maintain our own order" (65). This rhetorical position masks the division of social classes and ideologies that legitimate these very divisions. This does not go unnoticed by either Gabriel or Cámac, who uncover the perverse hatred disguised behind Pedro's logic. "I cannot hate men like Juan," replies Gabriel. "According to the very theory you have just described, Juan is beguiled, not a traitor, and I cannot hate him" (49). Nevertheless, Pedro finds justification in his circular rhetoric:

> "Hatred . . . is the sacred fire of the communist; without that weapon, without that invincible force, we will not shape the unity of all peoples, the eternal brotherhood. We will not transform the world.

> —And the hated? —I asked him.

> —Let them obey or die. APRA is only a passing fad in Perú, we Marxists constitute the future, the world force of renovation. We must burn without pity whatever obstacle in our path; without pity, but at the right time; too hasty or too late a move could jeopardize our advance, delay it for years. That is our responsibility. [67]

Gabriel finds this value-neutral logic difficult to assimilate, despite the fact that political leaders and economists submit themselves to it in the name of progress. Gabriel's attempt to save "the pianist" from his abusers represents his (Arguedas's) attempted subversion of the prison's (political) managerial-technocratic logic, a style favored by the circular (closed) modernizing world system. To be a social being, however, is not only to care for one's self (here, the "soul" of the Party), but to display solidarity with others. As Gabriel ironically admonishes: "Should I detest this flock of innocent and misguided people who called me Judas for having tried to help a dying man?" (67).

Both Gabriel and his homologous ego figure, Cámac, seek to address the problem of democratic order through moral and ethical commitment. From thence emerges their mutual concern for the lack of human rights in the prison, rights trampled upon by a dehumanizing institutionalized rationalism. With respect to the same, Cámac vents his native wisdom: "One should not trust entirely in the head. There are times when the intuition of the soul is also safe. There lies the difference between mountain and city dweller.... one must have, at times, [the ability to solve problems] by envisioning the solutions" (69). Paradoxically, while Pedro's political rationalization extends to a world beyond the prison walls, "the bigger struggle," "that of the world outside" (152-53), its future redemption must begin for both Gabriel and Cámac from within the prison itself. El Sexto and the evil it houses become for both Cámac and Gabriel an analogous referent of collective struggle for "transforming the world" for the better. Arguedas's metatestimonial discourse, as it emerges from the prison, reflects a loss of faith in the modern state and in its rationalizing politics to accomplish that transformation. As Norbert Lechner clarifies, however, it is not so much a question of "disenchantment with politics as such but rather with a specific way of doing politics, and in particular, with a politics incapable of creating [and maintaining] a collective identity" (1993, 132). The true struggle for Gabriel and Cámac must begin with the recuperation of moral human decency, nonexistent in the prison, and, by extension, in modern capitalistic Peruvian society.

As suggested earlier, it is the very perception of the presence of evil and its pervasiveness under the guise of different forms of oppression that motivate the search for an alternative paradigm of revindication for a culture that has been subjugated and silenced since the conquest and subsequent colonization. El Sexto prison mirrors this displacement, one equivalent to that abyss of destitution of which Heidegger speaks (1971), and from within which it is necessary to seek out the means of elevating oneself to new heights of human dignity. The utopic metaphorization of Andean reality, of original Andean social institutions and their forms of thought, may serve as essential recourse in that effort. This search does not represent merely the nostalgic reflection of a lost vision of the world (nostalgic Andean paradigm), one that, within the current process of (post)modernist rationalization, may no longer be valued. Rather, what Arguedas's text unveils is the attempt to reinsert these traditional Andean values within the very same process of (post)modernist rationalization—which is to say, to combine the mythical, the religious, and the ethical, with rational (reason-able) thought. This utopic actualization —utopic in its revolutionary sense, since it addresses the need for change—calls for a community sustained by what Anibal Quijano calls a "joyous intersubjectivity" (1993, 142).[19]

This utopic joyousness is partly echoed in the brotherhood that Gabriel shares with his indigenous cellmate, Cámac (in Quechua, he who creates), the miner-carpenter from the high region of Morococha, and later with Don Policarpo, the *piurano*, another apolitical mountaineer, who in the end assumes part of Gabriel's struggle. Aside from a shared geographical origin, the brotherhood of Gabriel, Cámac, and Don Policarpo is cemented on the sharing of cultural isomorphic structures. Even more, this geographic and ethnographic convergence acquires its strength in an ambiance in which beauty and goodness contrast with the entropic elements rampant in the social microcosm of El Sexto. A reading of this contrastive symmetry is possible in the eyes of Cámac. The latter, in fact, reflect symmetry with(in) opposition because one eye is healthy, clear, and serene whereas the other is sickly and continuously inundated with tears. In this same tropological vein, the latter eye would reflect entropic dystopia while the former a luminous utopia, not only as mirrored in the natural beauty of the higher Andean regions, which they reflect, but also in Cámac's "clear ideas," brilliant as the stars (13). Other contrasting, yet complimentary traits of Cámac's personality are manifest in concordances and divergences, as Gabriel himself attempts to describe:

> His face, his mannerisms; his way of treating me, now in the familiar, now in the formal; his bed of straw reinforced with newspapers; his coat and pants of simple peasant cut, bore no interconnection—that to which we are accustomed to see as corresponding in Lima—with

the clarity of his thought and the beauty of his language. He did not glean his terms, nor did he embellish them, as the politicians I had heard up to then. He was without a doubt an agitator, but his words named deeds directly, and ideas born of deeds, like the flower of the watercress, for example, that grows in the brooks. [17]

Cámac's words are not motivated by a deliberative rhetoric, but rather by a rhetoric understood in its judicial and epidictic sense. His words denounce directly and prophetically the social injustice and oppression of the workers on the part of foreign capitalists and investors, who only seek economic advantage at the cost of deculturized indigenous communities. Cámac's words clearly raise the necessity for an alternative that might include compassion and love toward the workers regardless of political affiliation. It is for this reason that, despite having been betrayed by the same Aprista miners, his moral principles remain firm:

> . . . to really hate a worker, perhaps it is necessary, but my heart cannot comprehend it. I hate the accursed gringos, and I will die fighting against them! But a misguided worker leader, only in his moment of betrayal; afterwards I get over it. I see them suffering equally, just like me; spat upon the same by the gringos and their bosses. [49]

Further on, he again admonishes:

> Thieves, vagrants, murderers!—replied Cámac—Is that the way a communist should talk, in that language? The Pianist was a poor innocent; he was worth more than you and I, comrade, because of his sufferings. . . . [65]

Words, particularly those of the criollos, do not always convey that sense of liberation that Gabriel and his cellmates clamor for in the prison. Moreover, implicated in Cámac's own death is their surplus of words (17). By the same token, the words of Luis, Pedro, and Gabriel also fail to convince the prison commissary to launch a purge of evils in the prison. The prison warden, as a puppet of the ideological state apparatus, interprets their request, not as an act of human solidarity, but rather as the mere political maneuver of *traidores a la patria* (traitors to the motherland) (102). Ironically, but in accordance with their ideological strategy, the political prisoners themselves separate moral and cultural concerns from political structure. Aware of this also, Arguedas turns to the indigenous populations as the true source of universal knowledge, that knowledge born of the daily practice of living with(in) nature. As such they are indeed guardians of an "integrated wisdom" (Quijano 1993, 151) of a holistic tree of knowledge.

Neither Gabriel nor Cámac is steeped in political party theory, and for this reason become targets of strong criticism on the part of the political leaders. Gabriel and Cámac, rather, speak through a cultural autochthonous language, such as that of music and dance. This is exemplified in Cámac's promise to construct a guitar for his friend in order to sing and to celebrate both his culture and his friendship. Sadly, with Cámac's death before the conclusion of the novel, this celebration of life is cut short. What is not curtailed, however, is the influence of Cámac's *fantasma protector* (guardian spirit) (69) who, in his brief role as guide in the Dantesque prison, awakens in Gabriel and in the other political prisoners a deeper social awareness. After Cámac's death, Gabriel assumes a militantly committed position, a stance in which prior contradictions are fused into new meanings and new visions. These new perspectives are embodied in a search for social contact within the microcosm of El Sexto, thereby subverting Pedro's initial claim for artificial and ideological separation of both classes and cultural groups. It is for this reason, as well, that Gabriel rejects political partisan affiliations, and instead, opts for a hybrid posture in which the visions of a mythic cultural past "percolate" more freely through the present, [20] as his words well illustrate:

> One must "sound out" an ancient culture. Humankind is worth as much for the machines [it] invents, as for the memory [it] has of its traditions. Cámac is not dead. . . .—My thought has never been clearer. [118]

The characteristics of this hybrid paradigm presuppose an "analectic," or systemic, manner of thinking that goes beyond the simple scientific rationalization of "dialectic" thought.[21] It is clear that "analectic" thought (unification in diversity) demands a praxis of jointly shared struggle, enriched by faith, compassion, and moral commitment. These ideas form part of an isomorphic global manner of thinking that subsists in cultures that struggle for liberation within a similar context of hegemonizing modernization.[22]

Within this perspective, *El Sexto* may be read as a discourse that resorts to a plurality of rationalities or manners of viewing the world, traditional and modern. This discourse emerges as a realization that neither capitalism nor socialism, neither the Left nor the Right, in themselves offer "a model" that summarizes the majority's aspirations, that is to say, a model representative of global consensus. In this sense, Cámac's words are enlightening: ". . . many others share the ideals of justice and freedom, perhaps better than the communists" (90). This vision is also reflected in the imaginary world of other inmates who, while lacking in political faith (80) like Gabriel, are capable of idealizing a more authentically Peruvian cultural and social structure. Pacasmayo, for example, speaks at one point of his desire to Peruvianize chess (*peruanizar el ajedrez*), to replace the traditional figures of the game with those of the Peruvian world: replace the king with the Inca, the queen with the "coya," the towers with the "torreones de Pucará" (large towers of Pucará), and the horse with the puma (76–77). It is interesting that Peruvian history serves as the base structure of this imaginary revolution, a proposal captured as cultural *mestizaje*, and subversive of the prevailing acculturating order that impinges from outside.

While all liberation movements have their beginning in the imagination, they are not accomplished merely through utopic desire ("wishful thinking"). Cámac himself appears aware of this when he says: "What good is the person who dreams while sitting down?. . . [What good] is he who does not commit and enter [the struggle] with fire in hand against the oppressor?" (94). Rhetoric and reason are not sufficient in themselves to sustain the individual and collective life that idealism presupposes. Required is a praxis similar to that "ventriloquated" in *El Sexto*, which is to say, one that speaks from within the system itself. The awareness of this impasse, acquired in his lived experiences in the Sexto prison, launches Arguedas toward an ideological and cultural strategy capable of assuring the survival of Andean paradigms in the face of accelerating world change. In other words, his vision is similar to that of Enrique Dussel, whose philosophy of liberation emerges from a locus where freedom is absent, which is to say from within a space(s) of oppression and suffering.

Toward the Recovery of a Paradigm of Redemption

> This place seems to be for no other purpose than to uncover what we thought did not exist. —Gabriel, *El Sexto*

Aníbal Quijano seems to mimic Arguedas when he states that in Latin America, "the real is rational only inasmuch as rationality does not exclude its magic" (1993, 151).[23] Nor its religious sense, we might add. Quijano's assertion could well translate the metaphysical discernment that emerges from *El Sexto*. While critics such as José Luis Rouillón Arróspide and Mario Vargas Llosa have touched on the religious symbolism and apocalyptic moral tone of this testimonial novel, few have commented on its teleological-metaphysical slant, which is to say, its final insight as redemptive possibility. The political paradigm that seeks to overpower the social pragmatics of the prison fails in this accomplishment. Political paradigms cannot replace the sacred mystical vision and image of the world (nor of apocalypse) because they simply cannot posit any ultimate (metaphysical) liberation. On the contrary, rationalizing political paradigms draw the Andean world toward a Heideggerian destitution that tarnishes all hope of salvation. This abyss of destitution, however, allows Gabriel/Arguedas to glimpse a redemptive hope by assuming the role of the poet of which Heidegger speaks in his essay, "What Are Poets For?" a role that Heidegger describes as that of penetrating the world of destitution and from within it making manifest the road toward a form of redemption.[24]

Indeed, El Sexto Prison is hell allegorized, a Godless world wherein theological amnesia and even madness carry eschatological significance, an image of the "excremental culture" (Kroker and Cook 1986) that denounces the social and masochistic perversions of a rotting world, and that reappear in other contexts, such as that of Chimbote in *El zorro de arriba y el zorro de abajo*. *El Sexto* portrays a Dantesque cosmos in its nine short fragmented or fractured chapters and in the six bridges, both multiples of the number three, also the number of floors in the prison. The bridges simultaneously both separate and communicate, sanitize and contaminate all social cells of the prison house, both horizontally and vertically.

From this vision there emerges for Arguedas a hybrid paradigm (composed of poetic, political, and ethical threads) that focuses the present through the past, through cultural memory projected toward a future of redemptive hope. An emblematic character in the novel who exemplifies this redemptive image, through acts of ethical solidarity, is the so-called *Ángel del Sexto* (angel of the Sexto). "We called him the Angel of the Sexto, the bread boy, because inside the bag he carried he would bring the prisoners letters and gifts from relatives, from sweethearts, and newspapers" (70). More than a bearer of trinkets, this angelic messenger is the epitome of both an apolitical moral and social praxis and a philosophical and social liberation that transcends simple political partisanship. Everyone seems to recognize his transcendent significance. As Gabriel continues to explain, "By a solemn agreement that no one broke, the 'ángel' was not [required] to carry or bring political messages" (70). The Angel embodies functions similar to those that Hopenhayn visualizes within a truly democratic society, such as the administration of scarcity, the mobilization of dispersed social energies, the de-hierarchization of production relations, the construction of collective identity, the socialized provision of basic necessities (education and other services), the maintenance and promotion of community participation, and "the search [for this same democracy] in small spaces" (107).

Political rationalization is still applicable within social conventions; however, Arguedas means to imply in *El Sexto* that politics no longer has validity as the sole means toward social equilibrium. Alongside political rationalization, the implicit utopic belief in a liberating praxis is maintained in the revolutionary struggle of popular movements against the hegemonic oppression and domination that assaults individual freedom. We recall here the concept of utopia as revolutionary form in the sense assigned to it by Karl Mannheim, that is to say, as radically transforming social praxis, and opposed to ideology as strategy used to maintain a given status quo (1985, 192–93). Even more, as utopian discourses from the time of Thomas More make manifest, it is disenchantment with a given order that awakens desire to a new, more just order. The implication, however, is not that a better future lies simply around the corner. The concluding lines of *El Sexto* point to an ambivalent existential space wherein the imaginary and the empirical, the ideal and the real are confused. As scholars of chaos have also noted, however, it is precisely from chaos (and its turbulence) that utopic ideals for new orders and new structures may emerge. In this light the utopic-revolutionary vision that Gabriel and Cámac outline in prison is genuinely Latin American, for contained within we discern the "echoes and fragments of past utopias whose present we can only perceive as a continuous crisis" (Brunner 1993, 53).

To reiterate, the modern (and postmodern) disenchantment that underlies Arguedas's novel does not cancel out utopic impulses within the Latin American cosmology. That is, it does not destroy hope in its revindication or in its coming into being, not at least within an imaginary terrain. As Aníbal Quijano and Xavier Albó both note, these impulses redefine themselves in the tension of uncertainty that opens before a renewed future for Latin America, which is to say, between the possibility of its coming into being, as perceived by Arguedas, and what it presently is. In this light, *El Sexto* as sociopolitical text raises more questions than triumphant utopic solutions: How, for example, do we reaffirm our identities, if we are no longer what we wanted to be? or How do we coexist, alternating with others, without allowing ourselves to be oppressed, if not by accepting ourselves as we are, but without ceasing to dream (our utopia)? We must recall here that *El Sexto* mirrors a poetic "analectic" vision— that is, a vision pointing toward the reconstruction of a new liberating movement of past identities emptied into new ways of thinking, of living, and of acting upon the world. It is not possible to understand this new manner of thought through Cartesian analysis alone, that form of rationalization that gave birth to the modern project of the Enlightenment. Rather, we must seek out the signifiers of an excessively fragmented reality in order to use them in the reconstruction of a more holistic vision, one that contrasts (while not clashing) with the historical sense imposed by the Enlightenment.

Finally, the crisis generated by a forced modernity cannot be resolved by ignoring other ways of thinking and other attitudes toward nature and culture itself. The contestatory position from which Arguedas writes, from and within social margins and crevices, between the literary and the autoethnographic, whether as actor, writer, or witness, allows him to plumb these social depths in the light of mythical, ethical, and cultural values, threatened by a technologizing instrumental reason and disseminated by a language of uniform technicality that Michel Serres refers to as "monosemic technolect" (1980, 87). For Arguedas, religion and other transcendental metaphysical domains (artistic, mystical and mythological) continue to discharge as important a role in the struggle for Latin American cultural liberation as instrumental reason. Therefore, and finally, Arguedas's redemptive vision necessarily calls for the inclusion not only of the reason of the Other, but of his or her inalienable Otherness as well.

Notes

1. A Spanish version of this essay authored by Ciro A. Sandoval is forthcoming in *Revista Iberoamericana*.

2. As José Joaquín Brunner explains, "exasperation" (as opposed to exhaustion) arises from modernity's "infinitely ambiguous effects, with its inevitable intentionalism, and its distortions, and with the problems that it bequeaths for the future of the region" (1993, 53).

3. Calderón further describes these times as tending "to a greater production of wealth and to a growing social marginalization and terrifying cultural homogeneity, a world of increasing non-communication between races, of cages, more legal than legitimate, of pastiche and of schizophrenia, which tends to completely negate the search for liberating identities" (1993, 60).

4. "At a moment in Latin America when we debate the ransom of [the Latin American] economy, spirit, and culture by imperialist domination, [at a time when] Peru struggles to unleash its own revolution, the work of Arguedas, because it is made of the substance of our problems, acquires a unique significance" (Larco n.d., 20).

5. By "ethnopoetic texture," we mean that ethnography cannot be sharply distinguished from literary practice, and from the text as linguistic production (according to Jacques Derrida, Roland Barthes, and Julia Kristeva mainly), which is to say, from writing itself. See, for example, James Clifford's introduction ("Partial Truth") to *Writing Culture: The Poetics and Politics of Ethnography* (Clifford and Marcus 1986).

6. Throughout this essay, the title of Arguedas's novel will always appear in italics, whereas the name of the prison (also El Sexto) will not be italicized.

7. All references are to the 1974 Editorial Horizonte edition of *El Sexto* (The Sexto prison). Unless otherwise indicated, all translations from the original Spanish (for all texts cited) are those of the editors.

8. Arguedas's word here is *cristianos*, literally "Christians," metaphorically "children of God" or people who abide by the word of God.

9. In "Razón de ser del indigenismo en el Perú" (Indigenism's reason for being in Peru), Arguedas speaks of his philosopher-mentor, José Carlos Mariátegui, who helped him recognize the structural correspondence be-

tween literature and the evolution of Peru, and create an affirmative awareness of its ethnic values as a function of class struggle (see Larco n.d.).

10. As Alberto Escobar clarifies, the work of Arguedas, "is not a *story* but
rather a *communication* whose discourse is intended to act upon the readers, in order to persuade [them] to accept the knowledge of the originator,
that is, of the very same *speaker*" (1984, 79; emphasis Escobar's).

11. The novel, of course, was not published until 1961, twenty-four years
after the actual incarceration it is based on. It was awarded the Ricardo
Palma Prize in 1962.

12. Biographers and critics claim that Arguedas himself was arrested in
1937 as a communist sympathizer. Others, like Mario Vargas Llosa, insist
that Arguedas was never "militant" in his political perspectives, and that his
incarceration of almost a year was essentially the result of a schoolboy
prank. Arguedas was involved, with other university students, in the dump-
ing of an Italian fascist general (General Camarotta, Mussollini's special
envoy to Perú) in a university fountain (Vargas Llosa 1980, 11). This incident
took place during the dictatorship of General Oscar Raimundo Benavides.
Sánchez Cerro was assassinated in April 1933 by a militant Aprista, and
Congress quickly elected former president Benavides to complete Sánchez
Cerro's five-year term.

13. The thirties, the decade in which the author begins his literary career,
constitute a critical moment for Arguedas and for the country, a moment in
which, according to Augusto Salazar Bondy, "a new way of perceiving life in
Perú is conceived" with the intervention of a group of intellectuals who represent, along with Arguedas, "the insertion of historical materialism in the
doctrinaire agenda of the national imagination" (1965, 308).

14. By this we mean the impossibility of arriving at definitive propositions on this same reality, whether scientific, ideological, social, or other. See
"The Utopianism of Roland Barthes" in Geoffrey Strickland's *Structuralism or Criticism?: Thoughts on How We Read*, 127–144.

15. This act of "accompaniment," for Arguedas, goes beyond a simple act
of human solidarity, as he himself exemplifies from an episode recalled from
his childhood: the parade of condors through his native village, in which

> four men, two on each side would open and extend their wings. The crowd
> accompanied the entourage in silence; only occasionally did they shout their

"vivas" to the motherland in their barbaric Spanish. . . . I contemplated in suffering the march of those condors, which they forced to walk by jumps and starts, while the gentlemen of the town applauded from the sidewalks and the balconies. . . . Their wings extended almost the entire width of the street. They moved forward jumping: I had the impression that their feet hurt, because as soon as they touched the stones of the road, they would lift them painfully. "Why are you crying? Why don't you leave?" they asked me. "I am accompanying [them]," I would tell them. [*El Sexto*, 62–63]

16. As Angel Rama tells us in *Transculturación narrativa en América Latina* [*Narrative Transculturation in Latin America*], the indigenous element continues to play a significant role in the cultural and biological inheritance of the mestizo. Social and cultural *mestizaje*, in turn, permeates throughout Latin America.

17. Arguedas's vision of this entity, as we point to later on, is very similar to Dante's allegorical construct. In Arguedas's rendition, however, it is Cámac who renders both roles simultaneously: that of Virgil, the enlightened guide and poet, and that of Beatrice, his angel or "fantasma protector" (69).

18. "Why do we have to fight in the Sexto as well? Aren't we all in prison for the same reason?" I asked. "Here separation and enmity are necessary for the Apristas," replied Pedro. "They will never allow for a doctrinaire elucidation. They only thrive by the heat of their hatreds; that blind hatred that cannot be extinguished. Ours is more lucid and includes the entire world; it is perfectly managed" (74–75).

19. According to Quijano this Andean social paradigm is characterized by "reciprocity, solidarity, the control of chance, and the joyous intersubjectivity of collective work and communion with the world" (1993, 142).

20. For French philosopher and social critic Michel Serres, time does not flow in the manner of a line or vector, in only one direction and as if it were made of continuous segments, as conceived in classical Newtonian physics. According to Serres, time is laminar-like. It flows, ripples in a chaotic, turbulent manner, and "percolates." From there, according to Serres, arise all our difficulties with historical theories—that is, with our classical manner of thinking of time as insufficient and ingenuous (see Serres 1992, 90–91).

21. The "analectic" according to Enrique Dussel, refers to

the real human fact by which every person, every group or people is always situated 'beyond' (ano-) the horizon of totality.... The analectical moment is the support of new unfoldings. . . . [it] opens us to the metaphysical sphere (which is not the ontic one of the factual sciences or the ontological one of negative dialectic), referring us to the other. . . . totality is laid open to question by the provocative (apocalyptic) appeal of the other. To know how to listen to the word of the other is to have an ethical conscience.... To know how to risk one's life in order to fulfill the demands of the protest of the oppressed and throw oneself into praxis for them is part of the process of the analectical moment. Theory is not sufficient in analectics. . . . The analectical moment is thus a criticism and a surmounting of the merely negative dialectical method. [1990, 158–59]

22. We recall, for example, an essay that points in this direction: "Creating Space for a Hundred Flowers to Bloom: The Wealth of a Common Global Culture" by the Kenyan poet, essayist, novelist and dramatist Ngugi wa Thiong'o (12–24). Only within the space of such a garden is it possible to imagine the forging of an incorporative solidarity and utopic intersubjectivity.

23. In the words of Arguedas himself: "There are not, therefore, many limits between the marvelous and the real . . ." (Escajadillo et al. n.d., 28). In his well-known acceptance speech upon being awarded the Inca Garcilaso de la Vega prize, "No soy un aculturado" (I am not acculturated), he tells us: "How well did I understand socialism? I am not sure. But it did not destroy in me my sense of the magical" (Appendix, *José María Arguedas: El Zorro de arriba y el zorro de abajo*. Ed. Eve-Marie Fell 257–58). See also *¿He vivido en vano? Mesa Redonda sobre* Todas las sangres (Have I lived in vain? Roundtable discussion on *All Bloods*): "There is no contradiction between magical and rationalistic conceptions; rather each character views the world according to his or her own human makeup" (Escobar 1985, 26).

24. Part of this vision for Gabriel is symbolized in the vagrants *(vagos)* of the first floor who suffer all manner of ignominy and humiliation. Gabriel sees represented in these individuals the figures of "martyrs" and "saints," as occurs, for example, with "El pianista" (the pianist) and "el japonés" (the Japanese): "En el cuerpo del japonés" (In the body of the Japanese) Gabriel

sees that "the world dragged itself along, there below; it carried his form, even his energy. . . . he carried an appearance that does not die. The pianist could hear the music, from outside, the kind invented by man, extracted from space and the surface of the earth. Man hears, brother, in the deepest sense . . ." (88–89).

Works Cited

Albó, Xavier. 1993. "Our Identity Starting from Pluralism in the Base." In *The Postmodernism Debate in Latin America: A Special Issue of* Boundary 2, ed. John Beverley and José Oviedo, 18–33. Durham, N.C.: Duke University Press.

Arguedas, José María. 1966. "La literatura como testimonio y como una contribución" (Literature as *testimonio* and as contribution). In *José María Arguedas*, 7–10. Lima: Juan Mejía Baca.

———. 1969. "La narrativa en el Perú contemporáneo" (Narrative in present-day Peru). In *Recopilación de textos sobre José María Arguedas* (Compilation of texts on José María Arguedas), ed. Juan Larco, 407–20.

———. 1970. "Razón de ser del indigenismo en el Perú" (Indigenous Peru's reason for being). In *Recopilación de textos sobre José María Arguedas*, ed. Juan Larco, 421–30. Havana: Casa de las Américas

———. 1974. *El Sexto* (The Sexto prison). Lima: Editorial Horizonte.

Beverley, John, and José Oviedo. 1993. *The Postmodernism Debate in Latin America: A Special Issue of* Boundary 2. Durham, N. C.: Duke University Press.

Brunner, José Joaquín. 1993. "Notes on Modernity and Postmodernity in Latin American Culture." In *The Postmodernism Debate in Latin America: A Special Issue of* Boundary 2, ed. John Beverley and José Oviedo, 34–54. Durham, N.C.: Duke University Press.

Calderón, Fernando. 1993. "Latin American Identity and Mixed Temporalities; or, How to Be Postmodern and Indian at the Same Time." In *The Postmodernism Debate in Latin America. A Special Issue of* Boundary 2, ed. John Beverley and José Oviedo, 55–64. Durham, N.C.: Duke University Press.

Clifford, James, and George E. Marcus, eds. 1986. *Writing Culture: The Poetics and Politics of Ethnography*. Berkeley: University of California Press.

Cornejo Polar, Antonio. n. d. "El sentido de la narrativa de Arguedas" (The sense of Arguedas's narrative). In *Recopilación de textos sobre José María Arguedas*, ed. Juan Larco, 45–72. Havana: Casa de las Américas.

Dorfman, Ariel. 1969. "Opiniones" (Opinions). In *Recopilación de textos sobre José María Arguedas*, ed. Juan Larco, 327–29. Havana: Casa de las Américas.

Dussel, Enrique. 1990. *Philosophy of Liberation*. Trans. Aquilina Martínez and Christine Morkovsky. Maryknoll, N.Y.: Orbis Books.

Escajadillo, Tomás G., Ariel Dorfman, and Alfonso Calderón. n.d. "Conversando con Arguedas" (Talking with Arguedas). In *Recopilación de textos sobre José María Arguedas*, ed. Juan Larco, 21–30. Havana: Casa de las Américas.

Escobar, Alberto. 1984. *Arguedas; o La utopía de la lengua* (Arguedas, or the utopia of language). Lima: Instituto de Estudios Peruanos.

———, ed. 1985. *¿He vivido en vano? Mesa Redonda sobre* Todas las sangres (Have I lived in vain? A roundtable on *All Bloods*), *23 de junio de 1965*. Lima: Instituto de Estudios Peruanos.

Fell, Eve-Marie, ed. 1990. *El zorro de arriba y el zorro de abajo* by José María Arguedas. Nanterre, France: Centre des Recherches Latino-Américaines.

Flores Galindo, Alberto. 1992. *Dos ensayos sobre José María Arguedas* (Two essays on José María Arguedas). Lima: SUR, Casa de Estudios del Socialismo.

Geertz, Clifford. 1988. *Works and Lives: The Anthropologist as Author*. Stanford, Calif.: Stanford University Press.

Heidegger, Martin. 1971. "What Are Poets For?" In *Poetry, Language, Thought*. Trans. Albert Hofstadter. New York: Harper and Row, 91–142.

Hopenhayn, Martin. 1993. "Postmodernism and Neoliberalism in Latin America." In *The Postmodernism Debate in Latin America: A Special Issue of* Boundary 2, ed. John Beverley and José Oviedo, 93–109. Durham, N.C.: Duke University Press.

Kroker, Arthur, and David Cook, eds. 1986. *The Postmodern Scene: Excremental Culture and Hyper-Aesthetics*. New York: St. Martin's Press.

Larco, Juan, ed. n.d. *Recopilación de textos sobre José María Arguedas* (Compilation of texts on José María Arguedas). Havana: Casa de las Américas.

Lechner, Norbert. 1993. "A Disenchantment Called Postmodernism." In *The Postmodernism Debate in Latin America. A Special Issue of Boundary 2*, ed. John Beverley and José Oviedo, 122–39. Durham, N.C.: Duke University Press.

Lévano, César. 1962. "Otras opiniones" (Other opinions). In *Recopilación de textos sobre José María Arguedas*, ed. Juan Larco, 315–16. Havana: Casa de las Américas.

Mannheim, Karl. 1985. *Ideology and Utopia: An Introduction to the Sociology of Knowledge*. New York: Harcourt Brace Jovanovich.

Ngugi wa Thiong'o. 1993. *Moving the Centre: The Struggle for Cultural Freedoms*. London: James Currey.

Quijano, Aníbal. 1993. "Modernity, Identity, and Utopia in Latin America." In *The Postmodernism Debate in Latin America. A Special Issue of Boundary 2*, ed. John Beverley and José Oviedo, 140–55. Durham, N.C.: Duke University Press.

Rama, Angel. 1987. *Transculturación narrativa en América Latina* (Narrative transculturation in Latin America). 3d ed. Mexico City: Siglo XXI Editores.

Rouillón Arróspide, José Luis. 1973. "El espacio mítico de José María Arguedas" (The mythic space of José María Arguedas). In *Nueva Narrativa Hispanoamericana* 3 (2):161–78.

Salazar Bondy, Augusto. 1965. *Historia de las ideas en el Perú contemporáneo: El proceso de pensamiento filosófico* (A history of ideas in contemporary Peru: The process of philosophical thought). Lima: Moncloa Editores.

Serres, Michel. 1980. *Le passage du Nord-Ouest*. Paris: Editions de Minuit.

———. 1992. *Eclaircissements: Cinq entretiens avec Bruno Latour* (Clarifications: Five conversations with Bruno Latour). Paris: François Bourin.

Strickland, Geoffrey. 1981. *Structuralism or Criticism? Thoughts on How We Read*. Cambridge: Cambridge University Press.

Vargas Llosa, Mario. 1980. "Literatura y suicidio: El caso de Arguedas *(El zorro de arriba y el zorro de abajo)*" (Literature and suicide: The case of Arguedas *[The fox from above and the fox from below]*). *Revista iberoamericana* 110–11 (January-June): 3–28.

Vidal, Hernán, and René Jara, eds. 1986. *Testimonio y literatura* (*Testimonio and literature*). Minneapolis: Institute for the Study of Ideologies and Literature.

Tricksters in the Fishmeal Factory

Fragmentation in Arguedas's Last Novel

Claudette Kemper Columbus

José María Arguedas's suicide in 1969 prevented completion of his last novel, *El zorro de arriba y el zorro de abajo* (The fox from above and the fox from below; hereafter referred to as *The Foxes*).[1] Yet even unfinished, this novel has won the reputation of a major twentieth-century work. This essay addresses chapter 3 of *The Foxes*, in which two kinds of trickster appear.

The main trickster in the scene is the mythic fox (from) below, named Diego—a composite being, although primarily human in form. Arguedas derives the fox in part from the dialogue between two foxes in the Huarochirí myth that serves as one of the pre-texts of *The Foxes* and that Arguedas modifies to close the novel's "First Diary," which precedes the its first chapter.[2] The fox below is also derived in part from pre-Columbian artifacts of foxes dancing by moonlight to honor a deity that may be the changeful moon goddess. This compound fox figure is juxtaposed to a bureaucratic industrialist, a contemporary type familiar to most of us: fat, vulgar, adulterous, egocentric Don Ángel Rincón Jaramillo. His mind sealed by avarice, Don Ángel represents the indifference of the low-level trickster, a "fox" possibly also derived from Andean folklore and a term applied to a shyster whose tricks are cheap.

The mythic fox below, Diego, presumably takes on the commercial shyster fox and his material circumstances, his emotional sterility and his social irresponsibility. These deficiencies attract the corrective potential of the high-level trickster Diego. But lamentably, the fox below discovers he cannot trick a person as hardened and vulgar as Don Ángel into dimensions of perception that include not only the arts and traditions of the native peoples of Peru but also the metaphoric agility of such a humane consciousness as Arguedas's own.[3] The avaricious, "angel" mobster with debased sexual tastes refuses change and will admit no divination, no aesthetic vision, no fecundating eroticism into the fishmeal factory. He shows himself so dehumanized and so denaturalized by his conscienceless acts of sexual and commercial chicanery that no playfulness on the part of the fox suggests better ways of life to him, in part because Don Ángel will neither recognize the traditions of the past that the fox below represents, and in part because greed and gross sexual appetite blind him. His is the indifference of a trickster of the lowest level.

The fox Diego, high-level exposer of conceptual and linguistic deficiencies, wears a cheap business suit that mimics Don Ángel's. His language also echoes that of Don Ángel. The fox introduces himself as an agent acting on behalf of the international mafia, with which Don Ángel is in collusion. By unmasking the viciousness of Don Ángel's consciousness, the fox unmasks the low-level trickery of the most powerful economic practices at work in the Peruvian port city of Chimbote, the main setting of the novel, an "instant city" inhabited by large populations of displaced rural and mining peoples. The fox bares the manager's inhumanity and obtuseness and their effect on Chimbote, and by extension, the effects of inhumane business practices on poor people worldwide.

The cap that the fox below wears changes colors whenever he breaks impulsively into a dance so removed from the conventional

behavior of typical businessmen and so incongruous in the office setting that Don Ángel more or less defends himself from the hyperreal
by ignoring both cap and dance. He ignores alternative ways of being
in the world offered him by the fox who, shamanlike, attempts to expand consciousness through a ritual dance that breaks down the
boundaries of the office setting. His dance transforms dead space
into culturally creative space. It is not only a metaphor for the natural
world that the fox represents but an expression of the fox's worship
of that world, in contrast to the fishmeal factory manager's social and
physical defilement of the natural world. By not remarking on the
dance, Don Ángel protects the narrowness of his perceptual field, occupied as it is with strategies for illicitly acquiring more capital and
with his plans to end this particular evening in a striptease joint.[4] As
a low-level trickster, he exposes, as the scene progresses, the cruel
ruses that irresponsible industrialists employ to cheat their workers
and to acquire political power. For Don Ángel, as a sort of minimalist
fox, represents the low-level trickster's base traits: vulgarity, crude
and careless sexual appetite, acquisitive deceitfulness. He mirrors
and echoes the conscienceless strategies of acquisition in international commercial transactions as they impinge on local industries.
Even the inappropriate name Ángel contributes to the darkness he
embodies and the disarticulative discourse of the low-level cheat. But
although the misnomer, which stands in contradiction to the de-
monism of his words and his acts, tips the reader off to low-level-
trickster deception on the verbal level, the text suggests no remedy
for the disjunctions he perpetrates between signifier and signified.

Overhearing the cryptic conversation between the Huarochirí
foxes of the deep past helps the mythic culture hero and shaman
Huatyacuri cure social and sexual problems because he is able to
learn from the high-level trickster foxes. The conversation between
the foxes reappears in modified form in Arguedas's "First Diary" and
also forewarns of cultural and sexual disturbances to come, both in
the narrative and in the world—except that, unlike Huatyacuri, the

Arguedas of the diaries represents himself as lacking confidence in his own vitalizing powers. For even the fox below, in the context of the modern world and of this novel, although he is a remnant of the mythic past alive in the present and although he is alive not simply as a memory but as a witness to contemporary depravity, is unable to influence Don Ángel, too corrupt to listen and to learn, his perceptual field too impoverished. No recognition of systemic psychosexual and social problems with their correspondent constraints on cognition and discourse (discourse defined in Foucaultian mode, as a set of culturally maintained representations), no verbal nor intellectual healing occurs through the medium of himself as an audience able to rise to cultural heroism by learning from a trickster dialogue in the way Huatyacuri could in the deep past.

The fox below attempts to open alternative spaces and discourses on such subjects as sexual deviance (rape, for instance) and the ruthless socioeconomic system. But his attempts fail. The sick system remains in place. He finds no culture hero in the outer office of a fishmeal factory. The reasons why affect us all.

Arguedas's novel contains a sociology of Chimbote that shows not only divisions of class and gender, but of different racial and ethnic groups speaking different languages, represented through highly individualized characters based in depth on identifiable, real-life people and situations.[5] Drawing so many of the characters in *The Foxes* from life underscores Arguedas's contention that there is no separation in his novels between fact and fiction; Arguedas intends the reader to perceive the mythic fox as an authentic agent in the "real"— that is, the disenchanted—world of conscienceless commerce, that world that casts its evil spells over almost every corner of life. Its most evil spell is its having won acceptance that it is the real world.

Traditionally, even the animality of the fox, exaggerated physical appetite in the raw, is potentially beneficial. Despite *fox* being a degrading pun for female genitalia,[6] in Peru as in other places, the fox trickster embodies healthy as well as diseased sexuality, and does so to this day.[7] Thematic in the domain of the pre-Columbian myths Arguedas invokes and in the action of this novel is the issue of healthy and diseased sensuality.[8]

Diego embodies a part of indigenous traditions that remains vital. As the figure of the artist, he is the polysemous and polyvalent representative of the disruptive and connective power of metaphor. The self-transformative dances Diego performs could be dances of fecundation. The foxes of myth dance in the springtime, the time of mating. The mythic culture and fertility hero, Huatyacuri (from *Huarochirí*), dances after his marriage. In addition to taking instruction from the mythic foxes' dialogue, the healer-trickster Huatyacuri uses panpipes taken from a fox to bring new dances, new music, and an expanded outlook to the people; he brings an environment of abundance. But the mobster Don Ángel remains uncomprehending. His obtuseness highlights the absence of a sense of the sacred and the dearth of principles of fecundation in factories productive of goods for sale that are not good in themselves.

The scene that unfolds between Diego and Don Ángel fragments conventions of genre. The scene combines the low mimetic elements of realism such as verisimilitude (the office is plainly no more than a contemporary office) with high mimetic elements, symbols that possess the power to alter material circumstances. The scene sets a figure from myth in dialogue with a businessman, a dialogue disrupted by such moments as when the fox below spins like a ball of colored glass in a disco and leaves the manager of the fishmeal factory nonplussed.

Chapter 3's assemblage of genre fragments could be deemed postmodern, were it not for Arguedas's deeply serious, reformist ethos, rooted in indigenous history. The interpenetration of past and present in the scene combines linear and cyclic time. The scene counterposes two radically different conceptual worlds. Don Ángel's sense of reality and his criminal sense of what is valuable enacts the "idiot" reality and defiling self-interest of low-level shysterism in the economic and political arenas—shysterism familiar to most of us. This nightmare reality dismisses ethical considerations as unrealistic. Ironically, realistically representing the nightmare chaos of the

Vietnam decade of the sixties renders verisimilitude indistinguishable from surrealism (a point Arguedas makes elsewhere in the novel).

No sooner does the fox with his letter of introduction from the "Fu Manchu" international mafia enter the office than the mythic-folkloric fox ruptures the "code" of realism that the office setting and the character of the manager of the fishmeal factory try to establish and maintain. Diego sports the horizontal whiskers of a fox, like the foxlike whiskers that identify flying shamans in Paracas textiles, and his fox ears move. His rough sandals and black trousers characteristic of the Andean Indian and the mestizo do not impress Don Ángel favorably; he recognizes the cheapness of the clothing but welcomes the fox because the fox bears credentials from the mafia. Therefore Don Ángel overlooks the strangeness of the fox's behavior; no businessman, mafia or otherwise, would behave as Diego does.

The fox observes Don Ángel's unfavorable reaction to his composite outfit and announces with tongue in cheek that it is no longer necessary for travel to wear such stylish dress as he has on. He explains that electronic conduits convey styles from around the world to backwater locales; hence his stylishness. Courtesy of cybernetic computers, the fox says he has seen Europe, Machu Pikchu (*sic*), and Miami Beach (86). His language claims he is wearing stylish, hybrid accoutrements and that he is worldly, but his language bears no relation whatsoever to his appearance.

The names of both characters (Ángel and Diego) are composites that signal the complexities of identification in the twentieth century as much as they signal the duplicity of the trickster. "Honorific Don Ángel Rincón Jaramillo" suggests a bizarre hybridization of religion ("angel") and industry (he "corners" the indigenous population by various ruses). Diego, or James, as in St. James, is a name once forbidden native Andeans, a sanction now flouted.[9] That these proper names have ambiguous and contradictory referents is but another indication of a loss of legibility, a loss of interpretational codes, disarticulation. Down-to-earth native traditions, folklore, myths, and tales are foreign to Don Ángel.

The fox's cap is itself a mixed symbol. On the one hand, it symbolizes the native Andean ostensibly taking a step "up" in life to become mestizo, frequently accomplished through change in dress. On the other hand, the cheapness of the cap gives away a wearer who is being exploited and de-cultured, except that, in this instance, the fox is "out of this world" and can be neither exploited nor extirpated.

Both Don Ángel and Diego are *bricoleur* operators of makeshift networks that are themselves enmeshed in the networks of international multiculturalism. Both are products of floating populations whose members perform ad hoc simulations of whatever seems the dominant power model. Both personify the counterfeit. But Diego as high-level trickster may be attempting to educate the uneducatable, whereas Don Ángel seeks to control only those workers whose faces he would erase (87). He would have all his workers be simulacra, modeled for the convenience of an invisible (and mafioso) power. Jean Baudrillard describes such erasure of the faces and persons of masses of people as a grinding "up into synthetic, deathless substance: an indestructible artifact that will guarantee an eternity of power" (91).

Although tricksters high and low use mimicry, although both Don Ángel and Diego are "unreliable witnesses" and are uninterested in accountability either in act or in language, they differ in that the fox below is free in space, time, and discourse: no sets of cultural practices either govern or explain him, and his language is polyglot. Don Ángel, prisoner of the system over which he has little power and less understanding, imitates it. He trots out several "run-downs" of political and economic situations for the fox. He reveals how he has fixed the company books, rigged elections, framed union leaders, cheated the workers, falsified figures—crimes assisted by urban anonymity.

As a low-level trickster and despite his know-it-all tone, Don Ángel shows no understanding of the ancient, educative function of the fox trickster nor of the native tradition. Although Don Ángel shows signs of recognizing the otherness of the spheres from which the fox hails ("Don Ángel's attention dwells on a trace of the extraordinary about the stranger's face," [85]), he plays a politics of nonrecognition. He acknowledges nothing between them save commercial conspiracy. He sees that the fox is transformative and hears him change his idiom and his metaphors, and yet pays no attention to what such flexibility might mean. Diego reveals nothing. To be a high-level fox is to be in the know, but what this fox Diego knows, readers must divine.

The wily Diego reveals himself to be extraordinary and yet remains in a space even less definable than that space between discourse and story in which Anne Doueihi situates trickster figures. For the high-level trickster tells no story and his words do not indicate his educative and potentially medicinal, creative, divinatory functions. Although Arguedas relates him to narratives and images in *huarochirí*, he remains an oracular and mysterious figure. In any event, anything resembling a real exchange between them is subverted by Don Ángel's elected obtuseness and by one convention of genre that does pertain: foxes do not "dialogue" with human beings any more than mafia agents converse free of a profane context. In this fishmeal factory, Bakhtin would seem a polysyllabic innocent.[10] That is to say, Bakhtin would look upon the medley of idioms, ideolects, and perceptions the scene contains as generating creativity. But in the diary section that follows chapter 3 of *The Foxes*, Arguedas claims that the foxes have gone beyond his comprehension and his powers as a writer (179). It is as if Arguedas in this passage is mourning the loss of the polyglot in cities subject to the machinations of low-level tricksters. Even tricksters of the highest order, masters of information and of discourse, seem unable to instigate change, no matter how brilliantly they perform.

Don Ángel remarks that the fox is like a spider, all eye.[11] And after the remark, the fox, like a spider, actually catches and kills a fly. Were this scene set in a realistic or naturalistic mode, one could "read" it as suggesting that the wily fox-cum-divinatory spider figure will kill the mafioso fly. But there is no textual and contextual support to suppose that the fox will kill the angel of the fishmeal factory like a fly. The author of this novel, no mean trickster himself, leaves the space between discourse and story disorientingly wide open.

Don Ángel gives the mythic-folkloric, inhuman/all-too-human fox a night tour of the fishmeal factory, an enormous fetish of a technology-triumphant civilization. As this high-level trickster, its face sharply aware and its discourse double-sided, this stranger who is also our unacknowledged selves, our unacknowledged knowledge, our forgotten past, tours the fishmeal factory, he thins the barrier between what we do not wish to know and what we allow to be conscious. The fox's very presence enacts contemporary denial of other ways of being in the world: ritual native practices and beliefs, the whole cultural heritage of the native peoples that progress extinguishes, the absence in corrupt technocrats of a sense of the sacred. Don Ángel, who calls the workers "worms," boasts about technology's march of "progress," and remains unaware of the contradiction between his use of the term *progress* and the word *worms*. It is because he remains unaware that the chapter raises the enormous issue of ersatz progress in the hands of low-level tricksters who eclipse space and time and whose deadly disarticulativeness defeats even the best among us.

Is Don Ángel unconscious of or does he will ignorance of all spheres save the manipulative and the exploitative? Indifferent to ethical awareness, this tour "guide" sees and refuses to accept the deeper wisdom that the fox below dances. He refuses the realms of folk experience from which the fox hails. Michel de Certeau mentions spirits and voices from other realms, proverbs, games, and tales as useful in tricking institutional order into art (26). Don Ángel, who has ears, does not hear the workers' cries, far less their tales. He has eyes and does not see the spirit of the realm from which the fox below appears. He preserves the falsehoods of self-serving and sleazy enterprises. If the mythic-folkloric fox could break open other spaces beyond Don Ángel's savagery through dance and discourse, there could be a role for art, for metaphor, for the sacred in the profane world of commerce.

As Anne Doueihi argues, the purpose of the [high-level] trickster is to play "in the space between discourse and story":

> trickster stories point to the way ordinary, conventional reality is an illusory construction produced out of a particular univocal interpretation of phenomena appearing as signs. This deeper wisdom about the linguisticality of our constructed world and the illusoriness of that construction is where trickster stories open onto the sacred. [198]

In *huarochirí,* the stories and the discourse of the trickster foxes and the trickster gods open onto the sacred. As a trickster artist, Arguedas inserts passages of extraordinary sensibility and oracular power among other passages of more familiar matter, the discourse of culturally maintained representations. (Some critics refer to these extraordinary passages as magical, but not, unfortunately, as if they understood the power of the "magical" to cure social and psychological disease.) The fox below shows himself expert at exposing low-level, trickster constructions. But his exposures bear no consequences.

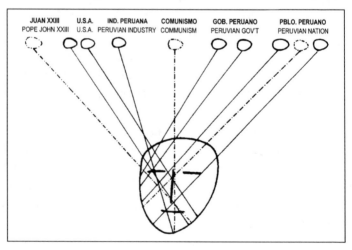

The positive aspects of deeper wisdom, such as an appreciation for the linguistic and musical potential for changing our constructed world, go unregarded. The high trickster is foiled by the low trickster; the low trickster is unchangeable because uncaring. Even the fox's dance, in which the very act of dancing produces colors and sounds—like the wings of mosquitoes, like blood spurting from an animal's cut arteries—cannot show Don Ángel gateways to creative life. The high trickster's other evocations of things not present—the aroma of the pollen of high-altitude flowers, for instance—are "magical" traces of the natural world absent from the office of the foul-smelling fishmeal factory. The fox's eyes luminous as high-altitude lakes—the unpolluted planet—are so transparent they make Don Ángel think he may discover some secret (104).[12] But like the Western critic criticized by Doueihi, it could be said that Don Ángel imposes "on Native American culture [his] own frame of concern":

> Western culture turns the discourse about the trickster into a discourse by Western culture about Western culture, with the trickster serving only in a nominal function so that the discussion may begin. [197]

Discourse as sets of culturally maintained representations organize lived experience and human perception—in most contexts. In this one, representations, discourses maintained in the native cultures are dismantled. For instance, Don Ángel decides to draw an "objective" diagram to show the fox what is going on in Chimbote and in Peru. Yet the profane sketch he draws divests state, religion, politics of their bases in justness.

"See," says Don Ángel, and he draws ten egg shapes, seven in white and three in red. (Egg imagery is a leitmotif in *The Foxes*, tagging crucial issues of fertility/sterility.) Don Ángel draws lines from these ten egg-shaped hollows that cross over the "the face of Peru" (107). These lines render the face masklike and inscrutable, shallow as thin paper. The eyes and the mouth are "closed" straight lines:

Don Ángel labels seven of the hollow eggs as if they numbered ten and claims the white "forces" as "we": "industry, the USA, the Peruvian government, the ignorance of the Peruvian populace, and the ignorance of the evangelical priests. The red forces are Pope John XXIII, communism, and the rage of the populace against the USA" (108).

Of the use of graphs to depict human situations, Certeau writes,

> However useful this "flattening out" may be, it transforms the *temporal* articulation of places into a *spatial* sequence of points. A graph takes the place of an operation. A reversible sign (one that can be read in both directions, once it is projected onto a map) is substituted for a practice indissociable from particular moments and "opportunities," and thus irreversible (one cannot go backward in time, or have another chance at missed opportunities). It is thus a mark *in place of* acts, a relic in place of performances: it is only their remainder, the sign of their erasure. Such a projection postulates that it is possible to take the one (the mark) for the other (operations articulated on occasions). [35; emphasis Certeau's]

Where the fox offers a *poiesis*, the man of crooked commercial practices makes marks that show the erasure of people and the shrinkage of space into a graph. Hollow eggs stand in lieu of the Pope and in lieu of protestant missionaries and in lieu of political parties. Don Ángel's orderly explanation codifies the chaotic as if his codification were an explanatory discourse, which it patently is not; as if it offered an "opportunity" for understanding, which it does not. The graph is a cover-up so transparent that it neither covers up nor explains anything. But it does take the place of "acts."

What we know about political and economic connivances helps us know what is going on in this scene. Criminal business interests block communication through negation, and even business practices that are not overtly corrupt subvert insight into humane options through the use of tables. "Statistics can tell us virtually nothing about the currents in this sea theoretically governed by the institutional frameworks that it in fact gradually erodes and displaces"

(Certeau 1984, 34). It is inefficient to think of people as giving access to knowledge, when the bottom line is profit and their agendas are not the social good but profit margins. The deployment of power through meaningless, "explanatory" graphs[13] is as disarticulative as the substitution of hollow oval shapes for "forces" and faces.

And Don Ángel knows the graph is demonic, for it makes him laugh as if he needed to release "guarded air" (a secret agenda? 109); he laughs as if emitting the eggs of a louse or a frog (109). "In the entire universe, very few command . . . hee hee hee!" (108). But after the fox dances again, Don Ángel finds it impossible to continue laughing, although he tries several times to resume "hee hee-ing." The fox casts a double shadow that dances more gracefully than the fox himself and causes Don Ángel to hear the heart of hearing, the soul of memory ("su oído de oír," "su oído de recordar" [109]). But, although he tries to imitate the fox's dance, he cannot. He then breaks into a song that jeers at life, and dog shit, and whores, and people he has trashed. Because he is unable to dance or to sing well, he sighs, "Poor mankind" (although he feels only for himself). He then remembers that he heard that phrase in "un disco long play" (112) and thus elevates his hate-filled ditty to the level of junk that salespersons pass on as art. Most music of this age of mechanical reproduction (Benjamin 1969)[14] represents the loss of memory of the past, the loss of the power of listening (the heart of the ear, the double shadow of the fox from below), the loss of the ability to sing and dance divinely. *Divine* is used in the sense that the artist feels rhythms connect the artist to the rhythms of the universe, except that the racket of technology in the fishmeal factory extinguishes any but its own, blunted universe of noise.

Contrast the shystering of fake information through the inscrutable and depersonalizing graph to authentic communicative fields, to the power of music, or dance, or myth, to a linguistics that places

at its center the operation of language *across* lines of social differentiation, a linguistics that focuse[s] on modes and zones of contact between dominant and dominated groups, between persons of different and multiple identities, speakers of different languages, that fo-cuse[s] on how such speakers constitute each other relationally and in difference, how they enact differences in languages. Let us call this enterprise a *linguistics of contact*, a term linked to Jakobson's notion of contact as a component of speech events, and to the phenomenon of contact languages, one of the best recognised challenges to the sys-tematising linguistics of code. [Pratt 1987, 60; emphasis Pratt's]

A situation of cross-cultural linguistics with zones of actual contact among peoples is of course precisely what Arguedas dreamed of for Peru and what the fox below represents. Arguedas's polyglot novel performs a few, splendid "polyglot" scenes of meaningful contact be-tween diverse cultures. But with the world becoming more and more like the fishmeal factory, even the power of *poiesis*, the powers of the artist Arguedas's foxiness and libido, his ability to elicit multiple meanings—and with them options—have been, and continue to be, fragmented by the refusal of those in charge of production to admit the damage they cause reproduction, an organic reproduction that acts to open alternatives to things as they are.

Notes

1. The page numbers cited come from the critical edition, coordinated by Eve-Marie Fell; all translations into English are mine. Frances Barraclough's translation of *El zorro* into English is to be published by UNESCO.

2. Arguedas translated the Quechua myths into Spanish as *Dioses y hom-bres de Huarochirí*; Frank Salomon and George L. Urioste translated them into English as *The Huarochirí Manuscript*. The fox myths used by Ar-guedas are from chapters 5 and 11.

3. Nancy Gray Díaz's informative chapter "Metamorphosis as Integra-tion" in her book *The Radical Self* shows how proficient use of metaphor can alter concrete situations resistant to change.

4. The situation between fox and functionary resembles Michel de Certeau's situation when he tries to hear "these fragile ways in which the body makes itself heard in the language, the multiple voices set aside by the

triumphal *conquista* of the economy. . . . my subject is orality, but an orality that has been changed by three or four centuries of Western fashioning" (1984, 131).

5. Arguedas calls for an urgent anthropology suited to cities that rise suddenly as if out of nowhere and that are sites of intense social struggles (1966a, 25).

6. Noted, for instance, by Martin Lienhard (1980, 188). Felicitas D. Goodman discusses *coyote* in terms of competent sexuality (1990, 184–85).

7. An Andean matchmaker, sometimes called a fox, would know that "one of the most widely cited talismans used to augment the attraction of the opposite sex is the tail of the fox. Young men must capture the animal, cut off the last vertebra of its tail, and release it alive. The tails of dead animals lack the necessary power, the 'cunning of the hunter,'" to turn young men "on the brink of becoming fully mature human beings" into mature human beings; see Luis Millones and Mary Louise Pratt (1990, 17); also see Gary Urton (1985).

8. In the Huarochirí myths, foxes gossip about sexual aberrations; a female fox figure entraps the shaman, medicine-man deity, Tutaykire.

9. In the sixteenth century, so many children were being named Diego that the church fathers realized St. James with his harquebus as a symbol of power was being used as a cover for the worship of Wiracocha, the deity of gunlike thunder and flashes of lightning; see, for instance, Irene Silverblatt (1988, 179–84).

10. Bakhtin argues for a "democratization" and pluralization of languages by "expunging the sacred and authoritarian word in general, with its indisputability, unconditionality, and unequi-vocality. Because of its sacrosanct, impenetrable boundaries, this word is inert, and it has limited possibilities of contacts and combinations" (1986, 133).

11. Since most early Andean cultures depict polymorphic figures, it seems evident that early, metaphoric cast of mind communicated a compound concept of being without difficulty. In the twentieth century, boundaries for self-conceptualization are far more limited and the strangeness of a fox-spider-person reveals an anthropocentrism that narrows metaphoric options for self conceptualization.

12. In the Andes, water preeminently symbolizes processes that further fertility, if its flow is balanced.

13. Certeau contends that graphs displace operations and erase territories:

(1) The "proper" is a triumph of place over time. It allows one to capitalize acquired advantages, to prepare future expansions, and thus to give oneself a certain independence with respect to the variability of circumstances. It is a mastery of time through the foundation of an autonomous place.

(2) It is also a mastery of places through sight. The division of space makes possible a panoptic practice proceeding from a place whence the eye can transform foreign forces into objects that can be observed and measured, and thus control and "include" them within its scope of vision. To be able to see (far into the distance) is also to be able to predict, to run ahead of time by reading a space.

(3) It would be legitimate to define the power of knowledge by this ability to transform the uncertainties of history into readable spaces. But it would be more correct to recognize in these "strategies" a specific type of knowledge, one sustained and determined by the power to provide oneself with one's own place. [1984, 36]

14. In "The Work of Art in the Age of Mechanical Reproduction" *(Illuminations,* 1969), Walter Benjamin examines the new functions and values of art in terms of exhibitionism and perceptual fragmentation.

Works Cited

Arguedas, José María, trans. 1966a. "La Cultura: Un patrimonio difícil de colonizar" (Culture: A difficult inheritance to colonize). In *Notas sobre la cultura latinoamericana y su destino* (Notes on Latin american culture and its destiny) by Francisco Miro Quesada Cantuarias, Fernando de Szyszlo, and Arguedas, 21–26. Lima: Talleres de Industrialgrafica.

———, trans. 1966b. *Dioses y hombres de Huarochirí: Narración quechua recogida por Francisco de Avila* (Gods and men of Huarochirí: Quechua stories compiled by Francisco de Avila). Lima: Siglo XX.

———. 1990 [1969]. *El zorro de arriba y el zorro de abajo* (The fox from above and the fox from below). Coordinated by Eve-Marie Fell. Madrid: CEP de la Biblioteca Nacional.

Bakhtin, M. M. 1986. *Speech Genres and Other Late Essays*. Trans. Vern W. McGee. Austin: University of Texas Press.

Baudrillard, Jean. 1983. *Simulations*. Trans. Paul Foss, Paul Patton, and Philip Beitchman. New York: Semiotext(e).

Benjamin, Walter. 1969. *Illuminations*. Ed., introd. Hannah Arendt. Trans. Harry Zohn. New York: Schocken Books.

Certeau, Michel de. 1984. *The Practice of Everyday Life*. Trans. Steven Rendall. Berkeley: University of California Press.

Díaz, Nancy Gray. 1988. *The Radical Self: Metamorphosis to Animal Form in Modern Latin American Narrative*. Columbia: University of Missouri Press.

Doueihi, Anne. 1993. "Inhabiting the Space between Discourse and Story in Trickster Narratives." In *Mythical Trickster Figures: Contours, Contexts, and Criticisms*, ed. William J. Hynes and William G. Doty, 193–201. Tuscaloosa: University of Alabama Press.

Goodman, Felicitas D. 1990. *Where the Spirits Ride the Wind: Trance Journeys and Other Ecstatic Experiences*. Bloomington: Indiana University Press.

Lienhard, Martin. 1980. "La ultima novela de Arguedas: Imagen de un lector futuro" (Arguedas's last novel: The image of a future reader). *Revista de Crítica Literaria Latinoamericana* (Lima) 6, no. 12: 177–96.

Millones, Luis, and Mary Louise Pratt. 1990. *Amor Brujo: Images and Culture of Love in the Andes*. Syracuse University Foreign and Comparative Studies, Latin American Series, no. 10. Syracuse: Maxwell School of Citizenship and Public Affairs, Syracuse University.

Pratt, Mary Louise. 1987. "Linguistic Utopias." In *The Linguistics of Writing: Arguments between Language and Literature*, ed. Nigel Fabb, Derek Attridge, Alan Durant, and Colin MacCabe, 39–66. New York: Methuen.

Salomon, Frank, and George Urioste, eds. and trans. 1991. *The Huarochirí Manuscript: A Testament of Ancient and Colonial Andean Religion*. Austin: University of Texas Press. [English and Quechua version of the *Manuscrito quechua de Huarochirí*]

Silverblatt, Irene. 1988. "Political Memories and Colonizing Symbols: Santiago and the Peruvian Mountain Gods of Colonial Peru." In *Rethinking History and Myth: Indigenous South American Perspectives on the Past*, ed. Jonathan D. Hill, 174–94. Urbana: University of Illinois Press.

Urton, Gary. 1985. "Animal Metaphors and the Life Cycle." In *Animal Myths and Metaphors in South America*, ed. Gary Urton. Salt Lake City: University of Utah Press.

Part Three

The Intersection of Subjectivities

As webbed knots composed of different strands, multicultural inter-textualities inhabit the workings of many Third (or Fourth—Indige-nous) World writers. The boundaries of these subjectivities have always been notoriously unstable. In a sense, therefore, this section tends to want to extend the notion of the textual well beyond tradi-tional notions of "literature" to raise cultural and psychological ques-tions attending to such issues as the degrees of exclusion and inclusion, of domination and sufferance, of complicity and resistance in the social sphere. These questions interrogate how the text is re-lated to mind (feelings, ideas, obsessions, repressions). This type of inquiry is usually directed toward two quite different aspects of the artistic process, one preconstructive and the other postconstructive, namely: How did the author's mind operate in the creation and the shaping of the work? and How does the mind of the reader or the au-dience respond to the work and contribute to its completion?

In his seminal work on Arguedas's "migrant condition," Antonio Cornejo Polar returns us to that overriding sense of *forasterismo,* or permanent cultural dislocation, that pervades Arguedas's textual pro-duction, which according to Cornejo Polar may well be defined as "the epic of the migrant." Arguedas's persistent move(s) from one culture to another is marked by a "precarious bilingualism," whose "ephemeral intertexts" mirror a displaced subject, functioning in a "fragmented, unceasing indeterminacy." Cornejo Polar's idea of "criss-crossing the ultimately syncretic mestizo-transculturation paradigm with the shifting syntax of the migrant" is indeed more inclusive and affirming of the "web of literary entanglements" that proliferate in necessarily incomplete modernities.

Julio Ortega's analysis of the "quandary of communication" in *Deep Rivers* insists on the "systematic plurality" and problematic position of the narrator of the novel, enunciated through three intermingling narrative voices: textual, cultural, and participatory, which also correspond to three types of discourse: novelistic, reportive, and biographical. This communicatory complexity, in addition to "extraordinary," is also revolutionary, as reflected in its powerful indictment against the usurpation of speech. Arguedas's "multiple communication," while encompassingly rich, opens up finally to an "ambivalent space" wherein "wandering," like the deep rivers that run in the "depth of origin," serves as counterpoint to a fixed state of being. Luis Jiménez treats a topic that Ana Maria Barrenechea still defines as incomplete, namely, Arguedas's relationship to women and the feminine (opening address, JALLA, 1995). In this final essay, Jiménez calls attention to the carnivalesque discourses represented by the female characters of Opa and Doña Felipa in *Deep Rivers*. In their passive-active representations, these female characters act out the writing of a text that "criticizes and censures the alienating situation of women" in postcolonial representations.

Migrant Conditions and Multicultural Intertextuality

The Case of José María Arguedas

Antonio Cornejo Polar

Taken as a whole, the work of José María Arguedas has been read as a splendid celebration of the epic of Indian and mestizo, in spite of its undeniable involvement with an intellectual and aesthetic process fraught with dramatic vacillations and ambiguities. [1] Basically, it reveals an uneroded faith not only in the values of the native culture but also in the ultimate historical triumph of that culture. For these same reasons, however, it frequently veers toward utopianism and myth. Except in a few instances when the writer is obliged to deal with impenetrable forms of resistance, or where strong skepticism infiltrates the text, the vast realm of Arguedean discursivity almost always looks with optimism at that strength or astuteness that Angel Rama calls "cultural plasticity" (1982). This quality has enabled the indigenous Andean population to assume attributes foreign to itself and at the same time to enrich its experience of the world through them.

In the modern Quechua Indian, Arguedas felt, there is almost no trace of the pre-Hispanic past, only that which has been imposed from outside or has been assumed, more or less freely, from other traditions. Consequently, the subject has become radically transformed in terms of performance and feeling, to a point that modern identity still continues to be uniquely indigenous.[2]

If, on the one hand, we take the question of identity from the pigeonhole in which it usually exhibits the stubborn traits of an immutable being and place it in a field that is flexible, we will have installed a convergent dynamic, one in which mixtures and hybridizations attain coherence and unity as a new synthesis. Such material must needs be the object of close study, but at this point mestizaje, with its neoplatonic yearning for the reconciliation of opposites, serves to establish a classic example of transcultural intersection. I am fully aware that this reductive schematization does not do justice to the discrete fluidity and ambiguous oscillations that enrich Arguedas's work, nor am I overlooking the fact that my association of mestizaje and transculturation should be dealt with in detail, and in a way that exceeds the needs of my current argument. It is necessary at this point to warn the reader that I do not intend to invalidate the almost consensual interpretation of Arguedas's work, which on several occasions has also been my own.[3] A recent glance at his disquieting posthumous novel *El zorro de arriba y el zorro de abajo* (The fox from above and the fox from below, 1971), however, has made me suspect that along with the previously discussed views, others capable of inciting new and perhaps even more stimulating readings still lie hidden. Consequently, I propose an examination of the subject that will not so much substitute for those readings as reposition them. I will look closely at the way in which a multicultural web has been woven that only partially obeys the codes of transculturation: namely, one concerning the figure of the migrant and the meaning of migration. As is known, Arguedas's last novel proposes, within the narrative strata it contains, an ominous social hermeneutic of the conversion of a modest village of fisherfolk into the greatest fishing port in the world, with a referent, Chimbote, that is scrupulously factual. Obviously, the demographic explosion of Chimbote can only be explained by massive migration, with protagonists of the most varied geographical provenance and of infinitely diverse social conditions: foreigners of multiple origin, coastal creoles, and Afro-Peruvians, but especially Andean Indians and mestizos. These have preferred to face the fearsome threat of the sea and of machinery they never imagined, and that also terrified them, rather than repeat their unending secular servitude. To depict such a chaotic rush of events, Arguedas elaborates a narrative rhetoric based on a primordial intuition, one he linguistically designates as a "boiling up" or "ebullition," or "eruption."

The migrant and migration form recurrent motifs in the novelesque stratum of the text and contribute equally to the global texture of the novel. They appear in the sequences reenunciating the ancient myths of Huarochirí that were first collected by Francisco de Avila about 1598 and translated from Quechua by Arguedas in 1966, and that involve, in particular, the restless legendary animals that give the novel its title. They also appear in the sections from the author's diary that are interpolated in the text, since this diary, with its frequent recourse to memory, sheds light on what is perhaps the decisive factor of the text as a whole, namely, the migrant condition of the narrator himself.

Although I risk falling into biographic fallacy, it seems to me inevitable to allude to the displacements, traumatic or pleasant, undergone by Arguedas from the time he was a child. He recalls first the hacienda belonging to his father and stepmother, the latter a landowner possessing vast territories that came with their feudal Indian serfs, the times spent in poor Quechua communities where the little fugitive was received lovingly, then his disoriented wandering through dozens of villages and towns in the Andes, and finally his sojourn in a Lima that still prized pure Spanish lineage and consequently despised the people of the sierra. Not surprisingly, Arguedas defined himself as a permanent stranger and elaborated subtle and tortuous considerations of what he called *forasterismo*, or the condition of being a stranger, the sense of unease experienced by a person who lives in several worlds but in the end is native of none and always exists in a state of confusion, a stranger in a strange land. I believe, in view of his final novel, in which the semantic mark of migration is so obvious, that all the work of Arguedas can be reread in this same key.

In fact, there is almost no Arguedean text that does not allude elliptically to migration or thematize it explicitly, and for this reason Arguedas's textual production might well be defined as the epic of the migrant. Although nowadays, when almost everything is classified as discourse and it is considered in bad taste to refer to real life, it still strikes me as appropriate to add that, along with violence, migration is one of the two outstanding phenomena of contemporary Peru. An internal migration from the country to the city, on many occasions compulsory, has in less than fifty years converted a rural country, 65 percent of whose inhabitants were classified as living off the land, into an urban one, where over 70 percent of the population live in the cities. To be sure, the migrant condition does not displace the ethnic categories of Indian and mestizo but engulfs them and others in an individual and collective historical movement. To migrate, after all, involves looking back from a present here and now that incorporates (or should incorporate) the many events and spaces left from the then and there, but which can be found, albeit in fragmented form, in the restless flow of memory, the now that runs on, even as it deepens vertically, in a condensation of time, accumulating but not synthesizing yesterday's experiences and spaces.

I wish to make clear that the migrant condition, although lived in a present that appears to amalgamate much previous activity, is, nonetheless, quite unlike the mestizo will to syncretize. Common preference apparently leans toward this synthesizing of ancestors on both sides, as can be perceived in the paradigmatic figure of the Inca Garcilaso, the true founder of mixed, syncretized lineage. The coherence striven for, however, has almost always become unraveled in conflicts that, even when they are buried, cannot be erased. The average migrant, one may assume, stratifies experiences and has neither will nor desire to merge a past and present whose lack of contiguity serves only to emphasize the diversity of those times and spaces and the values or defects of the one and the other. Fragmentation is perhaps the norm. In the beautiful Andean songs, for example, the migrant never confuses yesterday/there with today/here; on the contrary, one or the other is emphasized; they are distinguished and placed in opposition. Even when the migration has proved fruitful, one's place of origin is drastically other, a dwelling place for mythic experiences that condition and disturb the migrant but do not mix with the present; they serve to define the present as ruled by necessity but not by desire.

It would be easy, speaking of Arguedas's work, to find a plethora of unforgettable experiences from his childhood, of the times when, a fugitive from an unbearable world of the mistis, he took refuge in indigenous communities and which he contrasts, quite explicitly, with his experiences in the cities. Yet these latter quite often awaken his enthusiasm and, more important, fulfill his objective of revindicating the indigenous world. It is at this point that migration has its strongest meaning, namely, the move from one culture to another, and whose preponderant sign is its bilingualism.

Bilingualism, even when symmetrical, which it almost never is, can produce acute anxiety due to the hybridization of loyalties and acts, and due to a coexistence of language competencies that are rooted in a memory hewn into dissimilar geographies, histories, and experiences. These, it is true, are interconnected, but they rigorously preserve their links with the language in which they were lived. Arguedas used to say that it was almost impossible for him to express in Spanish what he had experienced in Quechua, from his relations with the Andean countryside to the ways of feeling primary emotions such as hate and love, emotions he shared as a child with his native protectors. It is revealing, in this vein, that Arguedas's poetry is entirely in Quechua.

At the risk of outlining a precarious psychology of the migrant, I prefer to ask myself tentatively if the migrant condition functions, as that of the mestizo certainly does, as an enunciative locus at which a more or less differentiated use of language is generated. Could such a language affect the constitution of an alienated, diffuse, and heterogeneous subject such as the migrant?

I shall now employ the terms *intertextuality* and *dialogism* with considerable freedom, aware that both terms provide a comfortable if unstable referent for those who speak from the mestizo perspective. All words form a constellation of meanings and can thus accommodate multiple voices. This operation, nevertheless, results in a discourse that is more or less centered on itself. The language of the mestizo does not de-problematize the balance that exists in its origins, but its linguistic politics repeats the syncretizing gesture that generates fusion at the level of "educated language," making it porous and capable of either (1) accommodating the other, albeit partially, or (2) performing an explicit translation. This involves a double linguistic play: if in the first language the signs preserve their origin and function within intertextual relationships or establish conflictive dialogic relationships to them, in the case of the second, the two or more linguistic sequences enter a space that is more dialectical than dialogical and produce merely the *effect* of harmonious conciliation.

I should like to mention as a case in point how Garcilaso tells of the reactions of the Indians and Spaniards at seeing a strange stone with gold inside. The Inca says, "In Cusco the Spaniards considered it a 'marvelous thing'; the Indians called it *huaca*, which means 'wondrous thing.'"[4] Although brief, this text uses two ancestral voices, "marvelous thing" and "huaca," and reveals mestizo language by translating the second as "wondrous thing," which is synonymous with "marvelous thing." This fully reveals the concept of synthesis informing all mestizo endeavors. The cost, however, is extremely high. *Huaca* has been deprived of its sacred meaning because its carefully achieved synonymity has been drastically obscured. For fusion of these terms to be possible, one of them must pare down its differences and move away from the intertext that culturally corresponds to it, and in this way facilitate the production of synthesis.

I believe that the language enunciated from the position of the migrant resembles the example given above, but it is also evident that notable differences exist. Of primary interest is the way in which the two fundamentally coincide; namely, in the formation of enjambed discourse in differing cultures, awarenesses, and histories. However, I must emphasize a decisive difference: the migrant's discourse normally juxtaposes diverse languages or sociolects, with no synthesis apart from the one formalized externally through a solitary enunciatory act. I should like to stress the centrifugal dynamic of migrant discourse and its command of multiple applications, denoting here and there and now and then. In an act that is almost symbolic it can set down limits and laugh at them at the same time, ridiculing, through the fluidity of a speech that can be taken in different ways, and always in passing, echoing, as it were, the unstable situation of the individual who is speaking. Naturally, this constant movement reveals the lack of a central fixed axis necessary for regulation, variability, and dissidence. The opposite is the case with the lack of a fixed place that fosters the dissemination of ubiquitous signs that have no established territories. Therefore, if the mestizo subject tries to re-harmonize the interrupted order of his discourse by molding it to the needs of an identity whose recognition of its fragility only makes it stronger, the migrant lets his language fragment, contaminating it with ephemeral intertexts whose irregularity is due to their primary figuration being a subject who is always displaced. From this perspective, I venture to say that in the first case the final sense is dialectic, with its internal rhetoric most likely favoring metaphor, while the second is characterized by open, inconclusive dialogue, with the preferential mode being, presumably, metonymy. The former functions in the solidity of a closed space framed by similarity, while the latter does the reverse and functions in a fragmented, unceasing indeterminacy.

The nature of migrant discourse makes it difficult to extrapolate quotations from the text, although it becomes quite obvious in longer passages. The following dialogue between two immigrants is taken from *El zorro*:

> "True," said don Esteban, "the evangelist missionary in Chimbote is, as you say, *¿desabridoso?*—it's got no flavor."

> "You mean *desabrido*—tasteless."

> "That's right. Quechua's clearer—*qaima*—but anyway, this fellow, even if he is *desabridoso-qaima*, he certainly makes you hear the prophet Esaías. He's terrific. . . ." [153]

Note the persistence of the anomalous *desabridoso*, in spite of the speaker having been told the correct word is *desabrido*. The speaker insists that the Quechua word *qaima* is better than the Spanish *desabridoso/desabrido*, and finally, the abrupt eruption of the biblical (not Catholic but Protestant Evangelical) intertext—in a Quechuafied phonetic "*E*saías" (in Spanish, *I*saías [Isaiah]) and the final inappropriate Spanish (given the context) "Grandazo es. . . ." ("He's terrific. . . ."). Note that, as opposed to the example from Garcilaso, *qaima* is not translated and is not an exact synonym of *desabrido*, while the speaker distinguishes at least three levels: he knows that *desabrido* is the correct word but insists on repeating *desabridoso*, yet points out that *qaima* is the best word for expressing his meaning. Obviously, this preference refers back to an earlier time and space; the corrected form belongs to the present, while the intermediary *desabridoso* illustrates graphically, as it were, the displacement of the subject. The linguistic situation is dramatized, with the entire sequence tied to the unclear newness of the message from the evangelical church. For the Quechua-speaking migrant, it is a matter of something *desabridoso*, but his verbal memory feels *qaima* to be a stronger word, and he fully recognizes that in spite of this, the intensity of the prophet Isaiah's words move him deeply when he hears them in sermons. True, this is not totally explicit in the brief passage quoted, but perhaps, in spite of its vagueness, it will serve to clarify how fragmented experience and language, while situated almost indistinctly in diverse points of the text, can rub shoulders and exercise the functions that correspond to their erratic condition.

Like the mestizo, the migrant is also a social subject. Although he is representative of a less-established group and with a tradition that is less firm, nonetheless, a founder figure and text can be found in Guamán Poma de Ayala and his *La nueva coronica y buen gobierno* (The new chronicle and good government). The section of that text entitled "Camina el autor" (The author's wanderings) is particularly pertinent, and the very vastness of the migrant presence in the cities at this time makes us reconsider a story that for centuries has involved endless migrations. Insufficient work has been dedicated to the topic, especially in the purely literary field, though the challenge that is implicit in *El zorro* should be sufficient to install the migrant subject, language, and system of representation at the center of new reflections on both Andean and non-Andean discursivity. If Arguedas's last novel narrates the rise of an almost integrally "transplanted" town, the author left evidence of his uncertainty lest an "*hervor*," a boiling up or ebullition, transmute his meanings to the unforeseeable rhythm of uncontainable avalanches.

Arguedas had, a few years earlier, published what was perhaps his first poem written in the Quechua language—it is a hymn or song in honor of the epic tale of the migrant. In "A nuestro padre creador Túpac Amaru" (To our father-creator Túpac Amaru), first published in 1962, Arguedas confers mythic origin and legitimacy on a very visible historical event: the conquest of Lima, the symbol of Spanish Peru and Spanish-speaking Peru, by immense masses of Indians who are, not with violence but with energy, turning a space that they had always found hostile and other into their own. With their spirit of old, the migrants are invading the city and profoundly changing it, bringing into being, paradoxically, from that very topos, the millenarian utopia, the "City of Joy." I quote the Spanish translation of some of Arguedas's lines:

> There are thousands upon thousands of us here, now. We have gathered together, town by town, name by name, and we are pressing against this immense city that used to hate us so, that used to despise us, that called us excrement. We must convert it into the town of folk who sing to the four regions of our world, into a joyous town, where each man works. We are an immense people that does not hate and is pure in heart like the snow on the god-mountains that the plague of evil has never reached. [1972, 24–25]

To be sure, Arguedas's utopian vision has not come to pass; harsh, unceasing poverty has impeded the fruition of his high ideal of social happiness for all. Still, there was much that has come true in his dream of a city on the plain where everyday men and women from the four suyos, or regions, of the pre-Hispanic cosmography heroically struggle to preserve their ancestral identity as they communicate with the others who are now their neighbors, while enriching themselves with their experiences. In their own way they have modernized, and this modernity, if it is authentic, can mean several things; it can be as many-faceted and varied as it is encircling. It can be said, with good reason, that massive transculturation or universal mingling of races is taking place, but the migrant is always a migrant, even when permanently installed in a given space whose image and appearance she modifies; always in the background there are experiences related to upbringing and an almost unshakable capacity to see existence in terms of the stages lived and barriers crossed before she could settle a place she no doubt finds as fascinating as it is frightening.

Although in this preliminary approximation I have insisted on the differences between mestizo and migrant, it is not my intention to formulate a dichotomy between the two, nor between their respective languages and intertextual insertions, but, rather, to establish two enunciatory positions from which articulation can and does take place. For the moment, I am excited by the idea of crisscrossing the ultimately syncretic mestizo/transculturation paradigm with the shifting syntax of the migrant, on the one hand, and the fragmentary multiculture possessed by that migrant on the other. Perhaps only from both perspectives, and certainly not excluding others, will we be able to affirm the web of literary entanglement, the vast, slippery discourse of a culture in which variations proliferate, in a plural and pluralizing universe whose condition, perhaps, is the chaos of a creation that is (cheerfully?) incomplete.

Translated by Alita Kelley

Notes

1. This article originally appeared, in Spanish, in *Revista de crítica literaria latinoamericana.* 21, no. 42 (2d semester 1995): 101–9. The translator has replaced terms like *he* and *mankind* with gender-neutral terms.

2. The theme is treated constantly, though with obvious variations, in Arguedas's texts collected by Angel Rama in *Formación de una cultura nacional indoamericana* (Formation of a national Indoamerican culture), Mexico City: Siglo XXI Editores, 1975.

3. The most recent bibliography, though not completely satisfactory, appears in José María Arguedas's *El zorro de arriba y el zorro de abajo*. Cf. my book *Los universos narrativos de José María Arguedas* (The narrative worlds of José María Arguedas) (Buenos Aires: Editorial Losada, 1973). I have dealt with this topic many times.

4. This episode appears in vol. 4, book 8, chap. 24, pp. 80–81, of Inca Garcilaso de la Vega, *Comentarios reales de los Incas* (Royal commentaries of the Incas), preliminary study and notes by José Durand, Lima: Universidad de San Marcos, 1967. It is a text I have worked on on several occasions. See my articles "La 'invención' de las naciones hispanoamericana: Reflexiones a partir de una relación textual entre el Inca y Palma" (The "inventing" of the Hispanoamerican nations: Reflections arising from a textual relationship between the Inca Garcilaso and Palma), in *Discursos sobre la "invención" de*

América (Discourse on the "invention" of America), ed. Iris Zavala, Amsterdam: Rodopi, 1992, and "El discurso de la armonía imposible" (The discourse of impossible harmony), *Revista de crítica literaria latinoamericana* 19:38.

Works Cited

Arguedas, José María. 1972. *Katatay/Temblar* (To tremble). Lima: Instituto Nacional de Cultura. [Bilingual edition, Quechua and Spanish.]

————. 1990. *El zorro de arriba y el zorro de abajo* (The fox from above and the fox from below). Coordinated by Eve-Marie Fell. Madrid: CEP de la Biblioteca Nacional.

Rama, Angel. 1982. *Transculturación narrativa en América Latina* (Narrative transculturation in Latin America). Mexico City: Siglo XXI Editores. [Cf. especially pp. 38–56.]

The Plural Narrator and the Quandary of Multiple Communication in *Arguedas's* Deep Rivers

Julio Ortega

Various fundamental aspects of *Los ríos profundos* (1958) by José María Arguedas (1911–1969), translated into English by Frances Horning Barraclough as *Deep Rivers* (1978),[1] have already received the serious critical attention they merit.[2] The chapter entitled "A Closed World" in Sara Castro-Klarén's *The Magic World of José María Arguedas* (1973), Antonio Cornejo Polar's *The Narrative Worlds of José María Arguedas* (1976), and William Rowe's *Myth and Ideology in the Work of José María Arguedas* (1979) deserve particular attention. I would like to focus on a central aspect of the novel, namely, its communicative system. That such a system is decisive in the production of the text will soon be evident, as will the way in which it informs the cultural perspective that inspires Arguedas's writing. In *Deep Rivers* the narrative conflict can be interpreted as a drama of communication, initially stratified in a social sense, then presented as the disjunctive product of different communicative systems, each of which assumes a different form of processing, transmission, and hierarchical stratification. The drama of communication involves the heart-rending forms of social existence itself and of cultural modes in conflict, which define the positional roles of individuals both in speech and in society. *Deep Rivers* may be read in this perspective as a "cultural text" (Lotman and Ouspenski 1973), whose semiosis or production of sense requires that the role of the agents in communication be redefined (Lotman and Ouspenski 1976; Lucid 1977).

Narration and Reading: Voices and Functions

In order to control competing and disparate information and to replace an oral, temporal telling of a tale with one that fixes meaning by the process of writing, the narrator of this novel must, at one and the same time, be one person and plural. In the greater space of the text, the narrator occupies the present time of the writing; he is an authorial "I" who establishes and fixes the story and gives it balance through a telling of the tale that exteriorizes it. In a second space within the text an "I" as witness can be found, an "I" who paves the way by producing reports and whose function is to make known the specific culture involved through discursive expansion and more pointed denunciation. Finally, within the dimensions of the story line itself, we find the "I" as actor in the form of the child protagonist in his then current-at-the-time-of-the-action situation and open to events and their dramaticity.

If the first narrator is responsible for writing a text, his act in emitting it takes the form of the *enunciation,* and a reading of his material presupposes the information has been organized, mediated, and processed as "something new." The second narrator illustrates the first's story as "truth" through cultural differentiation. The third, on the other hand, supports the enunciation of the first by occupying a role within the fiction. The plural narrator thus constructs a systematic implied reading: as author he produces a difference whose certitude is verified by the witness, and both co-inform an actor within the story line, with the latter being distinguished by his learning to process information (Barthes 1973; Charles 1977).

The interaction of narrative voices may be diagrammed as follows:

Narrator	Discourse	Reader	Function
"I" author	(novel)	textual reading	(discovery)
"I" witness	(report)	cultural reading	(truth)
"I" actor	(biography)	participant reading	(conflict)

The interaction of the three narrators is immediate, even simultaneous, since the text seeks to integrate them into the discourse concerning their own conflict, while at the same time the types of discourse (e.g., novel, report, or biography) behave inclusively and may move from one to another of the narrators. By the same token, the narrators are, obviously, all voices of one same narrator, and they imply a reading informed by the deepest sense of awareness within the text. This reading includes the authorial "I," who, being fully aware, will not resolve any conflicts but move toward his mask as actor (the child) and thus potentialize those conflicts. Finally, the term *function* refers to the way in which the relationship between narrator and reader is made meaningful through narrative strategy. Interaction of discourse certainly plays a major part: *bio-graphy*, for example, presupposes the "life of the actor" resolved as writing, and *dis-covery* presupposes an operation of the text, by which it can be clearly seen that in revealing himself as the author, the narrator submits to the actor's (the child's) conflict.

I must insist on the systematic plurality of the narrator of *Deep Rivers*, since some critics have spread a notion, redolent of obscurantism, that Arguedas was little more than a naive, or even "primitive," writer, and that this novel is an idyllic, Rousseauesque depiction of nature. Some have even gone so far as to suggest that the novel reveals an irrationalist perspective, namely, that it is a manipulation of myths invented by the author; yet, the rationality of myth within this text is quite evident, as I hope to show. The truth is more complex; it is also more interesting.

Already on the first page we see the multiple perspective in operation: the narrator-witness is such, primarily, through the relation of
the reader to the text, so when the word *colonos* (serfs, sharecroppers)
appears and clarification for the reader is required, the narrator produces a footnote: "Indians belonging to the haciendas" (3). It is interesting to note that the footnotes will, in most cases, gradually start
to be woven into the text itself.

Almost at once we read:

> They were relatives and hated each other. My father, however, had
> conceived some peculiar plan concerning the Old Man; and although
> he told me we were traveling to Abancay, we set out from a distant
> town for Cuzco. According to my father we were just passing through
> Cuzco. I was eager to arrive in the great city. And my first meeting
> with the Old Man was to be an unforgettable occasion. [3]

The introductions (see also, for example, the one at the beginning
of chap. 6, "Zumbayllu," 64), require one of the three narrative voices
to stand out, while the other two contribute. The rhetorical code
aims to prepare and assist the reader's receptive capacities, and a
study of the code will reveal the fine strategic work contained within
the text with the purpose of facilitating the intended reader's recep-
tivity.

In the case of the first chapter, after the introductory words of the
witness-narrator, we see the *author-narrator* appear from within the
story, with the text that introduces him serving, at one and the same
time, to present the story as it took place and to define the nature of
the action: "They were relatives and hated each other . . ." (3). If
the tenses of the narrative are noted, the way in which these voices
function will be clearer. In the next phrase, namely: "My father, however, had conceived some peculiar plan concerning the Old Man"
(3), the rhetorical code is implied (the promise of the future action of
the story) and the *author-narrator* is also implied, since the use of
the past perfect tense assumes the present of the writing. The following phrase, however, involves the *actor-narrator* in a temporal se-

quence—for example, the verbs: "he *told* me" "we *were traveling*" "we *set* out." The source of the information is thereby transferred to the father: "although he *told* me we *were traveling* . . . According to my father, we *were* just passing through . . ." (3); here the code is that of the *fable*, the sequence of action, with the longest sequence being that of the journey, with its erratic movement and indistinct space. The *actor-narrator* then changes the narrative tense: "I *was* eager *to arrive* in the great city" (3), with "I was" and "to arrive" realizing the action that the previous phrase already approximates to a tense that opens up present-in-the-past. The final phrase, "And my first meeting with the Old Man was to be an unforgettable occasion," (3) envelops both actor and author within an autoreferential code; the biographical perspective has been fulfilled through the textualizing of the recollection and the imminence of its telling. The abbreviated perspective of "an unforgettable occasion" reveals the *author-narrator*, implying the rhetorical code (once again a promise of the text: its interest); and finally, the interactive plurality of the voices. Thus, within the narrative, verb tenses in different remarks by the narrator serve as a source of information. This is also the case when context is pinpointed prior to its subsequent inclusion in the storyline. In chapter 4, following the introduction by the *witness-narrator* regarding landowners, we read that "Abancay is closed in by the lands of the Patibamba hacienda. The whole valley, from north to south, from one mountaintop to the other, belongs to the haciendas" (40). The *witness-narrator* uses the present tense to establish the nature of the space (the code of dual place) and to textualize that space immediately thereafter by the use of the imperfect tense:

> The grounds of the Patibamba mansion were better kept and larger than the main plaza of Abancay. . . . The house had a silent, white, arcaded porch. . . . A tall aviary stood in one corner of the garden. . . . The cage had several levels. . . . [40]

In the above, enumeration is temporalized as duration, revealing the broad gaze of the *author-narrator,* while the *actor-narrator* is incorporated within the telling as his gaze is reconstructed by the virtual and plural time frames that bind the two. "I often went to look in through the gate," the story line continues, but "only once did I hear the voice of a piano from that place" (40). It can be seen that the *author* perceives an event through the *actor*, and this immediately is brought into action as: "someone was playing it." Then the *actor* takes over the text and the space described intensifies the change to storytelling mode, with the inclusion of the adverb *already* announcing a switch to the immediate present: "A short distance from the owner's mansion the lane was already covered with sugar cane trash."[3]

And this same story line prevails: "The sun blazed down on the dried molasses" (41) in the present that the *actor* has recaptured. The interaction is not deductive, however, but is simultaneous; it is an alternating movement presented by the written drama and involving the subject.

Paradigms of Communication

The polar relationship with which the action of the novel begins, the Spanish *viejo* (chap. 1, "The Old Man") and *viaje* (chap. 2, "The Journeys"), signals the origin of the conflict in a text that will seek to remake the very meaning of communication. This duality is produced by a code of ambivalence, one that polarizes speakers, spaces, and groups through a disjunction of meaning. The Old Man, from Cuzco, the ancient center of significance, is the powerful relative, Ernesto's uncle, who extends his rule in the current distorted world of power with its own particular hierarchies and values. The Father, on the other hand, is the "wandering fool," the "madman" (41), a person of no fixed abode whose movements are emblematic of the break up of a genuine sense of reality, a sense that provides alternatives to perceptions that are socially sanctioned at the present time.

The beginning of the novel, with the return to a Cuzco occupied by the False Father, is symbolic in itself, with, presiding over the conflict, a figure who has usurped place and substituted different meaning. The return to the paradise of his forbears is frustrated for the boy: "This couldn't be the Cuzco my father had described to me . . ." (4). Place and sense have been exiled, and the text will be produced from their place of banishment to provide a radical revision of the models in dispute; it will take the form of the *Bildungsroman* that allows for the actualization of that dispute. Consequently, the reshaping of the motif of the world-made-anew is being put to the test by the reactions of a boy.

As in Juan Rulfo's *Pedro Páramo* (1955), a mythic schema underlies the Old Man's guilt; the leader's cruel way of being reflects the loss of the original space. The Old Man "shouts with the voice of the damned" and "stores up the fruit from his orchards and lets it spoil" (3), and the opposition between the two patriarchal figures (father/uncle) is reproduced in the configuration of the place itself—a white Spanish wall has been built upon the stone Inca rampart: "The white wall of the second story continued upward in a straight line from the Inca wall" (4).

Within the novel, the representation of space merits a study in itself. The Old Man's house is "on the same street as the Inca wall" (4), and even the tree in the courtyard is "low, with shabby branches" (5). It is in the courtyard that the boy meets the *pongo* (Indian servant); the *witness-narrator* tells us the meaning of the word in a footnote: "Hacienda Indians who are obliged to take turns working as unpaid servants in the landowner's house" (5). This meeting with the *pongo* will be paralleled with the boy's encounter with the Inca wall (7–8). Prior to his visit to Cuzco, Ernesto the *actor-narrator* was unacquainted with either of these paradigmatic signs of communication.

Now degraded to use as a public urinal, the street of the Inca wall is restored as communication and its fitted stones transformed by the boy's perception:

I touched the stone with my hands, following the line, which was as undulating and unpredictable as a river, where the blocks of stone were joined. In the dark street, in the silence, the wall appeared to be alive; the lines I had touched between the stones burned on the palms of my hands. [6]

The act of communication begins as a ritual act of recognition and with it the boy transmutes cultural matter (an Inca wall) into matter that is original (the guardian rivers of childhood). In this way he reestablishes order of origin; his model of culture will essentially be one of communication in which meaning will be organized so that it not only takes in the scenery (the natural world), but also the subject himself. It is not insignificant, therefore, that from the time of this ritual on, Ernesto confronts the misfortunes of his father's travels with the promise of place that is that of his father.

Initially, "when my father confronted his enemies . . . I would think of Cuzco. I knew that in the end we would arrive in the great city" (7). That promise was frustrated; however, the ritual by the Inca wall affirms the connection that verifies the foreshadowed meaning of the wall. Immediately thereafter, a dialog of recognition ensues in which speaker and intended reader identify by means of an encoding that utilizes the means of communication belonging to that model—that is, the original Quechua language:

Then I remembered the Quechua songs which continually repeat one pathetic phrase: *yawar mayu*, "bloody river"; *yawar unu*, "bloody water"; *puk'tik yawar k'ocha*, "boiling bloody lake"; *yawar wek'e*, "bloody tears". Couldn't one say *yawar rumi*, "bloody stone," or *puk'tik yawar rumi*, "boiling bloody stone"? The wall was stationary, but all its lines were seething and its surface was as changeable as that of the flooding summer rivers, which have similar crests near the center, where the current flows the swiftest and is the most terrifying. The Indians call these muddy rivers *yawar mayu* because when the sun shines on them they seem to glisten like blood. . . .

"Puk'tik yawar rumi," I exclaimed, facing the wall.

And as the street remained silent, I repeated the phrase several times. [7]

This beautiful passage is explicit enough. The ritual of communication involves the enunciation of the identificatory names of fundamental elements (water, stone, and blood). Through such naming, a primary statement is pronounced that establishes one mutual identity. Culture as information and as source of information is capable of reordering and reinstating plenitude of feeling through the very act of communication. Not by chance do the three voices of the narrator all yield to the word itself in their passing the use of language to each other.

From this instance on, Ernesto's perception will reorder and interpret information according to a different order of facts. "Papa, every stone is talking," he concludes (8), and, in the same way, he attempts to rework information concerning his father. The wall, he believes, might swallow up the tight-fisted lords of Cuzco (9); the cultural model is a moral one also, and the opposition of good and evil is proposed as a struggle for information when communication systems that signify by different means from the one in power are stifled. An antinatural power has been imposed, and this, as regards the social order, has given rise to present injustice, which, first and foremost, goes against the natural state of things.

Ernesto's emerging convictions, however, impose change according to his own beliefs. When the boy sees the cathedral, for example, we read that "it was the largest one I had ever seen. It was as if the arches were on the distant perimeter of some silent plain in the icy highlands . . ." and that "it was an immense façade; it seemed to be as wide as the base of the mountains that rise up from the shores of some highland lakes" (9). The cathedral, a cultural monument, is thus incorporated into the order of natural perception from which measure and value arise. Also faced with the appeal that he senses in the form of the cathedral—"Instead of being overpowering, it made me rejoice" (11)—the boy needs to respond: "I felt like singing in the doorway. I had no desire to pray" (11). Ernesto wants, like the Indians, to sing "a hymn," but, he stresses, unlike theirs, without tears. It is revealing that this Spanish monument is also built of stone. "We always call unhewn rock that is covered with parasites or red lichen 'living rock'" (12). The *author-narrator*, using the "we" of a culture while challenging its information, now tells us of the different types of apparently anomalous stone from which monuments can be built. The tour of other temples serves to strengthen the dispute between Inca and colonial walls. The stones of Huayna Capac's ruined palace "weren't bubbling or talking, nor did they have the spontaneity of those that frolicked in the wall of the palace of the Inca Roca; it was the wall who commanded silence . . ." (12). There communication had already been banned. But the conflict is not simply one between indigenous and Hispanic objects; the opposition depends, rather, on the perception and order in which the objects are situated culturally. The "song" of the María Angola, the legendary bell of the Cuzco cathedral, in spite of being a Hispanic object, functions within the cultural order upheld by the child. About its song we read that

> The world must have been changed into gold at that moment—I, too, as well as the walls and the city . . . the vibrations expanded slowly, at spaced intervals—growing stronger, piercing the elements. . . . [12–13]

The "message" of the bell immediately brings to Ernesto's mind other bells in Indian villages:

> I thought that those bells must be *illas*, reflections of the María Angola, which would change the *amarus* into bulls. From the center of the world the voice of the bell, sinking down into the lakes, must have transformed the ancient creatures. [13]

This passage is extremely pertinent, since it announces a religious synchronism implicit in a way of looking at reality that is made up of native and Hispanic elements, with both integrated to form a *mestizaje*, or mingling of cultures, whose organization, however variable, is always, basically, Andean. In this case the powerful song of the Spanish bell has turned a Quechua element, the *amarus* (serpents), into bulls—a Hispanic element. Such metamorphosis may be seen as allegorical, but the explanation continues to be mythical and belongs to the Andean way of thinking (Ossio 1973; Wachtel 1971; Millones 1979). It is equally evident, at the same time, that the bell's "song" also evokes "the image of my protectors, the Indian *alcaldes*" (13), a tutelary image from the real world, one that has incorporated bells into its mythic communication.

It can be seen, therefore, that this is not merely a dispute between the "indigenous" and the "Hispanic," but affirmation of two orders containing elements of one source of information as well as the other, with both incorporated within Ernesto's perception/modelization; Ernesto himself will live the conflict of defining one order in the space of the other.

Another communicatory figure no less illustrative and decisive in this debate is that of the *pongo* whom Ernesto meets in Cuzco. Arguedas has dwelt on this extraordinary emblem of the orphaned state of the indigenous people and the violence they have suffered at the hands of the hacienda system in the sierra of Peru, in the short story adapted from a Quechua tale and entitled "El sueño del pongo" (The Indian servant's dream). In it, the *pongo* is the principal actor in a delightful parable of the world-turned-upside-down and put to rights after death. Humiliation, the essential mark of the role of the serf, is a denial of the human condition: "one could sense the invisible weight that oppressed his breathing and the effort that he was making just to appear to be alive" (18).

Following the elevation of the *pongo* through greeting, contained in the first paradigm, the boy tries to communicate with him:

> I spoke to him in Quechua. He looked at me startled. "Doesn't he know how to talk?" I asked my father.
>
> "He doesn't dare," he told me. "Even though he is coming with us to the kitchen."

In none of the hundreds of towns where I had lived with my father were there any *pongos*.

"*Tayta*," I said to the Indian in Quechua, "are you from Cuzco?"

"*Manan*," he answered. "From the hacienda." [14]

The speaker makes use of his recourse to the common code of Quechua, but the addressee lacks any role within communication that will distinguish him as a specific being; as a serf, his role excludes him from speech itself. When he answers, he gives his state of belonging within an economic system (the hacienda) as his place of origin. For him, the use of speech as distinctive communication is prohibited. Social stratification distorts the very act of communication and establishes a practice of differentiation within the exercise of speech between human beings: some are sanctioned, others are manipulated. *Deep Rivers* contains a powerful denunciation of the usurpation of speech.

The Old Man clearly represents the dominant system that commits the usurping. After Ernesto and his father have slept in his house and suffered humiliation at his hands by being lodged in the kitchen—the servant's quarters—they still have to face the powerful landowner himself, whose distinguishing mark, his avarice, is yet another sign of distorted power. Ernesto settles the confrontation through an act of communication dramatized as follows:

"What is your name?" the Old Man asked, again training his eyes on me. . . .

"I have the same name as my grandfather, *señor*," I told him.

"*Señor*? Am I not your uncle?" . . .

"You're my uncle. It's time for us to go now, *señor*."

I saw that my father was delighted despite his almost solemn expression. [17]

Once again the substance of communication is revealed through naming. In this instance the appellations used impose a differentiation between the system of family relationships, in which a term of mutual recognition ("uncle") is pronounced, and the mark *señor* ("sir") distances the speaker. The latter appellation calls attention to the way in which an act of communication of an impersonal nature can reiterate a situation, and usage, which in this instance we can call *identificatory* because it puts the communicative functions to the test within the autoreferentiality of the communicative act itself. In this respect the passage is extremely eloquent. The speaker (the Old Man) and the addressee (the boy) are about to be defined through an identificatory situation: when the speaker, the Old Man, asks the boy his name—the communicatory act of asking someone's name signals the authority of the speaker—the boy replies by a subterfuge and refuses to give his name directly. Instead, he refers to the name of a superior patronymic authority, his grandfather. In this way, the addressee has placed in question the role assigned to him by the first speaker, who, in turn, immediately sees that his own role is being questioned in a subdiscourse in which an impersonal form of address has been imposed over the one that denotes the blood relationship between the speaking subjects. Alarmed, he demands to be defined not as "*señor*" but as "uncle," which denotes a family figure of authority and the one in command of this speech act. In another subterfuge that throws the identificatory act out of court completely, the boy uses both forms of address; he accepts the inescapable family relationship, "You're my uncle," then immediately distances himself again by addressing the Old Man as "*señor*" (17). In so doing, the communicatory act has made referents of both subjects, with the conflict inherent in the communicatory act involving both of them. In Hispanic usage, an act of identification must precede the setting up of a stable circuit through which information can be transmitted, but here it has been turned into an act complete in itself, and, moreover, one that brooks no continuation, since the addressee has rejected the moral role assumed by the speaker whose identity he has labelled as not genuine. With the *pongo*, Ernesto saw identification as a means to show that he recognized the role of both subjects in the speech act, but with his uncle, on the other hand, he has converted identification into a metadiscourse, both to challenge and reject.

That his strategy is employed prior to messages being transmitted reveals further social and ethnic stratification, since identification tacitly defines subjects in a valorative manner. It implies their social value, their source value, their ethnic value, and their very right to communicate in one discourse or another; the different types of discourse that correspond to speakers define each subject socially. Through the novel's use of stratified speech patterns, of mediated information, the drama of such discourse is revealed. That communication is informed by social situation is self-evident, but that the novel should reveal the way in which a hierarchy of values exists within the information transmitted, how subjects are ranked and norms established as to perception of meaning to the point of reenforcing and reproducing the structural violence of the society, speaks for its critical persuasiveness. It can, in this regard, be considered a denunciatory "social text." What is being denounced is the very social existence being depicted, along with all the heart-rending violence that constitutes it. And the denunciation is not only moral, it is rooted in the latent alternatives that exist in the social existence represented, and it seeks to legitimate the responsive capacity of a perception that is not merely Andean but Peruvian, a perception in which the Andean system reappropriates conflicting Hispanic information.

If Arguedas is seen as an indigenist or regionalist author, the extraordinary quality of his undertaking is being shortchanged; it is far more encompassing and fruitful. José María Arguedas faced, in his writing, some of the same cultural dilemmas confronted by the Inca Garcilaso de la Vega, Guamán Poma de Ayala, and César Vallejo. The redefining of an instrument of communication in order to transform

communication, the changing of writing into a product of reformulated communication, has affected the very nature of the text for these
Peruvian writers, and required them to reconstruct their textual un-
dertakings. For this reason, Arguedas might be considered not only
the most valuable Peruvian writer of this century, but the one whose
work reformulates the interactions of literature and culture in a text
that expands their functions through the power of its convictions.

Ernesto's Cuzco experience means the closing off to him of a legendary patriarchal space and the beginning once again of the wanderings that underline his figure that society defines as misfit and
outsider, a rootless adolescent. In the novel Ernesto assures us that
his perception goes back to his childhood, to the time he began to see
the world according to the communicative system that the Indians
had taught him, a paradigm of "natural" communication in itself. But
in Cuzco, Ernesto's education is confronted by new socially stratified
information. He is guided by his father, an impoverished "gentleman" whose concept of what is noble and ideal Ernesto has assimilated. A conflict is resolved when he is made certain that his own
perceptions are the right ones and that he will be required to take a
stand, to assume a critical, participatory position in order to fulfill his
social destiny. We are not dealing here with a simple "character in a
novel" but with a multidimensional subject, the "I" that does not reveal itself openly but which is, nonetheless, made manifest in the con-
structive and critical adventure that characterizes this text.

Multiple communication—namely, hearing things sing, naming
things, speaking to them, interiorizing them, and decoding their
meaning as one would with an alphabet—opens up a double, typically ambivalent space. One aspect of this space is joyful, the other
filled with suffering. Cuzco itself performs an act of redoublement
and includes the signs from the broken alphabet of the dominated
code, alongside the signs of the dominant one. "Nowhere else must
human beings suffer so much as here" (20), a passage concludes.
The buildings themselves form part of a struggle between two poles,

even within the dominant alphabet: together the churches of La Compañía and the cathedral mitigate the effects of that struggle. As the father and son read the monuments of the two cultures, they read a cosmic discourse both eschatological and moral, one formed from a way of perceiving reality that incorporates the lessons of the Andean world and the evidence offered by the Hispanic one. It is a way of seeing that we may call acculturated, without supposing it to involve homogeneous acculturation, which would imply a leveling "*mestizaje*" of both sources of culture; it is, rather, synchretic, and in the child it takes off from his structuralizing of semantic fields that are Andean in origin.

The following diagram might synthesize that journey, restarting from Cuzco:

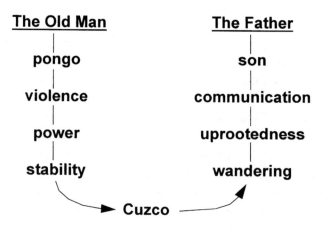

The Old Man   **The Father**
|
pongo   son
|
violence   communication
|
power   uprootedness
|
stability   wandering

Cuzco

If Cuzco, the "center of the world" for the pre-Columbian culture and a sacred place, has been usurped by the figure of the antifather, the miser, it means the original meaning has been marginalized and that wandering can be Ernesto's only space. As he leaves the city, a natural, protective figure appears once again: in counterpoint to the fixed state of being, the river offers free, purifying movement. Significantly, this is the Apurímac, the "God-who-speaks" (22), whose name assumes that the world the river runs through is a sleeping text that it awakens and the wanderer receives. It is a writing of the world that unfolds as a writing of memory:

> The voice of the river and the profundity of the dusty gorge, the sparkle of the distant snows, and the rocks that shine like mirrors all awaken in his mind primeval memories, the most ancient of dreams. [22]

Deep rivers run in this mythic depth of origin, feeding a promise of all-encompassing communication that defines the subject's pilgrimage. "The voice of the river grows louder, but doesn't become deafening; instead it makes one feel excited" (23), the text tells us, in its own characteristic way, which can be likened to an alphabet that the speaker receives, one that rearticulates natural objects and the subject, through the physical act of the dialog that has taken place.

Translated by Alita Kelley, with Julio Ortega

Notes

1. Quotations from the novel are cited from *Deep Rivers* (1978).

2. An earlier version of this essay was published previously in Spanish in *Texto, comunicación y cultura: Los ríos profundos de José María Arguedas* (Text, communication, and culture: *Deep Rivers* by José María Arguedas). Lima: CEDEP, 1982. See also Ortega, Julio, *Crítica de la Identidad: La pregunta por el Perú en su literatura* (A critique of identity: The question of Peru in its own literature). Mexico City: Fonda de Cultura Económica, 1989.

3. Translation by Alita Kelley. Barraclough, in her translation of *Deep Rivers*, omits the adverb discussed here by Ortega: "This lane was covered with sugar cane trash almost the whole way to the mansion" (40).

Works Cited

Arguedas, José María. 1958. *Los ríos profundos* (Deep rivers). Buenos Aires: Editorial Losada; *Deep Rivers*. Trans. Frances Horning Barraclough. Austin: University of Texas Press, 1978.

———. 1974. "El sueño del pongo" (The Indian servant's dream). *Relatos completos* (Complete stories). Buenos Aires: Editorial Losada.

Barthes, Roland. 1973. "Analyse textuelle de un conte de Edgard Poe" (Textual analysis of a story by Edgar Allan Poe). In *Sémiotique narrative et textuelle* (Narrative and textual semiotics), ed. Claude Chabrol. Paris: Larousse; Translation into Spanish in Renato Prada Oropeza, 1978. ed. *Lingüística y literatura* (Linguistics and literature). Xalapa: Universidad Veracruzana. [On the communicative act between author and reader.]

Castro-Klarén, Sara. 1973. *El mundo mágico de José María Arguedas* (The magic world of José María Arguedas). Lima: Instituto de Estudios Peruanos.

Charles, Michel. 1977. *Rhétorique de la lecture.* (The rhetoric of reading) Paris: Editions du Seuil.

Cornejo Polar, Antonio. 1976. *Los universos narrativos de José María Arguedas* (The narrative worlds of José María Arguedas). Buenos Aires: Editorial Losada.

Lotman, Y. M., and Boris A. Ouspenski. 1973. "The Semiotic Study of Cultures." In *Structure of Texts and Semiotics of Culture*, ed. Jan van der Eng and Mojmir Grygar. The Hague: Mouton.

———, eds. 1976. *Travaux sur les systemes de signes* (Works about systems and signs). Brussels: Editions Complexe.

Lucid, Daniel P., ed. and trans. 1977. *Soviet Semiotics: An Anthology.* Baltimore: Johns Hopkins University Press.

Millones, Luis. 1979. "Sociedad indigena e identidad nacional" (Indigenous society and national identity). In *Perú: Indentidad nacional* (Peru: National identity), ed. Cesar Arrospide de la Flor. Lima: Centro de Estudios para el Desarrollo y la Participación.

Ortega, Julio. 1989. *Crítica de la identidad: La pregunta por el Perú en su literatura* (A critique of identity: The question of Peru in its own literature). Mexico City: Fondo de Cultura Económica.

Ossio, Juan, ed. 1973. *Ideología mesiánica del mundo andino* (Messianic ideology in the Andean world). Lima: Ignacio Prado Pastor.

Rowe, William. 1979. *Mito e ideología en la obra de José María Arguedas* (Myth and ideology in the work of José María Arguedas). Lima: Instituto Nacional de Cultura.

Wachtel, Nathan. 1971. *La visión des vaincus: Les Indiens du Perou devant la conquête espagnole* (The vision of the vanquished: The Peruvian Indians and the Spanish Conquest). Paris: Gallimard.

Wo(men) in the Carnivalesque Discourse of Deep Rivers

Luis A. Jiménez

Besides Ernesto, protagonist and narrator in *Deep Rivers* (*Los ríos profundos*, 1958) by José María Arguedas (1911–1969), the figures of Opa and Doña Felipa also stand out in the novel.[1] Even though Opa could be considered a secondary character, her role is important because she represents the muted object of desire of the boarding students at the Abancay Catholic school who abuse her sexually. In contrast to Opa, Doña Felipa, the leader of the uprising of *chicheras* (makers or sellers of corn liquor), becomes the speaking subject of a sociopolitical movement in the southern Peruvian sierra. Her warlike spirit and opposition to the official discourse, chronicled by Arguedas, reaffirms her defensive posture toward the oppressed. Both women participate as object-subject of a "postcolonial discourse," according to the definition given by Sidonie Smith and Julia Watson (1992, xvi). In *Deep Rivers*, however, this sense of modernness reverts itself: the majority discourse that should belong to the Indian and mestizo population is appropriated by the minority discourse of the official white class in power.

From these two opposite poles, the adolescent Ernesto thoroughly narrates the participation of Opa and Doña Felipa, both active and passive. My analysis centers particularly on the relationship between Ernesto and Opa, and the protagonist's fleeting encounters with Doña Felipa as these interactions provide a broad explanation of the development of women's dynamics in the novel. A detailed analysis of these female characters' behavior offers two fragmented versions of the modern Andean woman, her culture and society within a low carnivalesque world that Arguedas portrays with a mocking laughter and even parody (para-ode).[2] Laughter in his archaic universe motivates the act of writing since it is innate to humankind. In his interpretation of Rabelais, Bakhtin explains that carnivalized literature shows how the rhetorical seriousness of discourse has transforming power (1965, 36–38). This carnivalesque sense of the universe unmasks irony and humor, satire and parody, which ambivalently mean to vividly reconstruct the "other side" of life that is recreated in *Deep Rivers*.[3] Furthermore, grotesque realism reaccentuates a modernization of laughter by using the popular festive mood of the crowd, thus recreating a ludic and eschatological image that Arguedas privileges to uncover the abuses perpetuated against lower class wo(men).

The well-informed and eclectic criticism of *Deep Rivers* sporadically points out the function of women in the novel. For William Rowe, the idealization of women is an "antidote" against Ernesto's feelings of hallucination, an absolute model that appears to be relegated to the margins of the natural order (1979, 170). On different grounds, Sara Castro-Klarén lucidly suggests that in Arguedas's narrative discourse there generally prevails a "patriarchal vision towards women" (1983, 55–56). In her viewpoint, the narrated facts are interpreted and judged by a traditional masculine voice that displaces and ostracizes female characters—above all, those belonging to the low social strata, like the *cholas* (Indian women who work as servants).

Apart from these specific comments, few critics dwell on the roles of Opa and Doña Felipa; roles that because of their dissimilar presentation could be considered diametrically opposed. My purpose is to elucidate how these two female characters act respectively as object-subject in the writing of a text that criticizes and censures the alienating situation of women. Nevertheless, it must be added that the presence of an adolescent narrator originates dialogical limitations: "I was fourteen years old; I had spent my childhood in an alien house, always tended by cruel people" (15). Ernesto's point of view is, therefore, quite limited, and it could be classified within the generic restrictions of the *Bildungsroman*. His narrative abilities only evoke episodes from the past by means of subjective memory. The questioning that pertains to the credibility of what an adolescent is relating does not imply Arguedas's intrusion either (Barthes's "death of the author").[4]

One of the most salient traits in *Deep Rivers* is the abundant description of characters. At times, the linguistic space lies on the speech act of men and women. By means of the orality of language, whether Quechua or Spanish, the reader recognizes the ethnia of the fictional character, an experiment that in Arguedas's text can be attributed to the "pluricultural bilingualism of the Andean zone" (Cornejo Polar 1973, 12). The character's discourse unfolds in hybrid constructions that contain two ways of speaking, two languages that link the character to a specific cultural stratum (Bakhtin's "situated utterance").[5] A close look at the text shows how two linguistic systems are split in search of dialogue: "He spoke to me in Spanish. When he spoke Quechua, he would take off his scarf or wrap it around his neck, as was proper" (36). In other instances, the narrator resorts to verbal portraits in order to present a physical or spiritual description, by means of which one knows if the character is white, Indian, or mestizo. Although in the novel Ernesto frequently focuses on the description of the eyes, broader facial expressions direct our attention to certain features of ethnicity and social domains that identify the fictional characters. Here follow two portraits from *Deep Rivers:*

... it seems as if rivers of tears might flow from his blue eyes. [7]

If I take Salvinia to my hacienda someday, they will say her eyes were made of that water; they'll say she is the daughter of the river. [105]

In the first statement the metaphoric illusion orients the reading to a double meaning: the gaze of Ernesto's father, a Eurocentric vision of the white man, and the image of the river that serves as the book's title. The paternal "blue eyes" call up racial imaginings. The reader sees in them the descendant of the postcolonial Spanish man residing in America. The autobiographical implications between Ernesto and Arguedas in the novel constitute a pivotal artifice for understanding the role of eyes and their expressions in the narrative of *Deep Rivers*. The image of the river recurs in the second statement. The language of nature describes a character on a figurative level, and this rhetorical and poetic mosaic is intertwined with the events in the novel.

It is worth noting that in Opa's description, the reader unmistakably notices her low ethnic origin and social role. The character's portrait takes the shape of a sick and smelly woman as the image conveys a possible physiological defect:

> On certain nights a feeble-minded woman who worked in the kitchen would come walking slowly into that playground. She was not an Indian; her hair was light and her face was white, even though it was covered with dirt. She was short and fat. [69]

On the one hand, fatness is usually associated with food; both fatness and food reaffirm the grotesque image of her body.[6] On the other hand, madness propitiates the incapacity to articulate her own discursive "I" for which the narrator relegates Opa to accept the rules of sexuality among the schoolboys. Moreover, within the novel's ironic universe, a pun can be depicted: Opa is called a "doncella" (58); that is to say, she is either a maid or a maiden woman who has never encountered a man intimately. At any rate, her real name, Marcelina, is not revealed until the end of the novel when she dies of the plague. By the brief act of naming Opa, Ernesto succeeds in humanizing the fictional character before her death.

Opa affirmatively responds to the initiative of sexual desire, an inherent appetite proving that the carnal act is not exclusive to masculine beings. In other words, "sex" is a biological factor while "gender" (masculine and feminine) falls within the parameters of culture (Stoller 1968, viii). Since Opa is not in complete control of her mental faculties, the character intensively enjoys her own body without really realizing the sexual ab/uses to which she becomes subject. Opa's prostituted body represents what Rauch (1988) calls woman as "allegory of modernity." Along with sex, madness is presented as a laughable spectacle, the amusement of participants and observers. In the novel, Opa is denied the right of articulated language, and the reader can only hear her guttural yet pleasing sounds: "Lleras had undressed the feeble-minded woman, and was urging Palacitos to throw himself upon her. [She] wanted him and moaned, beckoning to the boy with both hands" (53). Opa's contaminated body is more productive than her ailing mind. The pleasure experienced within the privacy of the boarding school's latrines cancels out on "moonlights when the feeble-minded woman did not go to the playgrounds" (52). The presence of the heavenly body, therefore, could be read as the absence of pleasure in the school's latrines.

A typical boy of pubertal age, Ernesto feels curiosity (or morbidness) toward his classmates' sexual relations with Opa. The protagonist acts as if he were a "voyeur" (Michel Foucault's "discursivation of sex"; cited in Dreitzel 1981, 218) "I contaminated myself watching them" (60). His endless interest in the description, cataloguing, and mapping out of the details of sexuality paradoxically starts out at the same time as the puritanical repression of actual sexuality in the Abancay Catholic boys' school. Ernesto shows his guilt as he evokes the latrines as satanical places and a mixture of excrement mingled with Opa's foul-smelling body. These latrines are the vantage point where sex is practiced: "the whole place concealed by the board fence was under a curse" (59), which causes Ernesto to search for redemption of his sins as he compares himself to a "river fish" swept into water muddied by an avalanche (59). The association to the natural world by means of this image shapes his ontological preoccupations as well as his relations with the environment. The assertion strengthens free movement ("river fish") and offers a pantheistic vision that parallels the purifying effect of water that liberates him from any carnal sin with Opa, as this violation never occurs in the novel. Ernesto claims his cleanliness in front of the priest Linares: "Don't get me dirty! The rivers might sweep you away; they're on my side" (211).

The narrator also discusses in explicit terms Chauca's acts of masturbation. Ernesto explains how, filled with remorse and guilt, this character represses his own sexuality by flagellating himself in front of the chapel door after having intercourse with Opa, thus showing off a masochistic attitude. The next morning he wakes up refreshed and cheerful, singing a lovely carnival song from his home village (59). Because of his pubescent age, it is logical to assume that Ernesto describes the sexual practices that go on in the parochial school of Abancay as episodes orchestrated through a code of lascivious rites, copulations, masturbations, and adolescent eroticism. All this is ironic since the Catholic church condemns and punishes such behavior and, at the same time, tends to encourage rather than limit sexual activity in the latrines. Being only fourteen, the protagonist enjoys commenting on the juvenile pastimes of his friends, who prefer to sneak out to the playgrounds to tell pornographic jokes and "stories about women" (50). However, the anxieties that motivate sexuality in these youngsters do not justify the enjoyment of Opa's body. Ernesto himself defends her, and unconsciously and grotesquely degrades her to an animalistic condition. The protagonist pities Opa, and it grieves him to remember how his classmates bang Opa's head against the board fence at the base of the latrines and how she runs down the passageway like a "hunted bear" (63). The metamorphosis (woman-bear) suffered by the madwoman is iconographically illustrated as a beast deprived of human characteristics and also exposed to physical ab/uses.

It must be added that the sexual initiation rites with Opa, whether *machista* or not, constitute part of the biological growing stages of Ernesto and his friends. Despite the negative vision of woman that Sara Castro-Klarén notes in Arguedas's patriarchal discourse, the narrator in *Deep Rivers*, half jokingly, half parodying, simply limits himself to expounding a paradigm of human conduct in general, which is typical in any postfeudal society in Latin America. A quick glance at Federico Fellini's film *Amarcord* explains on a grand scale this male pattern also present in contemporary European societies. Is not human sexuality a universal manifestation? H. P. Dreitzel, in turn, proposes a solution to this process that he calls "deritualism": "[We] shall attempt to overcome this bias by an historical consideration of changing attitudes towards the body and the emotions in modern societies" (1981, 205).

The physiological and sexual instincts of the students is regularly sated in the school's latrines. The latrine, a place that generally represents the suitable space for the act of defecation becomes, so to speak, an image that recalls copulation with Opa. As a point of fact, several anecdotes narrated by Ernesto compare the latrines to a carnivalesque procession similar to Roman Saturnalia, and characterized by physical violence, disorder and license to attain sexual gratification: "The biggest boys would come to blows trying to be the first to reach her or would stand guard near the *retretes* [toilet stalls] in a short line" (51). These violent and humoristic scenes parody (Sarduy 1980, 46–47) the brothel as an image commonly reflected in Latin American literature from *The Green House* (*La casa verde*, 1966) by Mario Vargas Llosa to more recently *The Imaginary Era* (*La era imaginaria*, 1987) by Cuban-born writer René Vázquez Díaz. The festive and public space that prevails in the latrines converted to brothels mocks and deceives the ecclesiastic order represented by the clerical power in Abancay.

While the schoolboys capitalize on sexual freedom to satisfy their erotic needs, Doña Felipa organizes a riot supported by the other *cholas*: "*mestizas*, dressed like the waitresses and owners of the *chicha* bars" (90). The participation of Opa and Doña Felipa in the novel thus assumes behaviors that mutually exclude each other: Opa is white, feeble-minded and belongs to the private and the hidden as sex is secretly performed at night in the latrines.[7] For Foucault, madness implies the absence of language, which leads to transgression (1965, 262). It turns out to be an involuntary silence that causes laughter and the mocking of those who observe a mad person and his or her irrational acts. In contrast to Opa, Doña Felipa is mestiza and part of the public and political sphere that carnivalesquely protests against the authoritarian discourse of those who govern the economy of the region. The object-subject split acquires, therefore, new meaning and implications that include "races" and different "classes" (Smith and Watson 1992, xiii).

If Opa's voice is never heard in the narrative discourse, Doña Felipa yells out the demands of the *colonos* that represent the Indian and mestizo peasant majority in the area. The feeble-minded woman acts during moonless nights impelled by her sexuality and is exposed to the laughter and the mockery of the students. Since the character's unspoken utterances seem to be pivotal in the novel, her silence is a provocation to the school's boarders that control her body and language. Doña Felipa struggles during the day for the right to obtain salt needed by the *colonos*. She is the only female character that, together with the rest of the *chicheras*, imposes her voice in the text and redefines her own culture and self. In order to achieve these goals, Doña Felipa appropriates the spoken word in Spanish and Quechua (*parole vive*, according to Derrida [1972, 89]) by means of dialogues with other revolutionary *cholas* and in her brief conversations with Father Linares, who pretends to silence her. In this context, we are relying on Jakobson's (1987, 66) semiotic theory grounded on the construction of oral communication, which is accomplished as linguistic contacts are verbalized (Doña Felipa's utterances), codified (Quechua language in this case) and received by the given receptors (the *cholas* or Father Linares) of the sociopolitical message. Doña

Felipa's speeches to the collectivity are part of a highly modern historical "politics of signification" at work (Bakhtin 1981) by which self and other rebel against the identity and affiliations granted by white hegemony and exploitation. In fact, language points to social systems that are never autonomous from cultural, political, and economic forces.

In keeping with change and social protest, Doña Felipa subversively acts as the spokeswoman of an ideology that mocks the economic monopoly in Abancay. Her oral discourse implies postcolonial violence and targets for decolonizing the act of writing controlled by a white minority that keeps the *colonos* on the margins of political discourse.[8] Central to this point is the lack of identity and self-awareness by the *cholos* while the *cholas* become the axis of economic productivity in the region. The *cholos* simply sing comical *huaynos* highlighted with outbursts of laughter while the *cholas* deploy language to turn the novel into a political text. As the subject of a historical moment, Doña Felipa is conscious that her behavior and that of her followers represent a threat to Abancay's society that sees in her the attempt to usurp of the cultural, economic, social, and religious space of a white minority in power. For all these reasons, the rebellious women are disparagingly classified as "thieves," "prostitutes," and "filthy *cholas*" throughout the novel. Doña Felipa's portrait is brief; her description depicts a mixture of corporal traits similar to those of Opa's: "her stout body completely filled the arch" and her ethnia is also identified with a concise lexical entry: "She was speaking in Quechua" (112). Although the initial emphasis on the descriptive element relies on the corporal image of the character, her identity is revealed through language, not through her body, a global trend subject to debate and revision within feminist circles of criticism (Jones 1985, 365–66). Nevertheless, the public manifestations by the *chicheras* accentuate with color and corporal movements a typical carnivalesque festival.

During the insurrection, the pictorial image of the event ambivalently reflects a double scenario that combines the serious and the jocular in the carnivalesque discourse (Bakhtin 1965, 122). Under the apparent festive and folkloric mood of the event, we perceive a socioeconomic testimony of the mestiza woman implicit in the written pages. The festivity is almost theatrical; the actresses are members of an exploited society that condemns white supremacy. For the spectator's diversion, the *cholas* begin to sing in a "carnivalesque dance," then the troop is transformed into a *comparsa* (parade with dancing figures) through the streets of Abancay (96). With this choir of polyphonic voices, the women collectively mock the exploiter. Even more, the *chicheras* form what can be called a typical "community of women" that dominate linguistic communication among themselves to prevent chaos: "they nudged one another, imposing order, trying to reach equanimity" (95). [9] The code that operates in this powerful alliance of women led by Doña Felipa is one of rebellion and resistance with a multiplicity of discourses and plurality of voices from the lower strata of society that the narrator repeatedly ties to the act of defecation.

Interacting with women's voices and songs, Ernesto discloses a high degree of carnivalization in the description of the euphoric and colorful march from Abancay's plaza toward the hacienda in Patibamba. By emphasizing the radical newness of the parade, the narrator illustrates how a particular literary discourse surfaces on a comical atmosphere that signals a hierarchical inversion (or subversion) of power: Doña Felipa turns from owner of a *chichería* to a *guerrillera* that protects and defends the *colonos*. At the same time, this inversion of political and economic values mocks, challenges, and satirizes the existing order in Abancay (Bakhtin 1965, 12, 119). The scenery invokes the culture of folk humor because even the mules that belong to the *cholas* dance in hyperbolic gestures: "the rhythm of the *danza* trotted along more gaily" (96). Laughter has its negative effects that ambivalently desacralizes the monologic discourse of the dominant white class. [10] It is interesting to add that the carnivalesque episode with the mules is similar to the medieval "feast of the donkey" which also appears in the legends of Saint Francis of Assisi.[11]

Time and again, a collective event such as the humorous dancing of mules and *cholas* together serves as an illusion to the "carnival grotesque" (Bakhtin 1965, 36–38) imagery whereby the lower strata of Andean society that the *colonos* represent react against "official, formalistic and logical authoritarianism." The narrator relates his experience in the carnival once he joins the popular insurrection led by Doña Felipa: "The sour odor of human excrement swelled within my veins. I should have liked to sing, through tears of blood, that Patibamba carnival song to which *we* had come down this same road" (98, 100). Interestingly enough, his words allow the reader to associate the carnival with the act of defecation that Ernesto identifies through his own sense—a smell that fills his "veins." Along the same lines, the pluralization (we) employed by the literary persona magnifies the function of the narrative "I" (Benveniste 1971, 203) as the first person plural pronoun is located at the core of a political situation that interlaces characters, cultures, and languages. It becomes, therefore, an amplified and more solemn "we" (Ernesto and the *chicheras)* but it also suggests the ambiguity that the protagonist portrays embedded in his condition of "man of two worlds" in *Deep Rivers* (Cornejo Polar 1973, 138). In its tonalities, the shift in subject position compromises the "I" to mingle with the "other" in a ludic interaction that reveals the communicative efficacy of dialogism under fictional historical events.

With the arrival of the army to Abancay, the revolution is finally placated and the *chicheras* end up being incarcerated, vexed, and mistreated. The punishment the guards inflict on them consists of stuffing "excrement into their mouth" (140). One of the *cholas* insults the Colonel: "Don't make me swallow the little Colonel's shit! It is shit. Did they bring the shit from Cuzco?" (140). All these examples reiterate the defecating function of language spoken by low-strata characters in the text. They accurately register bodily functions in a gaily Rabelaisian fashion whereby the humorous and the grotesque fuse people and beasts alike: "A festive, holidaylike hubbub could be heard in the dirty street. The ground is hard; they sprinkle it every day—wide damp patches in the dirt alternate with the urine stains from horses and men" (101). These bodily functions in the novel negate coercion and imposed values in an explicit positive presentation of an Indian world, a world capable of creating language. Although grotesque, excrement is a discursive referent that inspires laughter and mocking by Abancay's white community. Doña Felipa's apparent triumph concludes when the *colonos* share the needed salt as she evaporates in the face of the struggle. Her escape, however, implies a victorious return that cannot be materialized in *Deep Rivers*. Ernesto suggests the possibility of her return when, in his inner speech, he compares the rebellious woman to the river: "And you will return. We'll put the idiot in a convent" (153). The narrator's assertion deals with the need of cleansing Opa's body by means of a physical and spiritual confinement.

In her escape, Doña Felipa abandons her orange Castilian shawl on the stone cross of the Pachachacha bridge. In a symbolic attempt and struggle to recapture the "sign" (to paraphrase Barthes 1977), Opa escalates the cross "like a bear" to rescue the lost item and then disappears moaning "like a lost soul" (152). The narrator informs the reader about Opa's speech habits and patterns: "She wasn't mute but that [bellowing] was the only way she could shout" (152). The stress in the next lines links the negation of language to the stereotyping of the character: "She bellowed in the tone of voice that is typical of short-necked, fat people" (152). Once in the possession of the desired object, the woman plays with the shawl as if she were in a comical representation of a *danza*. Once again, she is described as a savage animal: "She wiggled her feet like a puma switching its tail" (188).

Meanwhile in Abancay, Father Linares prays in the church for the safe return of the sociopolitical order that the *chicheras* have violated. Ernesto, in turn, parodies the priest's prayer with his own improvised humorous prayer whose disparity causes the parishioners to laugh. In the parodic effect of the prayer, the narrator distances himself from the religious reality of the moment to create an illusion by linking the two women: "the idiot from the school has your shawl; dancing, dancing, she came up the hill and now she doesn't go to the courtyard at night . . . she has to suffer yet" (159). Suffering occurs in the last chapter of the book as people panic with the mysterious apparition of a plague epidemic. The disease haunts, invades, and corrodes Opa's body, the first victim to succumb in the school. Ernesto is terrified of contamination but in a cumbersome exercise of kindness visits the feeble-minded woman in her hovel next to the "foul water from the toilets" (208). The description of the dying woman is grotesque: "The idiot's hair and blouse swarmed with lice; they crawled along slowly" (208). In *Deep Rivers*, the plague becomes a spiritual metaphor of Opa's liberation from sin and purification of her ab/used body. In the text, lice can be interpreted as a synonym of evil that possesses Opa:"Now you will put a light in her mind, you will make her an angel and have her sing to your glory, great Lord. . . !" (209). As Susan Sontag points out, "the melodramatics of the disease meta- phor assume a punitive notion: of the disease not as a punishment but as a sign of evil" (1977, 87).

In *Deep Rivers*, José María Arguedas invites the reader as a participant in the construction of a grotesque vision of the lower strata in Andean society. Beginning with Ernesto's linguistic antagonism, passing next to Opa in the school latrines and Doña Felipa in the *chichera*'s insurrection and up to the plague that destroys half of Abancay, the author always compenetrates, sympathizes, and fights in defense of destitute women that suffer sexual and political violence within the carnivalesque world in which they live. In my thesis I have proposed that masturbation, copulation, and defecation are simply tropes that become an appropriate vehicle for a dramatic satire that culminates with Opa's death and Doña Felipa's vanishing from

Abancay. Significantly, only the timeless rivers that we constantly see flowing in the novel can bear witness to humor, satire, and the mocking truth that act as self-destructive ingredients in the text's political and social protest.

Notes

1. All quotations are taken from *Deep Rivers* (1978).

2. Parody implies a song next to another, a countersong. For an interesting study of parody in Latin American literature, see Jean Franco (1975).

3. Martin Lienhard (1981, 105-39) underlines this textual strategy as he analyzes Arguedas's *El zorro de arriba y el zorro de abajo* (The fox from above and the fox from below).

4. Roland Barthes affirms that the rhetoric of writing distances the creator from his work of art in favor of the participation of a reader who reconstructs narrated events (1977, 142).

5. For Bakhtin, the language of characters in a novel, how they speak, is verbally and semantically autonomous: "each character's speech possesses its own belief system, since each is the speech of another in another's language" (1981, 315).

6. See Bakhtin's interesting connection among grotesque imageries of the body, food, and the sexual life of an individual (1965, 309).

7. The word *opa* is a synonym for idiot, which comes from the Greek *idiótés*, which means private person.

8. For the rhetoric of violence in *Deep Rivers*, see Ismael P. Márquez (1995).

9. For the ties between women, see Nina Auerbach (1976), which contains an abundant bibliography on the topic.

10. I am basing this example on the negative function of laughter set forth by Bergson and in opposition to the positive nature in Rabelais that Bakhtin favors for considering it "folk humor" (1975, 71).

11. It can also be associated with the feast of Saint Lazarus in Marseilles.

Works Cited

Arguedas, José María. 1978. *Los ríos profundos* (Deep rivers). Trans. Frances Horning Barraclough. Austin: University of Texas Press.

Auerbach, Nina. 1976. *Communities of Women: An Idea in Fiction.* Cambridge, Mass.: Harvard University Press.

Bakhtin, Mikhail. 1965. *Rabelais and His World.* Trans. Helena Iswolsky. Cambridge, Mass.: M.I.T. Press.

———. 1981. *The Dialogic Imagination: Four Essays.* Trans. Caryl Emerson and Michel Holquist. Austin: University of Texas Press.

Barthes, Roland. 1977. *Image, Music, Text.* Trans. Stephen Heath. New York: Hill and Wang.

Benveniste, Émile. 1971. *Problems in General Linguistics.* Trans. Mary Elizabeth Meek. Coral Gables, Fla.: University of Miami Press.

Bergson, Henri. 1975. *Le rire: Essai sur la signification du comique* (Laughter: An essay on comic meaning). Paris: Presses Universitaires de France.

Castro-Klarén, Sara. 1973. *El mundo mágico de José María Arguedas* (The magic world of José María Arguedas). Lima: Instituto de Estudios Peruanos.

———. 1983. "Crimen y castigo: Sexualidad en J. M. Arguedas" (Crime and punishment: Sexuality in J. M. Arguedas). *Revista iberoamericana* 49 (January-March): 55–65.

Cornejo Polar, Antonio. 1973. *Los universos narrativos de José María Arguedas* (The narrative worlds of José María Arguedas. Buenos Aires: Editorial Losada.

Derrida, Jacques. 1972. "La Pharmacie de Platon" (Plato's Pharmacy). In *La dissémination* (Dissemination). Paris: Editions du Seuil.

Dreitzel, H. P. 1981. "The Socialization of Nature: The Western Attitude towards Body and Emotions." *Indigenous Psychologies: The Anthropology of the Self,* ed. Paul Heelas and Andrew Lock, 205–23. London: Academic Press.

Foucault, Michel. 1965. *Madness and Civilization: A History of Insanity in the Age of Reason.* Trans. Richard Howard. New York: Vintage Books.

Franco, Jean. 1975. "La parodie, le grotesque et le carnavalesque: Quelques conceptions du personnage dans le romans latino-américain" (Parody, the grotesque, and the carnivalesque: Some conceptions of character in the Latin American novel). In *Ideologies, littérature et societé en Amérique latine* (Ideologies, literature, and society in Latin America). Brussels: Editions de l'Université de Bruxelles.

Jakobson, Roman. 1987. *Language in Literature*. Cambridge, Mass.: Harvard University Press.

Jones, Ann Rosalind. 1985. "Writing the Body: Toward an Understanding of l'Ecriture Fémenine." In *The New Feminist Criticism: Essays on Women, Literature, and Theory*, ed. Elaine Showalter, 361–77. New York: Pantheon Books.

Lienhard, Martin. 1981. *Cultura popular andina y forma novelesca: Zorros y danzantes en la última novela de Arguedas* (Andean popular culture: Foxes and minstrels in Arguedas's final novel). Madrid: Latinoamericana Editores.

Márquez, Ismael P. 1994. *La retórica de la violencia en tres novelas peruanas* (The rhetoric of violence in three Peruvian novels). New York: Peter Lang.

Rauch, Angelika. 1988. "The *Trauerspiel* of the Prostituted Body, or Woman as Allegory of Modernity." *Cultural Critique* 10:77–88.

Rowe, William. 1979. *Mito e ideología en la obra de José María Arguedas* (Myth and ideology in the work of José María Arguedas). Lima: Instituto Nacional de Cultura.

Sarduy, Severo. 1980. "Parodia, homenaje y violencia" (Parody, homage, and violence). *Lecturas críticas* 1, no.1 (December): 46–47.

Smith, Sidonie, and Julia Watson, ed. 1992. "De/Colonization and the Politics of Discourse." In *De/Colonizing the Subject: The Politics of Gender in Women's Autobiography*. Minneapolis: University of Minnesota Press.

Sontag, Susan. 1977. *Illness as Metaphor*. New York: Farrar, Straus and Giroux.

Stoller, Robert J. 1968. *Sex and Gender: On the Development of Masculinity and Feminity*. New York: Science House.

Testimonial Portrait

Images of José María Arguedas

Pedro Lastra

In 1984, Carlos Germán Belli interviewed me for a brief article that appeared in Lima's newspaper *El Comercio* on December 2, the fifteenth anniversary of José María Arguedas's death. [1] One of his questions had to do with what he considered "my absence" from literary criticism of Arguedas's work, of which we had talked before. Carlos Germán Belli, like other friends, was surprised that Arguedas was not present in my literary reviews. At that time, I answered the following:I have asked myself several times why I have never written anything about José María. Juanita [my wife] also often reminds me about that. But I feel that presence so closely that it is hard for me to dissociate the person I knew from the writer I read and from the one who motivates certain literary reflections. I feel that I can't express in critical or academic discourse what the reading of his works suggests to me. It is always necessarily bonded to the memory of an intense fraternal relationship. Perhaps, I could express it under the form of a very open testimony, not subordinated to chronological order, a sort of historical reconstruction of a friendship. [15]

I apologize for citing myself, but those words briefly explain and situate the purpose of presenting some images of Arguedas as a person, since I will take for granted that our relationship began in early readings, like the one I did of his short story "Warma Kuyay" in an anthology of Peruvian short stories published in Chile. That piercing story of a multiple experience of the marginality of a group, of love, society, and reality itself allowed me to perceive, if not critically at least emotionally, that it was the voice of a poet. Such an emotion never left me again; it was accentuated by my reading, maybe in 1956, of "Diamantes y pedernales" (Diamonds and flint) and "Agua" (Water), in the 1954 edition that the university bookstore in Santiago sold. That is why, when the novel *Los ríos profundos* (Deep rivers) appeared in 1958, I read it in one afternoon. Then, the next day I gathered my close friends from the philosophy and education department—I was doing my Spanish studies at the University of Chile—and I asked them to listen to passages like this one, in which Ernesto stands before an Inca wall:

> I walked along the wall, stone by stone. I stood back a few steps, contemplated it, and then came closer again. I touched the stones with my hands, following the line, which was as undulating and unpredictable as a river, where the blocks of stone were joined. In the dark street, in the silence, the wall appeared to be alive, the lines I had touched between the stones burned on the palms of my hands.
>
> . . .
>
> The wall was stationary, but all its lines were seething and its surface was as changeable as that of the flooding summer rivers that have similar crests near the center, where the current flows the swiftest and is most terrifying. [6–7]

I was studying literature and I knew about the impertinence of identifying a fictitious narrator with the real author of a novel, but I felt that such a principle did not work well with Arguedas. I wanted to meet that author. Without any basis for such an assumption, I thought the real author had to be very similar to the main character of his short stories and novels. In January 1962 I had the opportunity to confirm my feeling.

Gonzalo Rojas organized a conference of Latin American writers at the University of Concepción. Several young writers, including myself, were in Concepción to participate in a literature workshop sponsored by the Ford Foundation and the university. The conference was a continuation of previous meetings organized by Gonzalo in 1958 and 1960. Also present were Alejo Carpentier, Augusto Roa Bastos, Carlos Fuentes, José Bianco, Pablo Neruda, Mariano Picón Salas, Fernando Alegría, Benjamín Carrión, Héctor Pablo Agosti, Mario Benedetti, José Donoso, José Miguel Oviedo, Claribel Alegría, among others. Those were days of great cultural effervescence in Concepción, and it was an opportunity for the younger writers to learn by opening a dialogue with the masters we admired. I remember that one afternoon Roa Bastos got together with a group of beginners and listened with great attention to a reading of poems and short stories. I am still moved by the endless patience and great enthusiasm with which the author of *Hijo de hombre* (Son of man, 1965), a book that was quite familiar to those attending, endured the event. *He* was even allowed to read some poems from his unpublished book *El naranjal ardiente* (The burning orange grove).

José María was one of the writers invited to the conference. I did not see him arrive and I do not know why I feared he was not going to be present. I was glad, then, when I suddenly heard his name, and also to hear him in a short intermission during the opening dialogue. But at the end of the meetings we would always lose sight of him. At some point I saw him at a distance, talking to Agosti. Later, he would tell me how much he admired the calm eloquence of the Argentinean essayist and politician. And this story has a little coda, because I mentioned that impression to Agosti, in Cuba in 1966, when we were judges at the Casa de las Américas contest: "If José María knew how much that eloquence costs me," Agosti said to me, "I start getting sick as soon as I learn I have to speak."

One of those afternoons during the conference, Gonzalo organized a little expedition to a nearby tourist site, La Laguna de San Pedro, where the participants were entertained. Everyone was talking to each other, but José María, perhaps rather tired, remained alone by a window. I approached to greet him and I started, with difficulty, what I now remember more as a monologue. I told him that the editors Mejía Baca and Villanueva's idea of compiling the short stories of "Agua" and "Diamantes y pedernales" in a single volume was a great one. He was surprised I knew the book, and that encouraged me to add that I also knew *Yawar Fiesta* and *Los ríos profundos*. We kept on talking in the bus during our return to the city. We made plans to see each other in Santiago. He told me to look for him at the historian Rolando Mellafe's house, where he was going to stay for about ten days. That is how a dialogue that never ended began.

José María had brought to Chile some copies of his novel *El Sexto* (The Sexto prison), published the year before, and he gave me one in Santiago. That book, which transfers to fiction a real experience of extreme violence, made an impression on me. It dealt with the experience of the confinement of José María in a prison in 1937, due to a student protest provoked by the visit of General Camarota, envoy of Mussolini, to Lima. We talked extensively about the novel during his stay in Santiago, considering also its relations to other books on the subject: *Memoirs from the House of the Dead* by Dostoyevsky, for example, the reading of which Arguedas considered personally decisive. At some point we also talked about *Hombres sin Mujer* (Men without wives), by the Cuban writer Carlos Montenegro. That book had circulated in Lima during those years, in one of the collections of the Cruzada Latinoamericana de Difusión Cultural, edited by José Bonilla and the writer Enrique Congrains Martín. Montenegro's book irritated Jose María in a particular way and the conversations about that disappointment showed me again, in the flesh, what was already clear in his writing: his acute sensitivity to human corruption or degradation, and the consciousness of a tenacious and permanent struggle between the forces of good and evil, which is a main attribute of his work. He perceived, accurately, that Montenegro's novel did not transcend the mere confirmation of degrading or simply degenerate behaviors that abounded in the prison described by the Cuban narrator. Montenegro had similarly suffered confinement in prison, but not for political reasons, according to some biographers. As is obvious to Arguedas's reader, in *El Sexto* the overwhelming presence of sordidness, violence, and degradation does not weaken hope: it strengthens it: ". . . anger gives me hope," says Alejandro Cámac, " a carpenter from the mines of Morococha and Cerro in the Mantaro Valley, ex-peasant from Sapallanga," Gabriel's cellmate. This character-narrator unmistakably substitutes for the real author. One af-ter-noon we talked about Cámac. I had marked, in my copy, the following paragraph:

> What was most impressive about Cámac? His clarity in terms of the image he had of the world or the few, the very few, resources he had used to come to such categorical and cruel discoveries? His appearance, his manners, his way of addressing me here in a formal way, there in a familiar one; his bed made of straw reinforced with newspapers, his jacket and trousers of rural cut? None of these seemed to correspond, according to what we were used to in Lima, to the clarity of his reflections and the beauty of his language. He didn't seek meticulously for his words, neither did he groom them, as the politicians he had heard did. He was undoubtedly an agitator, but his words named facts directly, and the ideas that were born from the facts were just like the watercress flower, which grows in the brooks. . . . [17]

I pointed out to him the integrity and wisdom of Cámac and the plasticity of his speech; they seemed to me memorable aspects of the novel. And then, he told me how by studying the folklore of the Mantaro Valley, he had been able to determine the peculiarities of speech of this unforgettable character, which he had in mind since his years in prison. He was excited by my interest in the subject and he promised me a copy of a 1953 issue of the magazine *Folklore amer-*

icano, in which he had published an extensive collection of magic-realist short stories and traditional songs from the Mantaro Valley and the Jauja and Concepción provinces. "When you read those stories you will remember Cámac," he told me. In a letter dated February 20, 1962 he announced the esteemed gift: "I am sending you, by regular mail, the first issue of *Folklore americano*. Excuse me for the poor condition of the copy; it is the only one we have left, and we used to lend it frequently."

The collection (actually a complete book: 193 pages out of the 322 in the entire magazine) is notable for several reasons. Thirty years later, looking over the pages of *Folklore americano*, I not only remember Cámac but I also uncover—in a work remarkable for the novelty of its subject, for the solidity of its information, and for its scientific knowledge—the lyrical tension that gives life to its descriptions, such as in the following paragraph about the geographical landscape of the area he was studying:

> The luminous and splendid valley and its fruits stand out in contrast to the solemn aspect of the mountains. This sensation of contrast awakens in the spirit of the sensitive traveler the constant latent inclination to magic, to the magical aesthetic. Here is a hummingbird as shiny as an emerald, its wings glittering in a gigantic maguey flower, its small body resplendent against the deep blue mountain range in the distance! Nevertheless, this valley doesn't have the shadows of the fields of Cuzco, which reflect the mythical appearance of Andean orography. Neither does it show the extreme contrast between the ardent sugar cane that grows in the Apurimac's deep ravines and the perpetually snow-capped high mountains that surround them. . . .
> [*Folklore americano,* 108]

Years later another excerpt from that collection would seem disquieting to me, to say the least. It is the series of stories about the damned, from which José María created a "special category" (that's what he called it) of "suicide stories." In that type of story, the person who commits suicide appears as a "kind character, a tender and poetic figure who expiates the guilt of a sin of the Christian sort . . . by performing services for his family." One of them, loving and sad at parting, leaves behind, at home, as a souvenir, "flowers and stones from the afterlife." Another one begs his mother: "Do not cry, because when you do, the river takes away my immense sugar cane plantations and my beautiful flowers." (Rereading these lines again with Juanita, my wife, we inevitably think of our friend's farewell note, which we found inside an envelope with documents he entrusted to me, and which was supposed to be opened only in the event of "some fatal accident. And don't forget me; remember me with joy. I was happy.")

There is in this important volume of stories a chapter which should be emphasized here, because it gives an account of José María's ways of approaching manifestations of folklore in music and dance and of the naturalness with which he incorporated them into his life. I am referring to the part about "Canciones de trillas nocturnas" (Songs of nocturnal threshings), where he briefly recounts how he had encountered, around 1927, a first version of the piece: "Trilla de alberjas en Pampas" (Threshing of green peas in Pampas), which he recorded in 1969 for the book and record we published at the Editorial Universitaria in Santiago, Chile. This is his account:

> In the small valley where the town of Pampas lies, I heard, at night, the songs for the threshing of green peas. I got close to the threshing floor and I could see, for some minutes, the work: a group of women was singing by the floor's edge:

Saruykuy saruykuy	Pisa Pisa	Tread tread
chakichaykiwan	con tus pies	with your feet
saruykuy. . . .	pisa, aplasta. . . .	tread, crush. . . .[2]

> The men were crushing the dry husks of the green peas with their feet in step. It was the night of a full moon and there was a transparency that made the silhouettes of the trees and the people stand out, almost shine. The women's voices were characteristic of all Indian women who sing ritual songs; they were of extremely high pitch. At that time

I was sixteen and I could not stay to see the process of threshing. But I learned the lyrics and music of the song. No instrument accompanied the singing. . . . The threshing of green peas I saw in Pampas was carried on in an ambiance of self-communion, of ceremony. The melody is of an imploring character, old Jarawi, regardless of its dancing rhythm. That song evokes in me the image of the little valley with all its attributes. [239, 241]

The importance that music and singing had for José María has been pointed out several times. There are excellent works about this in relation to his literature and his life, among them a study by Angel Rama ("*Los ríos profundos*, opera de pobres," [1987]) and the testimonial pages of John V. Murra's "José María Arguedas: Dos Imágenes."[3] Murra comments on a revealing letter.

According to him, Arguedas had given a talk at the Agricultural University, which he thought had gone very badly. In order that the people who had come from so far might not feel disappointed, he sang them the song of the threshing of green peas. Three weeks later he was invited to the Engineering University, and that talk seemed to him to have gone well. But the engineers had heard that he had sung for the agronomists. . . .What about us? No, he said, the talk was good, and I don't have to compensate you with a song. And he didn't sing. [54]

The John Murra story I quoted above refers me to a Santiago episode. Halfway through 1967 we started the series *Letras americanas* with an edition of *Los ríos profundos* at the university press. For us, it was an important event; moreover, José María was willing to give a talk at the University of Chile's main auditorium, in which he would analyze his own work: "Realidad humana y experiencia literaria" (Human reality and literary experience). It was my turn to introduce our guest to a considerable audience of academicians, writers, students, and private fans, so to speak (José María was already a very well known and highly appreciated author in the country). Things began well enough, but suddenly he felt overwhelmed by such a large audience and he started his lecture in a manner as vacillating as chaotic. I was devastated. I blamed myself for putting my friend in such a situation and I began to sense imminent disaster when José María suddenly stopped and said with extremely unusual energy, "All I have said is totally useless; I will start again." The audience, who truly admired him, received that declaration with a recognition that was translated into immediate and general applause. The talk was brilliant, without a doubt the best of those he gave in Chile, and he knew clearly—as Murra tells it—that his presentation had been very well received.

That night we were going home to have dinner with three other people, but José María was so happy that, upon leaving the university, he invited three or four more friends. When Juanita asked him how the presentation had gone, he answered, "Just imagine, they applauded me as a movie star."

We had the opportunity to see and experience what singing meant to him on many occasions, but nothing was more revealing than what happened one afternoon in 1969 when he showed up at our house very discouraged. He talked to us about it. We worried about his moods, but we also knew how affection and the companionship of friends suited him well. At sundown, a mutual good friend, Doctor Eugenia Serrano, joined the family reunion. The dialogue became animated; José María told some entertaining stories and at one point he said he wanted to sing. Singing transformed him. Juanita reminded him that just a few hours earlier he had said that he was very depressed, and he promptly answered, smiling, already transported to another region of reality, that it was true, but that he was "a happy depressed person."

True to my purpose of presenting these images without linear chronology, I will return to March 1962, when José María returned to Chile, after his trip to the Latin American Writers' Conference at the University of Concepción. He then stayed several weeks at Nicanor Parra's house, near the mountains, a house from which it is easy to go down into the city, something José María would do every day. At that time he visited us frequently, or sometimes I would go looking for him. During those months his circle of Chilean friends started to expand.

At the entrance to Nicanor's singular country house (those peculiarities are the matter of another meticulous description) there is a big willow tree, very old no doubt, whose branches fall until they almost touch the waters of a small brook that runs down from the highlands. That willow tree dazzled José María. He would talk to us about it. The first time we came down from the house together, he stopped briefly to look at it and said with unforgettable intensity, ". . . this tree is a god."

But the purpose for those trips back and forth to the city were peculiar, according to Nicanor. During his morning stroll he used to accept the invitations he received, but it was evident that in the afternoons his enthusiasm faded. Years later I would accompany him as he slid his notes of regrets under the doors of his prospective hosts from the night before. "Ah! José, I know those little notes quite well," I told him once, because I had found one at home, soon after I had met him (it must be from January 1962. I have it and it reads thus: "Dear Pedro: I am totally exhausted, I beg you to excuse me for not coming to your house tonight. I couldn't get out of dinner at Neruda's, which was very fatiguing and ended very late last night. I beg you to give my regrets to your dear friends and guests. Could we meet Tuesday morning, or at six in the evening?"). That's why Nicanor used to say, "José María goes into town in the mornings to make appointments with people, and returns in the afternoon to cancel them."

Among the letters I received from him that year, there is one dated July 8, from which I include a paragraph that seems to me of special importance:

> Since I arrived in Santiago I have written 150 pages of my thesis, a series of articles and a haylli-Taki (hymn-prayer) in Quechua to Túpac Amaru. I have translated it and it is going to the printer's this week.

243

It's the first time I venture into formal writing in Quechua. My friends are enthusiastic about this piece and a worker at the museum—half illiterate—to whom I read the poem had to make an effort not to burst into tears. I have written it in present-day Quechua.[4]

I think that this image of José María would be incomplete without a reference to his poetic writing, which he started with "A nuestro padre creador Túpac Amaru" (To our father creator Túpac Amaru) and followed with "¡Qué Guayasamín!" (What a Guayasamín [an Ecuadorian painter]!), "Oda al Jet" (Ode to the jet), "Temblar" (To tremble), "Llamado a algunos doctores" (Appeal to certain intellectuals), and "A Cuba" (To Cuba).[5] Even though he emphatically pointed out in a conversation with Chester Christian that Spanish was not the means of expression of his poetic feeling,[6] it is evident that in spite of us not being able to appreciate the difference, the translations he made of his own texts (only "¡Qué Guayasamín!" and "A Cuba" are not totally his) come to us as authentic poems in Spanish.

From the first time we met, José María made it his purpose that I get to know Peru. He and Celia planned for me to visit Peru in 1962, but I couldn't make the trip until November 1964. It was not possible at that time for them to receive me as their guest, so they arrived at the unique solution of turning me into a "museum piece" during the time I stayed in Lima.

Alicia Bustamante Vernal, José María's sister-in-law, was the creator and owner of a great museum of popular art, which filled the rooms of a large old house at Plaza San Agustín. It was a famous place: Pancho Fierro's *peña* (meeting place), which is even talked about in travelers' guides, such as Concha Meléndez's *Entrada al Perú* (Doorway to Peru, 1941). They put me up there for more than a month; I even wrote part of the lecture I gave in Lima there. It was a curious, fascinating feeling to walk during the night through those rooms crowded with altarpieces, little bulls from Pucara, and many other pieces of Peruvian popular imagery from different parts of the country. Since then, those images have remained affectionately with me. According to José María I was a mobile piece of the museum that could and should be moved to other regions, so he insisted on planning a trip for me to Cuzco. I went there to repeat my talks on Chilean literature, and José María lent me his coat, which became clearly necessary on one of those cold Cuzco nights. I will relate just one episode from that extremely intense experience because of the consequences José María inferred from it, which he later brought to my awareness.

One day I visited Pisac's ruins, high on a mountain that softly rises from the banks of the Vilcanota River (the name of the Urubamba River in the Cuzco region). I was accompanied by three young Peruvian physical education teachers whom I had met some days before in Machu Picchu, and who were in Cuzco participating in a conference related to their discipline. The famous Inca fortress is truly impressive. From up there one can see the whole area surrounding the town of Pisac, famous for its animated Sunday fair. The climb to the fortress was arduous, a slow trip of several hours from which I returned exhausted. My traveling companions, who were very agile, took off ahead of me when we reached level ground, so I stopped to talk to an old Indian man who suddenly came out of the first house at the entrance to the town. I told him I came from another country, that it was the first time I was visiting these parts, and that the ruins of that fortress had made a big impression on me. He accompanied me to the little plaza where my friends were waiting for me.

José María was impressed by that simple story, and I know from Alberto Escobar that he related it to other people more than once. "You don't know," he told me, "what it must have been like for that Indian to walk next to a young gentleman who talked to him as if to an equal. He will tell it later among his own people, and they won't believe him."

Few things were as vividly revealing of the social inequalities of caste in that world. José María wrote all his works about and against these inequities.

I began these images by remembering the writers' conference in

Concepción. I will close them, for now, by talking about what happened at another meeting of Latin American writers in Chile in August 1969, organized by the Writers' Society and sponsored by the Ministry of Education and Chilean Universities. Among the numerous articipants were Juan Rulfo, Mario Vargas Llosa, Juan Carlos Onetti, Carlos Martínez Moreno, Rosario Castellanos, Marta Traba, Leopoldo Marechal, Angel Rama, Alberto Escobar, Carlos Germán Belli, Emanuel Carballo, and many writers from Europe.

I took part in the organization of that event and that explains why I have kept some papers from that meeting. Among them, one José María dictated to me on August 6, which I kept in my file after reading it at the designated session. It is a letter addressed to the president of the Writers' Society, where he thanks him for the invitation to the conference which would start on August 18. The final paragraph reads:

> I have been in Santiago since February under special medical treatment. Consequently it will not be necessary for the society to cover the expenses of my trip and accommodations. However, my presence at conference meetings will be unavoidably restricted by my poor state of health and the recommendations of the specialist in charge. Nevertheless, you can be sure I will do as much as possible to contribute to the success of an event so generously and diligently organized.

He did not come, however. He told me he was not in the mood for meetings, and the best he could do was to go to Valparaiso for refuge at some friend's house during the time of the conference. He probably left on the 21st, because the last version of "¿Último diario?" (Final journal entry?) of *El zorro de arriba y el zorro de abajo* (The fox from above and the fox from below) is dated Santiago, August 20. He just wanted to see Juan Rulfo, the Latin American writer he most admired and loved.[7] He left me a note for him, with instructions to hand it to him very privately, and also to let him know the phone number of the house where he would be staying. He was hoping to meet Rulfo again, and he was sure that Rulfo would be willing to go to Valparaíso at the end of the many sessions programmed for the conference. At home, we would exchange jokes about that little conspiracy and we certainly had fun with it.

When Rulfo received the note and the information I included, he agreed with the suggestion, because he was worried about José María's emotional state, which we talked about.

But as often happens, there was a change in the conference program. Soon after it started, the Writers' Society received a tempting invitation from the municipality of Viña del Mar and the universities in Valparaíso to continue the work in those neighboring cities. There was enthusiastic agreement to proceed with the idea, which we soon put into practice.

I let José María know about this change and he was greatly disturbed by the news: "I will have to confine myself to this house," he told me, "but we will try to meet, and I hope I can also see Juan." In fact, I met him a couple of times at the restaurant of the Hotel Victoria in Valparaíso, a place that had once been prestigious but was now on the decline; the writers would not come there.

I would seek out some pretext or other to get out of the conference—something Rulfo couldn't do—and I would meet José María, who used to show up with his face muffled in a scarf and his head covered by a Basque beret, a semidisguise that was indeed functional. Suddenly the swinging door would open and my muffled friend would look around stealthily. He would make sure I was alone and then approach me without apprehension. The situation ended up amusing him, because I would point out to him that he could have been a perfect conspirator. Juan Rulfo, in turn, would play a similar role by approaching me the following day to ask me about José María. They did not get a chance to meet, but they often talked on the phone.

I have retold this little episode because of what it reveals. It tells us about José María's character inasmuch as it shows that his emotional conflicts were coming to a head and that his decisions were becoming extreme. "¿Último diario?" is the declaration of his defeat. His escape to Valparaíso around the same time, an escape announcing the refusal or rejection of all or almost all literary connections, was nothing less than a foreshadowing of that defeat.[8]

Translated by Angela María Pérez

Notes

1. This essay was originally published in a special Spanish version as "Imágenes de José María Arguedas" in *Escritura* (*Teoría y crítica literarias*) 33–34 (January–December 1992): 47–59. All quotations were translated for the present edition unless otherwise specified.

2. The original text transcribed here and its translation into Spanish are slightly different from those he sent me on October 5, 1969, for the book and record. In that version he adds the stanza that starts, "Corriupis cartay kachkan. . . / Dicen que tengo una carta en el correo. . ." (They say there is a letter for me at the post office. . .). The 1969 translation of "Carnaval de Tambobamba" for the book and record also has some changes from the previous versions, such as *Poesía quechua*, Serie del nuevo mundo (Buenos Aires: Editorial Universitaria, 1965).

3. Both articles were published in 1983, in a special issue of *Revista iberoamericana* 122 (January–March).

4. José María's Ph.D. thesis, "Las comunidades de España y del Perú," (The communities of Spain and Peru) was published at the University of San Marcos in 1968. He obtained his degree in ethnology the following year.

5. These poems can be found in the book *Temblar/Katatay y otros poemas* (Temblar/Katatay and other poems), with a prologue by Alberto Escobar and notes by Sybila Arredondo (Lima: Instituto Nacional de Cultura, 1972). There is a Cuban edition that includes "El sueño del pongo" (The Indian servant's dream) (Havana: Ediciones Casa de las Américas, 1976). In his prologue Escobar correctly comes to the following conclusion: "Arguedas . . . was essentially a poet."

6. "I can write poetry in Quechua and I can't do it in Spanish, which shows me that my mother tongue is Quechua" (228). "Alrededor de este nudo que es la vida: Entrevista con José María Arguedas" (Concerning this

problem called life: An interview with José María Arguedas), *Revista iberoamericana* 122 (1983).

7. The feeling was mutual, as evidenced in an interview by Ernesto Parra Escobar with Juan Rulfo published in *Quimera* (Barcelona) 103–4 (1991): 112–17. Rulfo answers Parra's question about his Hispano-American preferences: "First, Juan Carlos Onetti; he is a fundamental author for me. Then, José María Arguedas from Peru." Parra mentions the success of *El Sexto* and Rulfo adds, "He has another excellent novel, *Los ríos profundos*; a great writer, José María Arguedas" (115).

8. While writing these "images" I am reading some memorable pages by José Miguel Oviedo, "El último Arguedas: Testimonio y comentario," (The latest Arguedas: Testimony and commentary) *Cuadernos hispanoamericanos* (Madrid) 492 (June 1991): 143–47, which he wrote regarding his critical edition of *El zorro de arriba y el zorro de abajo* (Madrid: Colección Archivos, 1990). His reading of the book is very acute and its value is increased by the personal relationship between the author and critic that preceded it.

Works Cited

Arguedas, José María. 1953. "Folklore del Valle del Mantaro. Provincias de Jauja y Concepción. Notas de José María Arguedas. Cuentos mágico-realistas y canciones de fiestas tradicionales" (Folklore of the Mantaro Valley. The provinces of Jauja and Concepción. Notes by José María Arguedas. Magic realist stories and traditional festival songs). *Folklore americano* 1 (November). [Contains "Folklore del Mantaro," 101–29; "Cuentos," 130–236; "Canciones," 237–93.]

———. 1965. *Poesía quechua* (Quechua poetry). Serie del nuevo mundo. Buenos Aires: Editorial Universitaria.

———. 1972. *Temblar/Katatay y otros poemas* (Teblar/Katatay and other poems). Lima: Instituto Nacional de Cultura.

———. 1974. *El Sexto* (The Sexto prison). Lima: Editorial Horizonte.

———. 1981. *Deep Rivers*. Trans. Frances Horning Barraclough. Austin: University of Texas Press.

Christian, Chester. 1983. "Alrededor de este nudo que es la vida: Entrevista con José María Arguedas" (Concerning this problem called life: An interview with José María Arguedas). *Revista iberoamericana.* 122:221–34.

Germán Belli, Carlos. 1984. "Entrevista con Pedro Lastra" (Interview with Pedro Lastra). *El Comercio* (December 2): 15.

Murra, John M. 1982. "José María Arguedas: Dos Imágenes" (José María Arguedas: Two images). *Revista iberoamericana.* 122 (January–March): 43–54.

Parra Escobar, Ernesto. 1991. "Entrevista con Juan Rulfo" (Interview with Juan Rulfo). *Quimera* (Barcelona) 103–4: 112–17.

Rama, Angel. 1987. "*Los ríos profundos, ópera de pobres*" (*Deep Rivers,* a work of the poor). In *Transculturación narrativa en América Latina* (Narrative transculturation in Latin America). Mexico City: Siglo XXI Editores, 1987.

Afterword

Monica Barnes

If you walk Andean trails, sooner or later you will encounter José María Arguedas. Some, like Pedro Lastra, have met him in the flesh and formed personal relationships. Others know him only in the luminous spirit glimpsed through his writing.

My own knowledge of Arguedas is of the latter type. My understanding comes directly from his works, and, to a lesser extent, from the reminiscences of people who knew Arguedas as friend, lover, relative, teacher, or colleague. Yet, this is not entirely true. I also know Arguedas through a link to the land he loved, the mountains and punas with their mysterious lakes, mestizo towns, and Indian communities.

From 1978 to 1981 I conducted archaeological research in the valley of the río Soras, a rushing river that forms part of the boundary between the Peruvian departments of Ayacucho and Apurímac. I shared, to some extent, the lives of the people around me, and got to know many of the cities and towns mentioned by Arguedas in his novels and anthropological essays. These included Pampachiri, Larcay, San Juan de Lucanas, and Puquio, the setting of *Yawar Fiesta*. Beyond them I traveled to Andahuaylas, where José María was born. There an elderly notary proudly showed me vellum-bound tomes, the records of a seventeenth-century predecessor. Such documents are fairly common in Peru, but these were remarkable in that sections were written in Quechua. If I mentioned Arguedas's name, a look of pain and discomfort still crossed the faces of older people. I took the road from Andahuaylas east to Cuzco and west to Huamanga (Ayacucho), both landmarks in Arguedas's world.

It was at this period that I discovered Arguedas's novels and had the special pleasure of reading them for the first time while living my everyday life in a mixed mestizo-*runa* (Quechua peasant) community. Not only did I peruse *Yarwar Fiesta*, I lived it. Twice I had the privilege of participating in a mountain celebration of the July Fiestas Patrias culminating in the bull-and-condor fight made illegal by Peruvian law, and famous by Arguedas. This was not in Puquio, but in Pampachiri, an old colonial town in Andahuaylas province (Barnes 1994), known to readers as the home of one of Ernesto's fellow boarders in *Los ríos profundos*. Here I witnessed dramas of rivalry, love, and hatred, much like those felt and described by Arguedas.

In these years I shared a sacred world where no important event—birthday, funeral, or journey—passed without prayer and offerings. Friends taught me to join in the rites. Indeed, they seemed anxious that I participate, both for my own spiritual protection, and theirs. I learned where to stop on the road so that an important *apu*, one of the revered mountain deities, could be propitiated. No animal, be it so small as a guinea pig or so large as a bull, was ever merely killed. It was sacrificed. Two people were needed—a sponsor, who provided the animal, and a dispatcher, who did the killing. Prayers to the earth, to God and the major saints, and to the spirits of surrounding mountains were said in reverence. The sponsor and dispatcher sprinkled *chicha*, beer, or cane alcohol on the ground, to honor Pachamama, and on the animal to be killed, to honor and dedicate the beast. We drank toasts to one another before the victim's throat was slit. The setting was sometimes as intimate as an adobe kitchen, or as public as the plaza during a fiesta. Both women and men performed this ritual.

I was a popular sponsor, being known to have enough money to purchase animals. Everyone appreciated the meat liberated for human consumption by this ceremony.

I have many other memories: the sadness of seeing a newborn wrapped within her dead mother's shroud, or the satisfaction of finding my own, personal *illa* or luminous sacred object, as beautifully described in *Los ríos profundos.* This was under the instruction of Mama Cruz, elderly cook and *curandera.* Although I knew no Quechua at the beginning, and she had no Spanish, we somehow managed to communicate. Mama Cruz's prognostications often reflected warning rumors. In exchange for her wisdom, I shared my knowledge of sulfa ointment, a substance that seemed magical to her.

In this Arguedian world I read of the world of Arguedas. I consumed the novels set in the sierra, and the short stories as well. To this day I can never reread "Agua" or "Warma Kuyay" without hearing the voices of certain old friends conversing in my head.

This direct, experiential approach to Arguedas's work is only one path out of many. In this book focused on José María we find others well worth following. Pedro Lastra shares his reminiscences of Arguedas from their first meeting in 1962. Lastra cautions himself, and us, not to make the old mistake of equating an author's personality with that of his narrators and protagonists. Nevertheless, Lastra, probably joined by all other admirers of Arguedas, sensed from his first readings that among Arguedas's work are several romans à clef. Subsequent friendship confirmed this impression, which has also been noted by critics (e.g., Landreau). Like the wisest of his characters, Arguedas had an "acute sensitivity to human corruption or degradation" (Lastra) and saw the struggle between good and evil as a permanent one.

Arguedas was not often an overtly political actor, his early imprisonment notwithstanding. Nevertheless, his oeuvre has profound political implications. There is no better portrayal of Peru's poisonous class system at mid-century. As Ciro Sandoval and Sandra Boschetto-

Sandoval note, the Sexto prison, setting of the novel of the same name, provides a model of Peruvian society and its competing ideologies. *Yawar Fiesta* and *Los ríos profundos* unfold as struggles among conflicting interests in large mountain towns. *El zorro de arriba y el zorro de abajo* exposes the stresses of explosive growth in the context of an abusive capitalism. As Arguedas himself pointed out, in "La novela y el problema de la expresión literaria en el Perú" (The novel and the problem of literary expression in Peru), social classes, not individual characters, are in some sense the protagonists of his novels. Arguedas clearly lived and worked in particular political, social, and economic contexts.

When Arguedas was coming to maturity as a writer, the dominant Latin American economic paradigm was Dependency Theory, especially as developed and promulgated by Raúl Prebisch, an Argentine planner. According to Prebisch and his followers, the industrialized countries formed a sort of center, often called the First World, a term coined by progressive French journalists in the 1950s. The communist nations, stagnating under Stalinist influences, were the Second World, although seldom referred to as such. Therefore, the underdeveloped portions of the globe comprise the Third World.[1] Unless relations could be reforged, the First World would always exploit the less developed dependent nations. Capitalist countries buy the Third World's raw materials cheaply, selling manufactured goods back to them in the form of high-priced, value-added products. Thus most of Asia, Africa, and Latin America could be seen as the "periphery," dependent on richer countries.

To break this cycle of dependency and its concomitant poverty and political and economic domination from outside national borders, Prebisch proposed government ownership of all important means of production along with import substitution. Only the state was strong enough to produce goods efficiently and without exploitation. By barring imports, usually through duties one or more times their base retail price, Third World nations could develop internal markets and the manufacturing capacity to fulfill their demands. This would break the cycle of dependency and lead to true national autonomy and an end to pernicious exploitation.

So persuasive was this model that most Latin American countries had adopted it, in one form or another, by the 1970s. However, the anticipated prosperity did not follow. Corrupt and inept bureaucrats proved unable to plan and manage efficient production. Furthermore, with the possible exceptions of Mexico and Brazil, national markets were not large enough to support a full spectrum of industries. Priscilla Archibald touches on some of these issues at the beginning of her contribution to this volume, and Rita De Grandis still finds dependency theory a useful analytical framework.

However, there was a competing development model promulgated in the fifties and sixties. This one derived its impetus from the First and Second World countries rather than from within the Third World itself. In this second model well-to-do nations extended help to poorer countries in the form of aid (both money and commodities), loans, and expertise. Latin American nations were cast in a client-patron relationship with the United States, the Soviet Union, and certain European countries, as well as with international institutions. Applied anthropology projects that were part of this model have been much criticized for their heavy-handed ethnocentrism. One, discussed by Archibald, was the Vicos Project, operating in the northern Peruvian coastal valley of the same name and sponsored by Cornell University. Groups with superficially dissimilar ideology such as the Summer Institute of Linguistics also adhered to this guided Westernization model.

As Archibald points out, there is a disjunction between the cultural insensitivity of these Westernization projects and the high values Arguedas placed on history and tradition. Arguedas's insight led him to emphasize the cultural dynamism of the Colonial Period, rejecting the structuralist ahistoricity that dominated the anthropology of his day. He saw the Andean experience as one constantly adapting to changing conditions.

This view is also underlined by Landreau in his remarks on the

process of transculturation as perceived by Arguedas. Just as traditional culture can creatively absorb and transform elements of the
modern, Peru's Hispanic sector has integrated aspects of indigenous
Andean thought. This is especially apparent to people like Arguedas
who have studied both Andean and Iberian cultures. In short, Arguedas was not inclined to make the still common mistake of assuming that pre-Hispanic beliefs and customs passed essentially
unchanged from Tawantinsuyu (the Inca empire) to the present. Neither was he willing to take assertions of pure Hispanicism at face
value, or to assume that modernization precluded the traditional.
Archibald reminds us that Arguedas rejected versions of Andean
tales that removed "what were regarded as extraneous, nonindigenous elements." One such version is Julio C. Tello's publication of a
portion of Guaman Poma's famous letter, in which Tello removed all
references to Christianity. In his celebration of mestizo culture, Arguedas was swimming against the prevalent current of his time. Not
only in Peru, but even in Mexico, Indians were subjected on the one
hand to pressure from intellectuals and connoisseurs to return to the
supposedly pure practices of their ancestors and on the other hand,
by bureaucrats and developers to abandon their way of life in favor of
Westernized modes.

Since the death of Arguedas, economic and political paradigms
have shifted. The Sendero Luminoso (Shining Path) revolutionary
movement was inspired by Maríategui and Mao but was essentially
sui generis. It was much criticized, not only for its violence, but for its
frequent disregard of indigenous values.

Now that the Sendero Luminoso has suffered military defeat,
Peru, led by Alberto Fujimori, has entered a phase of deregulation,
privatization, and almost laissez-faire capitalism. Academic economists, trained, for the most part, in the Prebisch paradigm, have
offered critical predictions that, again for the most part, have not
been fulfilled. Probably because of the prohibitive cost of accessing

detailed, real-time economic data, academic analysts are usually up to five years behind the present in their assessments. Thus, Arguedas studies have not yet taken full account of these paradigm shifts.

One can appreciate Arguedas's wisdom in illuminating the widest possible social, economic, and political issues. Arguedas, through following his own passions, created an oeuvre that is truly classical. While rooted in the social conditions of his day, it nevertheless addresses universal concerns. One of the challenges for Arguedas scholars is to reinterpret his message in the light of changing economic, social, and political conditions.

Alita Kelley has already begun that enterprise. In her essay "The Persistence of Center: José María Arguedas and the Challenge to the Postmodern Outlook," Kelley argues that Arguedas's last novel, *El zorro de arriba y el zorro de abajo,* represents an ultimate rejection of postmodernism. Although postmodernism encompasses a spectrum of perceptions and styles, according to Kelley, "the postmodernist can find no redemptive forces, nothing in which to place hope of transcendence: all metanarratives have failed, God is dead, belief in historicism is not justified, reason has let us down, science dooms us to chaos." Most of the contributors to this volume seem to agree that nothing could be further from Arguedas's world, infused, as it is, by the sacred.

Living as he did in a bilingual, multicultural milieu, for Arguedas the Spanish language was not a default choice. He struggled to fulfill his deep inclination to portray Indian and mestizo experience in the Quechua language through which it is lived. Nevertheless, to do so would limit his audience to the few people able to read *runasimi* (as the Quechua people refer to their language). Spanish presented greater possibilities for diffusion, both inside and outside Peru. In searching for a solution to this dilemma, Arguedas experimented with transforming the cadence and rhythms of Quechua into Spanish. Success was elusive, as it was for Frances Barraclough when she translated the Andeanized Spanish of *Los ríos profundos* into the English of *Deep Rivers*, taking us one further remove from Quechua speech and thought.

Arguedas's rejection of literary Spanish for his artistic purposes was a radical move. "Correct" grammar and usages retained a stranglehold on Spanish longer than in English, and the "proper" manner of writing Quechua is still under some dispute. Nevertheless, we must remember that as recently as 1885, the year *Huckleberry Finn* was published, Twain's great novel was not criticized for its alleged racism or weak ending chapters, as it is today, but for its use of dialect and for the cynicism that infuses it.

Possibilities for writing in Quechua fortunately have expanded since Arguedas's death. In this volume Martin Lienhard outlines the state of contemporary Quechua poetry, arguing that Arguedas and later Quechua poets were not simply expanding the corpus of sung *runasimi* verse. Rather, Arguedas created avant-garde free verse, and his successors continue to write in this style. Their poetry is not directed to the monolingual villager, but rather to the sophistical bilingual people of Lima and other cities and towns. Nevertheless, traditional Andean music and singing were fundamental to Arguedas. To apprehend the transformative power of music one only has to think of how a person's visual reaction to a film is deliberately amplified, contradicted, or foreshadowed by the soundtrack. In this volume William Rowe muses on the roles music and other sounds, or rather the memory of such, play in Arguedas's work.

Problems of translation are central to the papers by Landreau and by Lienhard, and are discussed in most of the rest. Landreau focuses on "the complex relationship in Arguedas's writing between autobiography and translation." Indeed, Landreau goes so far as to assert that "[cultural translation] motivates Arguedas's entire literary and intellectual project." Here we are reminded of Pedro Lastra's early intuition that Arguedas's protagonists and narrators reflected his own experience and personality to a greater degree than with many writers of similar sophistication. However, Landreau cautions us against a naïve view of the autobiographical aspects of Arguedas's work. "Autobiography legitimates a story, told lyrically, but it does not make the story a form of unmediated testimony." Rather, experience is transmogrified and fitted into genera such as the novel, the poem, or even the anthropological essay. Literal fact is turned by the author into literary fact.

Sandoval and Boschetto-Sandoval note that *El Sexto* is a "meta-testimonial" novel, revealing the multilayered complexity of Andean identity and society. Julio Ortega points out that there are really three interacting first person narrators (from the point of view of point of view) in *Los ríos profundos*. These are the author, witness, and actor. Nevertheless, the three narrators are voices of one narrator, a perception that mirrors Christian ideas of the Trinity. Ortega also highlights other communicators active in the Cuzco portion of the novel. Included are human characters such as Ernesto's uncle's humble servant, as well as striking aspects of the environment, notably the marvelous Hatunrumiyoc wall, part of the *cancha* (compound) of Inca Roca. Quechua, English, and Spanish all share a concept of "living rock" from which the Hatunrumiyoc was fashioned. We are intuitively equipped to understand Ernesto's perception of a moving, active wall.

As Archibald points out, Arguedas the anthropologist received a cool critical reception while he was alive, and for a while afterward. In part this is because Arguedas was ahead of his time, a reflexive anthropologist in an age vainly striving for objectivity. I am struck by the contrast between the obscurity into which Arguedas's anthropological writings slipped after his death and the appreciative reviews Catherine Allen received some two decades later with *The Hold Life Has*, another lyrical portrait of an Andean society presented, without apologies, from the subjective viewpoint of a particular observer.

Arguedas's Quechua poetry and prose, the latter in the form of letters, give rise to another set of translation problems. Wide accessibility requires translation directly into Spanish, English, and other languages. Literary translation in general is practiced in an intellectual setting where many scholars, critics, and general readers have excellent knowledge of both the original and target languages. Most chicano novels, for instance, are available in both English and Spanish versions, often "translated" or rewritten by the author of the original text. However, while there is a growing readership conversant with both Spanish and Quechua, few people can understand Quechua and English, or Quechua and German, to give just two possible combinations. Thus, many readers can have access to Arguedas's Quechua writings only in translation. Although Arguedas himself "translated" many of his own poems into Spanish, in effect these are often new variations on the same theme.

Nevertheless, as in all translations, choices must be made, and a word's original semantic field never entirely overlaps with that of the word chosen to represent it. Thus, in Landreau's English version of "Huk doctorkunaman qayay" (Appeal to some intellectuals) the following phrase occurs: "They say too that my heart is weak." In Quechua this is "Manas sonqoykupas allinchu," literally "they say, too, that my heart is not good." Landreau has undoubtedly caught the spirit of this line. The speaker is not accused of having a bad heart in the sense of an evil one, but one that is insufficient in some way. Nevertheless, it is easy to see that choices other than "weak" are possible, and that the inevitability of decision leads the reader to particular readings of the poem.

Of course there is much more to translation than a good fit of synonyms. A grammatical choice can be seen in Harrison's translation, cited by Landreau, of the first lines of "Huk doctorkunaman qayay." There, in translation, references are in the first person plural. Landreau makes them singular. A grammatical argument can be made for either position. Likewise, Lienhard in this volume explores the possibilities presented by the two forms of "we" available in Quechua. One, *nokanchik* (or *nokanchis*) includes the person being addressed.

The other, *nokayku*, excludes the addressee. We see from these examples that a translated poem is inherently a study of a poem. As more of this is done, a corpus of perceived meanings will emerge.

The intractability of Arguedas's language dilemma was brought home to me as I worked on this afterword, listening to volume 1 of John Cohen's "Huayno Music of Peru (1949–1989)." About half the songs on this record are in Spanish, and most of those lyrics are transcribed and translated into English. However, the other half, sung in Quechua, were not put down on the printed page, either in transliteration or translation, although they are translatable.

In the appendix to Lienhard's contribution there are Quechua and English versions of Arguedas's "Túpac Amaru kamaq taytanchisman," as well as Quechua poems by our contemporaries Dida Aguirre, Eduardo Ninamango Mallqui, and Isaac Huamán Manrique. While I applaud the republication of their poems, I am discouraged to see that they have been translated, not from Quechua, but from (omitted) Spanish versions. Perhaps this is why there are differences in the order and arrangement of the English and Quechua lines of Dida Aguirre's first poem. Line 23 in the Quechua version, "Lliu llapallanchipa," is apparently left unconsidered in the English rendition. This is a very strong line emphasizing absolute completeness and perfection. Furthermore, there is a shift from the plural "chay yana sonqo mistikunam / those men of evil heart" to the singular "he is spying on us, circling," that does not seem entirely justified by the original. Likewise, the evil people are not just any men, but *mistikuna*, upper-class exploiters. Much can be lost in translation, and the meaning can be subtly shifted, as a work passes through an intermediary language.

However well grounded in a particular political and social matrix, and however well problems of translation and transculturation are solved, Arguedas's oeuvre would not work its durable magic without a mastery of content. Claudette Kemper Columbus focuses on the theme of tricksters in Arguedas's last, and unfinished novel, the punningly titled *El zorro de arriba y el zorro de abajo*. (*El cerro de arriba y el cerro de abajo*—the hill above and the hill below—is a common locational phrase, in use both in Spain and in the Andes at least by the seventeenth century.) Trickster figures, usually in the form of animals, are common in folktales from both the old and new worlds. These have been well studied by anthropologists and Arguedas was surely aware of such stories. As Columbus indicates, he was particularly familiar with trickster figures in the early-seventeenth-century Huarochirí manuscript that Arguedas translated from Quechua into Spanish. Columbus sees the fox from above as a cheap trickster, Don Ángel Rincón Jaramillo, a fat, avaricious, vulgar, adulterous, and egocentric industrialist who runs a fishmeal factory. The fox from below is Diego, a corrective, higher trickster who helps one enter a more human consciousness in which traditional people and their accomplishments can be appreciated. Diego exposes and protests exploitation of any kind. Columbus's reading is an insightful one that integrates Arguedas the novelist and Arguedas the scholar into one creative thinker capable of dissolving boundaries between genera.

Antonio Cornejo Polar takes up the theme of the migrant in *El zorro*. For Cornejo Polar the migrant appears caught in a "multicultural web . . . that only partially obeys the codes of transculturation . . . ." Cornejo Polar concentrates on language and experience.

Luis Jiménez draws our attention to women and the carnivalesque in *Los ríos profundos*. In particular, he examines the characters of la Opa ("idiot" in Quechua), a sexually abused and degraded drudge at the Abancay boys' school, and of Doña Felipa, a *chicha* seller turned political activist. Jiménez looks at how these two female characters are both objects and subjects in a world quite alienating to women, especially those of low social position.

Ciro Sandoval and Sandra Boschetto-Sandoval view another of Arguedas's novels, *El Sexto,* as a socioethnographic corpus inviting "reflection on alternative paradigms of individual and cultural liberation from oppression." Such expositions of themes and meanings must continue in the light of new insights. As Cornejo Polar writes, "along with the previously discussed views, others capable of inciting new and perhaps even more stimulating readings still lie hidden."

When I left the physical world of Arguedas, not to return for almost eight years, I lingered for many months in his mental universe. Indeed, I have visited it frequently ever since. I see now, more clearly, that a complex subject can never be exhausted. So it is with Arguedas's works. One must continue to study them in the light of emerging theories and perspectives. When Arguedas died, the second wave of feminism had barely washed the shores of North America and Europe, let alone the rest of the world. Yet feminist views of Arguedas, unanticipated by him, are certainly enlightening. In this essay I have expressed my strongly held opinion that Arguedas can, and should, be reexamined in the context of evolving political and economic systems. In many ways the twentieth century has been a vast ideological and practical experiment, or rather, series of experiments, with results ranging from magnificence to almost unspeakable horror. The world is very different now than at mid-century, and we need to see Arguedas's testimony and philosophy in the light of what we have learned.

Future Arguedas studies will greatly refine the analysis of his Quechua corpus, both poetry and letters. These must be studied in the original, whether by literate, bilingual speakers of that language, or by those of us who have acquired our knowledge in the classroom and field. This project is made more possible by increasing literacy in the Andean countries, and by improved language acquisition materials. Translations should proceed, of course. In fact, multiple translations are a good vehicle for probing the dimensions of meanings and metaphors.

Studies of content and form will not be neglected. These can only be enhanced as our understanding of the Andean world develops. Finally, as unlikely as it may at first seem for a well-beloved author now dead some thirty years, we can strive to expand the Arguedian corpus. Like John Keats, Arguedas was a correspondent who could bore into the deepest levels of his friends' consciousness with a few exultant or painful words. John Murra has very recently published collections of Arguedas's letters. I believe that there still exist, in private hands and the Ortiz family, other correspondence that would speak to the general reader, if published. We can hope that this will be done and that José María will sing to us, once again, in his full voice.

Note

1 At first the "third world" *(le tiers monde)* was a utopian (revolutionary) concept, one associated with the "third estate" (the powerless) at the time of the French Revolution. The connotations of this term have changed over the decades. The former colonial countries, once independent, could develop into prosperous, nonaligned peaceful nations free of the abuses of both capitalism and communism. When that did not happen, the "third world" began to connote the poor.

Works Cited

Arguedas, José María. 1996. *Las cartas de Arguedas* (Arguedas's letters). Ed. John V. Murra and Mercedes López-Baralt. Lima: Pontificia Universidad Católica del Perú, Fondo Editorial.

Barnes, Monica. 1994. "The Yawar Fiesta of Pampachiri, Apurímac, Peru." *NAOS* 10.–3:13–18. Pittsburgh: Department of Hispanic Languages and Literatures, University of Pittsburgh.

Ortiz Rescamiere, Alejandro, ed. 1996. *Jóse María Arguedas : recuerdos de una amistad* (Jóse María Arguedas : memories of a friendship). Lima: Fondo Editorial de la Pontificia Universidad Católica del Perú.

Chronology of José María Arguedas

1911 Born José María Arguedas Altamirano, January 18 in Andahuaylas, in southern mountains of Peru; son of Victor Manuel Arguedas Arellano, lawyer from Cuzco, and Doña Victoria Altamirano Navarro (from distinguished upper-class family). Augusto B. Leguía (1908–1912) governs the country. Machu-Picchu discovered.

1912 Guillermo Billinghurst is elected president with support of the popular movement. Latin American Students Congress in Lima.

1913 Workers of Callao are granted 8-hour workday.

1914 Mother dies; José María left in care of his paternal grandmother. Father travels constantly through various districts of the sierra. Colonel Oscar R. Benavides overthrows Billinghurst government. Indigenous uprising in Puno. Repression on Llancan hacienda. Outbreak of World War I.

1915 Political, union, and peasant unrest. José Pardo elected president. Ultraconservative party of José de la Riva Agüero formed. José Gálvez publishes *Posibilidad de una genuina literatura nacional* (Possibility for a genuine national literature).

1916 Minimum salary legislated for indigenous workers. *Tiempo* (Time) appears (newspaper in which José Carlos Mariátegui will soon begin to preach his socialism).

1917 Father marries Grimanesa Arangoitia, rich widow and owner of several haciendas. José María moves to Puquio to live with stepmother. One of her sons, Pablo Pacheco, is ill-fated presence in the writer's childhood, as evident in *Amor mundo*

(World love). War declared on Germany. First workers' union and Student Federation organized. Russian Revolution.

1918   Studies in San Juan de Lucanas. Stepmother forces him to live with the Indian servants—a milestone for Arguedas. Workers strike in Lima.

1919   Several visits to Cuzco with father. Entire family visits Lima for first time. Enters fourth grade in religious school in Abancay. Haya de la Torre is elected president of Student Federation. Mariátegui edits *La Razón* (Reason), and same year is forced into exile in Europe because of his beliefs and Marxist ideology.

1920   Second brief trip to Lima. Continues living in San Juan de Lucanas. New constitution legally recognizes indigenous communities. Vial Conscription Law aggravates indigenous situation.

1921   Lives in Puquio. Family situation becomes unbearable. Runs away with brother Arístides to Hacienda Viseca to live with uncle. There meets Felipe Maywa and other Indians that will later serve as characters in his works. First Indigenous National Congress.

1922   Conflicts arise between Cerro de Pasco Corporation and the indigenous communities in center of the country.

1923   Returns to Puquio. Undertakes extensive trips with father through most of sierra range (recalled in *Deep Rivers*). International problems arise with Chile. Haya de la Torre forced into exile in Mexico. Indigenous uprisings in Huancané and La Mar. Mariátegui returns from forced exile in Europe.

1924   Following a trip to Ica, settles in Abancay; there studies in a religious school. These experiences recounted in *Los ríos profundos* (Deep rivers). Haya de la Torre founds APRA (Alianza Popular Revolucionaria Americana) party in Mexico.

1925   Accident results in atrophy of two fingers of right hand. Completes primary education. Mariátegui publishes *La escena contemporánea* (The contemporary scene).

1926   Begins secondary education in religious school in Ica. Its scenery and legends will serve as material for "Orovilca." Political repression. In Cuzco "Resurgimiento" movement is formed in defense of the Indian. Mariátegui's magazine *Amauta* appears, in which he encounters ideological stimulus that directs him to socialism and indigenous movement.

1927   Continues in Ica with frequent trips to the sierra. First love experience (Pompeya) frustrated. Persecution and deportation of union leaders and leftist intellectuals. Political and cultural repression. *Amauta* shut down (reappears in December), and Mariátegui, its founder, persecuted.

1928   Travels with father to Huancayo, where he enters third year of secondary school. Known for pensive, solitary air. First literary efforts appear as articles in student journal *Antorcha* (Torch): "The Dehumanization of Art" and "Indian Present and Past." Also writes a "600-page novel" that he claims "the police confiscated." Official formation of APRA as a Peruvian party leads to definitive rupture between Haya and Mariátegui. Mariátegui founds Socialist Party, which will later become the PCP (Communist Party of Peru). Union newspaper, *Labor*, appears. Mariátegui publishes *Siete ensayos de interpretación de la realidad peruana* (Seven essays on the interpretation of Peruvian reality).

1929   Enters merchants' school in Lima. Frequently travels to Yauyo to visit father. Eventually spends more time there than in Lima. Peace treaty signed between Peru and Chile. Return of Tacna to Peru. Founding of General Confederation of Peruvian Workers. *Labor* is shut down. Archaeological monuments declared state property. Intellectual revision of Peruvian history and literature begins.

1930   Intense political and social agitation. Commander Sánchez Cerro overthrows Leguía government. New government continues repression. Mariátegui dies. Victor Andrés Belaúnde publishes *La realidad nacional* (The national reality) in response to Mariátegui's *Seven Essays*.

1931   Returns to Lima and enters University of San Marcos to study letters. Lives with brother Arístides, from whom he is inseparable. Violent confrontation between APRA and government. Haya de la torre publishes *Teoria y práctica del aprismo* (Theory and practice of Aprismo) and Cesar Vallejo, his novel *Tungsteno* (Tungsten). The latter leaves a strong and lasting impression on Arguedas.

1932   Father dies; brothers lose financial support. José María obtains position in postal department through influence of a friend of his father. Failed presidential assassination attempt: execution by firing squad of eight sailors. University of San Marcos closed down until 1935. Aldous Huxley publishes *Brave New World*.

1933   Studies singing. First edition of "Warma Kuyay" appears in magazine *Signo* (Sign). Probable encounter with Moisés Saenz, Mexican diplomat, author of various works and architect of ethnographic investigations, and with whom Arguedas establishes important working and personal relationship. Sánchez Cerro assassinated by a militant Aprista. Congress elects General Benavides president. Political amnesty declared; APRA initiates public activities. Acute polemic between Apristas and Communists, a central theme in *El Sexto* (The Sexto prison, 1961).

1934   Publishes in *La Calle* and *La Prensa* (Buenos Aires). J. L. Rouillon publishes some of these stories in 1973 under the title *Cuentos olvidados* (Forgotten stories). Repression against APRA, which is forced underground. Ciro Alegría, another indigenous writer, deported. Mariátegui's *Defensa del Marxismo* (In defense of Marxism) is published.

1935   *Agua* (Water), a collection of three stories (in their second edition), appears, winning second prize in international competition sponsored by Revista Americana of Buenos Aires. Enrolls in anthropology course in Department of Biological, Physical, and Mathematical Sciences. Political repression continues. Numerous APRA articles published, the most important being "El anti-imperialismo y el APRA" (Anti-imperialism and APRA) by Haya de la Torre.

1936   With other writers, founds magazine *Palabra, en defensa de la cultura* (Word, in defense of culture). With Aprista support Eguiguren wins presidential elections. These are annulled and Congress extends Benavides's presidency by three years. Notable archaeological finds.

1937   Completes literary studies. Visit to San Marcos campus by Mussolini envoy General Camarotta provokes student protest. Arguedas is arrested and spends eleven months in Sexto prison. Loses position at postal service. "El despojo" (Spoilation) published in fourth volume of *Palabra*; will later appear as second chapter of *Yawar Fiesta*. Aprista leader assassinated.

1938   *Canto kechwa*, translations of indigenous songs and an essay on Indian and mestizo art, appears in September. Museum of Anthropology founded.

1939   Prepares thesis, "The Mestizo Popular Song: Its Poetic Value and Possibilities," for degree in humanities. Never presents it. For doctorate he submits "The Problem of Language in Peru and the Poetry of the Mountain and Coastal Regions." Becomes professor of Spanish and Geography at Mateo Pumaccahua Boys' School in Sicuani, Cuzco. Marries Celia Bustamante Vernal, sister of Alicia Bustamante, painter, popular-art collector and first to organize an exhibition of Sabogal indigenous art. Manuel Prado wins presidential elections, despite opposition from APRA. Outbreak of World War II.

1940   Travels to Mexico to represent Peruvian educators at Inter-American Indian Conference in Pátzcuaro. Spends two years in Mexico. Serious economic crisis. Rupture of the Latin American countries with Germany, Japan, and Italy.

1941   Promoted to a position in Ministry of Education "to aid in the reform of secondary education programs." Publishes first novel, *Yawar Fiesta*. Continues to publish articles on folklore and indigenous customs in *La Prensa*. Armed conflict with

Ecuador. Ciro Alegría publishes his internationally acclaimed indigenous novel *El mundo es ancho y ajeno* (Broad and alien is the world).

1942   Completes his educational reform work. Becomes professor of Spanish at Alfonso Ugarte High School. Peace treaty signed with Ecuador. First Communist Party Congress. Magazines *Folklore* and *Revista del Instituto Americano de Arte* (Cuzco) first appear.

1943   Works at Our Lady of Guadalupe and Alfonso Ugarte schools. Major fire at National Library; heavy losses.

1944   Suffers psychological crisis, resulting in writer's block for almost five years. Creation of National Democratic Front, with participation of Communist and APRA parties. Violent strikes in Lima and Callao over workers' salary demands.

1945   Continues as Spanish professor. Democratic Front assures election of José Luis Bustamante y Rivero as president. Law of National Security abolished. Political amnesty granted. Democratic process begins. Ministry of Artistic Education and Cultural Extension (Folklore and Popular Art) created. Armistice signed; World War II ends.

1946   Internal conflicts in Democratic Front. Economic crisis. Creation of Museum of Peruvian Culture.

1947   "Denounced" as communist by Aprista newspaper, *La Tribuna*. Appointed Director General of Folklore, Ministry of Education. Undertakes with Francisco Izquierdo Ríos national survey to collect stories and legends. Together they publish *Mitos, leyendas y cuentos peruanos* (Myths, legends and Peruvian stories). Democratic Front collapses, with APRA passing to the opposition. State of siege. APRA blamed for assassination of Francisco Graña, publisher of *La Prensa*.

1948   Begins teaching courses on Quechua at San Marcos. Secretary of Inter-American Committee on Folklore. Publishes essays on Quechua literature, both ancient and modern. Fragment of *Deep Rivers* appears. English translation of *Canto kechwa*. Military government takeover: General Odría deposes president Bustamante. Eight-year dictatorship begins.

1949   Publishes *Canciones y cuentos del pueblo quechua* (Songs and stories of the Quechua peoples). Suspected of being a communist, loses position at Colegio Mariano Melgar. Fierce repression against the left and APRA. Haya de la Torre takes refuge in Colombian embassy. Law of National Security reinstalled.

1950   Publishes *La novela y el problema de la expresión literaria en el Perú* (The novel and the problem of literary expression in Peru), a fundamental text for understanding his position on literature. Obtains diploma in ethnology from San Marcos. Returns to Ministry of Education as head of Department of Folklore and Popular Art. In Education Department, teaches Quechua and "Problemas Funamentales de la Cultura Peruana" (Fundamental problems of Peruvian culture). Odría becomes "Constitutional president" by fraudulent election. Popular rebellion in Arequipa. Government agents assassinate union leader Negreiros. Complete works of Mariátegui published.

1951   Travels to La Paz. In Cuzco studies festival of Inti Raymi. Law of National Security vigorously applied.

1952   Studies Puquio area. Widespread opposition to Law of National Security. Popular uprising in Arequipa. "Social poets" actively intervene in struggle against the dictatorship.

1953   Studies folklore in Mantaro valley. Appointed head of Institute of Ethnological Studies in Museum of Culture. Secretary of Inter-American Committee on Folklore based in Peru; edits its official journal, *Folklore americano*. Publishes anthology of Quechua poetry. Government of dictator Odría appoints him Director of Cultural Affairs; he declines.

1954   Publishes *Diamantes y pedernales* (Diamonds and flint), which includes the stories of "Agua" plus two new stories and an introductory note explaining his difficulties (and progress) in rendering Quechuan world in Spanish. Studies folklore in Ayacucho. Adopts, for writing of Quechua, graphs proposed by Indigenist Congress of La Paz. North American corporation and capital investment increases in Peru. Labor unrest.

1955   Receives prize from *El Nacional* of Mexico for story "Death of the Brothers Arango." Publishes translation of an anonymous Quechua elegy on death of Atahualpa. Christian Democratic Party founded.

1956   Travels to Puquio once again, and publishes results of his investigations, including myth of Inkarrí. Publishes *La evolución de las comunidades indígenas* (The evolution of indigenous communities).

1957   Publishes "Hijo solo" (Lonely son) and study on the fair of Huancayo. Obtains university degree in letters.

1958   Professor at University of San Marcos, Department of Ethnology. Receives Fomento a la Cultura prize for his thesis "La evolución de las comunidades indígenas." Travels on fellowship to France and Spain. *Deep Rivers* published, affords him considerable international notoriety. Labor unrest. In Lauricocha oldest archaeological remains are found: 9,325 years.

1959   Receives Ricardo Palma Prize for *Deep Rivers*. Continues to publish translations of Quechua texts. Serious economic crisis: devaluation of the sol.

1960   Named Secretary of International Folklore Committee. Attends Third American Book Festival in Buenos Aires. Government awards major concessions to International Petroleum Company: popular demonstrations in protest. Peasant unions grow in force. Popular demonstrations in favor of Cuban revolution.

1961   Travels to Guatemala to study popular art. From this experience he conceives "El forastero" (The stranger). Publishes testimonial novel *El Sexto* (The Sexto prison). Peasants invade haciendas. Leftist political activism. Some prepare for armed struggle.

1962   Receives Ricardo Palma Prize for *El Sexto*. Travels to Berlin to attend First Conference of Iberoamerican and German writers, organized by the journal *Humboldt*. "La agonía de Rasu Ñiti" (The agony of Rasu Ñiti), considered his best story, is published. Also publishes poem "A nuestro padre creador

Túpac Amaru" (Hymn to our father and creator Túpac Amaru) in bilingual (Spanish-Quechua) edition with introductory note on literary potential of Quechua. Haya de la Torre wins presidential elections, but Armed Forces intervene. Government of General Pérez Godoy. Influence of Latin American "boom" writers felt internationally.

1963   Appointed director of Casa de la Cultura. Receives doctorate in ethnology with thesis "Las comunidades de España y del Peru" (Communities in Spain and Peru). Promoted to full professor at University of San Marcos. Edits *Cultura y pueblo* (Culture and nation) and later *Revista peruana de cultura* (Peruvian journal of culture). General Lindley replaces Perez Godoy. Government decrees agricultural reform measures. Guerrilla movement begins. Fernando Belaúnde wins general elections. Moderate-conservative alliance wins majority in Parliament. Government repression begins against peasant workers who invade haciendas throughout Peru.

1964   Resigns from Casa de la Cultura to assume directorship of National History Museum. Edits first issue of *Historia y Cultura* (History and culture). Travels to Mexico to attend inauguration of several cultural sites. Professor at Agrarian University of La Molina. Publishes *Todas las sangres* (All bloods). Lectures at University of San Marcos on "Comparative Regional Cultures." Government conflicts with International Petroleum. Political crisis between legislative and executive branches of government.

1965   Separates from Celia Bustamante. Participates in Colloquium of Latin American Writers in Genoa and in Primer Encuentro de Escritores Peruanos (First meeting of Peruvian writers) in Arequipa. Makes appearances at major universities in United States. Travels to Chile and France. Publishes bilingual edition of "El sueño del pongo" (The *pongo*'s dream) a "Quechuan story," in booklet form, as well as poems and numerous articles. Participates in roundtable discussion on *Todas las sangres*, organized by Instituto de Estudios Peruanos. Guerrillas in Cuzco y Junîn (MIR) and in Ayacucho (ELN). Armed forces unleash extermination campaigns. State of siege.

1966   Appointed full-time professor at La Molina Agrarian University, where he has taught part time since 1962. Attends 37th International Conference of Americanists in Argentina. Visits Uruguay. First attempts suicide. Travels to Chile, where he consults with his psychiatrist, Dr. Lola Hoffman. Keeps a suicide diary (later incorporated into last novel). Guerrilla movements end. Problems with International Petroleum continue.

1967   Travels to Puno in February to attend festival of the Virgen of La Candelaria, as a judge in folklore competitions. Participates in conferences in Guadalajara, Santiago (Chile), and Burg Wartenstein (Austria). Lectures at San Marcos: "Peruvian Culture in Oral and Written Literature." Marries Sybila Arredondo. Publishes "Amor mundo" (World love), which he says was "not written for publication," but "on doctor's orders." Economic crisis: devaluation of the sol. Executive and legislative branches begin to collaborate. Intense popular campaign against International Petroleum.

1968   Heads Department of Sociology at La Molina. Travels to Cuba to serve on selection committee for Casa de las Américas Prize. Receives Garcilaso de la Vega Prize. Pronounces now well-known "I am not acculturated" speech. Publishes numerous articles on anthropology, folklore, and Quechua literature. Three trips to Chile, to consult with psychiatrist and to continue writing *El zorro de arriba y el zorro de abajo* (The fox from above and the fox from below). Belaunde signs Talara Act with International Petroleum amid heavy protest. Led by General Velasco Alvarado, Armed Forces topple Belaunde. "Peruvian Revolution" commences. Talara occupied militarily and International Petroleum expelled. Government describes itself as "humanistic, socialist, and Christian." Diplomatic tension with United States.

1969   Publishes new edition of "The Pongo's Dream" in *El sueño del pongo: Canciones quechuas* (The *pongo*'s dream: Quechua songs) (which includes a recording of Arguedas reading from the texts). Travels to Chile four times. Writes *El zorro de arriba y el zorro de abajo*, forwarding original manuscript to Editorial Losada in Buenos Aires. Fires shot into his head on November 28 and dies on December 2. Leaves several letters explaining motives for his suicide. Agrarian reform decreed under following slogan: "Peasant: the patrón will no longer eat from your poverty." Other reforms announced. Andean Pact constituted. North American Indian culture influential in publication of Ursula Le Guin's *Left Hand of Darkness*.

Bibliography

Selected and Updated Publications of José María Arguedas

Ethnography and Folklore

BOOKS AND MONOGRAPHS

(1947) *Cusco*. Ediciones "Centur" 1, no. 3. Lima: Corporación Nacional de Turismo.

(1954) *Música y danzas del Valle del Mantaro* (Music and dances from the Mantaro valley). Introductory remarks by Mildred Merino. Commentary by José María Arguedas. Lima: Universidad Nacional Mayor de San Marcos, Centro Federado de Letras.

(1957) *Estudio etnográfico de la feria de Huancayo* (Ethnographic study of the fair at Huancayo). Lima: Oficina Nacional de Planeamiento y Urbanismo.

(1966) *José María Arguedas* (Biblioteca Perú vivo) (José María Arguedas: "Peru vivo" Series). Lima: Editorial Juan Mejía Baca. [Includes "El testigo de la transformación del país: Las grandes perspectivas" (Witness to the transformation of the country: The broader perspectives), "El Perú y América Latina" (Peru and Latin America), "La literatura como testimonio y como una contribución" (Literature as testimony and as contribution).]

(1968) *Las comunidades de España y del Perú* (The communities of Spain and Peru). Lima: Departamento de Publicaciones de la Universidad Nacional Mayor de San Marcos.

(1969) *El sueño del pongo y canciones quechuas tradicionales: Interpretación y lectura de José María Arguedas* (The Indian servant's dream and traditional Quechua songs: Interpretation and reading by José María Arguedas). Chile: Editorial Universitaria. [Book and phonodisc.]

PROLOGUES, SELECTIONS, AND TRANSLATIONS

(1938) Introductory note to *Canto kechwa: Con un ensayo sobre la capacidad de creación artística del pueblo indio y mestizo* (Quechua song: With an essay on the Indian and mestizo capacity for artistic creation). Lima: Ediciones "Club del Libro Peruano." [Bilingual text; partial translation in *The Tiger's Eye* (New York) 5 (1948): 93–106].

(1947) Selection and notes for *Mitos, leyendas y cuentos peruanos* (Myths, legends, and Peruvian stories), ed. Jóse María Arguedas. Colección Escolar peruana. Lima: Editorial de la Dirección. [Includes "Algunas consideraciones acerca del contenido y finalidad de este libro" (Some considerations regarding the contents and purpose of this book), 9–20].

(1949) Translation and notes for *Canciones y cuentos del pueblo quechua* (Songs and stories of the Quechua people). Lima: Editorial Huascarán. [Partial translation in *The Singing Mountaineers: Songs and Tales of the Quechua People*, ed. Ruth Walgren Stephan. Austin: University of Texas Press, 1957.]

(1955) Translation for *Apu Inca Atwallpaman* [anonymous Quechua elegy]. Lima: Editorial Juan Mejía Baca and P. L. Villanueva.

(1957) Selection, translation, and notes for *Ollantay: Cantos y narraciones quechuas* (Quechua songs and stories) (anonymous), 51–123. Lima: Patronato del Libro Peruano.

(1959) "Traducción y Nota Preliminar" (Translation and introductory note). *Ijmacha* [anonymous Quechua song]. Lima: Ed. La Rama Florida.

(1960) Prologue to *Bibliografía del folklore peruano* (Bibliography of Peruvian folklore), by Mildred Merino de Zely and César Angeles Caballero, ix–xv. Mexico City: Publicaciones del Comité de Folklore de la Comisión de Historia del Instituto Panamericano de Geografía e Historia.

(1964) "La crisis de la cultura actual del Perú y esta selección de estudios" (The crisis of current Peruvian culture and this kind of study). *In Estudios sobre la cultura actual del Perú* (Studies on current Peruvian culture), 5–7. Lima: Universidad Nacional Mayor de San Marcos.

(1964) Series prologue to *Visita hecha a la provincia de Chucuito por Garcí Díez de San Miguel en el año 1567* (Visit to the province of Chucuito by Garcí Díez de San Miguel in 1567), ed. Waldemar Espinoza Soriano,1:vii–viii. Documentos Regionales para la Etnología y Etnohistoria Andinas (Regional documents for Andean ethnology and ethnohistory). Lima: Casa de la Cultura del Perú.

(1965) Introductory note to *El sueño del pongo, cuento quechua* (The Indian servant's dream, a Quechua story), trans. Arguedas, 3–4. Lima: Ediciones Salqantay.

(1965) "La poesía quechua" (Quechua poetry). In *Poesía quechua* (Quechua poetry), ed. Arguedas. Buenos Aires: Editorial Universitaria.

(1966) "Introducción a Dioses y hombres de Huarochirí" (Introduction to Gods and men of Huarochirí). In *Dioses y hombres de Huarochirí: Narración quechua recogida por Francsco de Avila (¿1958?)* (Gods and men of Huarochirí: Quechua stories compiled by Francisco de Avila [1958?]), ed and trans. Arguedas, 9–15. Lima: Museo Nacional de Historia y el Instituto de Estudios Peruanos.

(1966) Introduction to *Panorama de la Música Tradicional del Perú: 53 piezas trascritas de grabaciones tomadas directamente en el lugar, con su letra y glosa* (Panorama of traditional Peruvian music: 53 compositions transcribed and recorded directly on site, with individual characters and glosses), 7–8. Lima: Ministerio de Educación Pública, Escuela Nacional de Música y Danzas Folklóricas, Casa Mozart.

(1966) Introductory note to *Mesa redonda sobre el monolingüísmv quechua y aymara y la educaciøón en el Perú* (Roundtable on Quechua and Aymara monolingualism and education in Peru), 7–9. Lima: Casa de la Cultura del Perú.

(1967) *Poesía y prosa quechua* (Quechua poetry and prose), ed. Francisco Carrillo, 5–10. Lima: Biblioteca Universitaria.

(1969) "Discurso del señor José María Arguedas a nombre de los participantes" (A lecture by Mr. José María Arguedas on behalf of the participants). In *Primer encuentro de narradores peruanos: Arequipa 1965* (First meeting of Peruvian writers: Arequipa, 1965), 265–67. Lima: Casa de la Cultura del Perú.

CONTRIBUTIONS TO JOURNALS AND COLLECTIONS

(1940) "El wayno y el problema del idioma en el mestizo" (The *huayno* and the problem of mestizo language). *Educación (Revista de pedagogía y orientación sindical)* (Mexico City) 4, no. 6: 109–12.

(1944) "Carnaval de Tambobamba. Una valiosa contribución para Folklore. Interpreta con profundo sentido José María Arguedas" (The carnival of Tambobamba. A valuable contribution to folklore, movingly interpreted by José María Arguedas). *Folklore* 3, no. 12: 299–300.

(1944) "Un método para el caso lingüístico del indio peruano." (A method for the linguistic case of the Peruvian Indian). *Historia* 2, no. 6: 28–33.

(1945) "Notas para el estudio de las fuentes indígenas del arte peruano" (Study notes on the indigenous sources of Peruvian art). *Historia* 3, no. 10: 221–28.

(1947) "Dos cuentos quechuas" (Two Quechua stories). *Las moradas* (Lima) 2:124–34.

(1947) "El folklore y los problemas de que se trata" (Folklore and problems concerning it). *El Educador Peruano* 2:8–12 and 3:5–8.

(1948) "La literatura quechua en el Perú. La literatura erudita. Las Oraciones e Himnos de Origen Católico" (Quechua literature in Peru. Erudite literature. Prayers and hymms of Catholic origin). *Mar del sur* (Lima) 1:46–54.

(1951) "Folklore" (Folklore) in *Peru, Ayer y Hoy* (Peru: Past and Present), ed. Herbert Kirchhoff, 111–16. Buenos Aires: Talleres Gráficos Kraft.

(1952) "El complejo cultural en el Perú y el primer congreso de peruanistas (lo indio, lo occidental y lo mestizo): Los prejuicios culturales, la segregación social y la creación artística" (The Peruvian cultural complex and the first conference of Peruvian writers [Indian, Western, and mestizo issues]: Cultural prejudices, social segregation, and artistic creation]). *América indígena* (Mexico City) 12, no. 2:131–39.

(1953) "Folklore del Valle del Mantaro. Provincias de Jauja y Concepción. Notas de José María Arguedas. Cuentos mágico-realistas y canciones de fiestas tradicionales" (Folklore from the Mantaro valley. Jauja and Concepción provinces. Notes by José María Arguedas. Magical realist stories and traditional festival songs). *Folklore americano* 1 (November) [Includes "Folklore del Valle del Mantaro" (Folklore from the Mantaro valley): 101–29; "Cuentos" (Stories): 130–236; "Canciones" (Songs): 237–93]

(1955) "Los himnos quechuas católicos cuzqueños. Colección del Padre Jorge A. Lira y de J. M. B. Farfán. Estudio preliminar" (Catholic Quechua hymns from Cusco. Compiled by Father Jorge A. Lira and J. M. B. Farfán. Preliminary study). *Folklore americano* 3:121–66.

(1956) "Industrias populares en el Valle del Mantaro" (Popular industry in the Mantaro valley). *Fanal* (Instituto Peruano de Cultura) 12, no. 46: 6–11.

(1956) "Puquio, una cultura en proceso de cambio" (Puquio, a culture in the process of change). *Revista del museo nacional* (Lima) 25:184–232.

(1957) "Evolución de las comunidades indígenas: El valle del Mantaro y la ciudad de Huancayo, un caso de fusión de culturas no comprometida por la acción de las instituciones de origen colonial" (Evolution of indigenous communities: The Mantaro valley and the city of Huancayo, a case of cultural fusion uncompromised by early colonial institutions). *Revista del museo nacional* 26: 78–151.

(1958) "Historia de Miguel Wayapa" (Story of Miguel Wayapa) and "La amante del condor" (The condor's lover). In *Narraciones y leyendas incas: Antología de cronistas y autores modernos* (Stories and Inca legends: An anthology of chroniclers and modern authors), ed. Luis E. Valcárcel, 41–52. 2d ed. Lima: Editorial Latinoamericana.

(1958) "Notas elementales sobre el arte popular religioso y la cultura mestiza de Huamanga" (Preliminary notes on religious popular art and mestizo culture in Huamanga). *Revista del museo nacional* 27: 140-94.

(1960) "Cambio de cultura en las comunidades indígenas económicamente fuertes"(Cultural change in economically strong indigenous communities). *Cuadernos de Antropología* (Universidad de San Marcos) 2, no. 2: 33–38.

(1960) "Mesa Redonda y Seminario de Ciencias Sociales" (Social sciences roundtable and seminar). *Etnología y arqueología* (Universidad de San Marcos) 1:237–88.

(1961) "Cuentos religoso-mágicos quechuas de Lucanamarca" (Religious-magical Quechua stories from Lucanamarca). *Folklore americano* 8–9:142–216.

(1961) "Textos quechuas" (Quechua texts) (with Jorge A. Lira). *Revista del museo nacional* 30:41–59.

(1964) "Conclusiones de un estudio comparativo entre las comunidades del Perú y España" (Results of a comparative study between the communities of Peru and Spain). *Visión del Perú* (Lima) 18:17–25.

(1965) "Breves selecciones de insultos quechuas" (Brief selection of Quechua insults). *Folklore americano* 13:228–31.

(1965) "El joven que subió al cielo" (The young man who ascended into heaven) (with Jorge A. Lira). *Folklore americano* 13:127–40.

(1965) "El mestizaje en la literatura oral" (*Mestizaje* in oral literature). *Revista Histórica* 28:271–75.

(1967) "La difusión de la música folklórica andina: Clasificación de un catálogo de discos" (The spread of Andean folk music: Classification of a record catalog) (with Milton Guerrero). *Cuadernos de folklore* (Agrarian University) 1:17–33.

(1967) "La posesión de la tierra: Los mitos posthispánicos y la visión del universo en la población monolingüe quechua" (Poetry of the earth: Post-Hispanic myths and the vision of the universe in the Quechua monolingual population) (with Alejandro Ortíz Rescaniere). In *Les problemes agraires des Amériques Latines* (Latin American agricultural problems) (1965 conference, Paris), 309–15. Paris: Editions du Centre National de la Recherche Scientifique.

(1968) "Análisis de un genio popular: Violeta Parra, hacen artistas y escritores" (Analysis of a popular genius: Violeta Parra, making artists and writers). *Revista de educación* (Santiago, Chile) 13:66–76. [Roundtable discussion.]

POSTHUMOUS TEXTS AND CONTRIBUTIONS

[1969] "No soy un aculturado . . . Palabras de José María Arguedas en el acto de entrega del Premio Inca Garcilaso de la Vega" (I am not acculturated . . . Words of José María Arguedas upon receipt of the Inca Garcilaso de la Vega award) (1968). *Cultura y Pueblo* 15–16:3.

[1970] "Razón de ser del indigenismo en el Perú" (Indigenous Peru's reason for being). *Visión del Perú* 5:43–45.

[1975] *Formación de una cultura nacional indoamericana* (Formation of a national Indoamerican culture). Introduction, selection, and prologue by Angel Rama. Mexico City: Siglo XXI Editores.

[1976] *Señores e indios: Acerca de la cultura quechua* (Lords and Indians: Concerning Quechua culture), ed. Angel Rama. Buenos Aires: Arcas/Calicanto. [Includes "José María Arguedas transculturador" (José María Arguedas transculturator), by Angel Rama, 7–42.]

[1977] *Nuestra música popular y sus intérpretes: De lo mágico a lo popular* (Our popular music and its interpreters: From the magical to the popular). Lima: Mosca Azul y Horizonte.

[1982] Selection of fifty-five transcribed unedited texts. In *José María Arugedas et la culture nationale dans le Péru contemporain (1939–1969)* (José María Arguedas and national culture in contemporary Peru [1939–1969]). Lille, France: Atelier de Reprod. des Theses.

[1985] *Indios, mestizos y señores* (Indians, mestizos, and lords). Lima: Editorial Horizonte. [Includes "Carnaval en Tambobamba" (Carnival in Tambobamba), 151–55.]

Literature

(1935) *Agua. Los escoleros. Warma Kuyay* (Water. The schoolboys). Lima: Compañía de Impresiones y Publicidad. [Includes Quechua glossary.]

(1939) *Runa Yupay.* Ed. A. Arca Parró. Lima: Comisión Central del Censo. [Quechua text.]

(1941) *Yawar Fiesta.* Lima: Compañía de Impresiones y Publicidad. [Revised edition. Lima: Librería Juan Mejía Baca, 1958.]

(1954) *Diamantes y pedernales* (Diamonds and flint). Lima: P. L. Villanueva and Juan Mejía Baca. [Includes author's note, "Diamantes y pedernales" (Diamonds and flint), "Orovilca," "Agua" (Water), "Los escoleros" (The schoolboys), "Warma Kuyay."]

(1958) *Los ríos profundos* (Deep rivers). Buenos Aires: Editorial Losada. [Expanded as *Los ríos profundos y selección de cuentos* (Deep Rivers and other stories). Caracas: Biblioteca Ayacucho, 1978.]

(1961) *El Sexto* (The Sexto prison). Lima: Librería J. Mejía Baca y Tip. Santa Rosa.

(1962) *La agonía de Rasu-Ñiti* (The death agony of Rasu-Ñiti). Lima: Talleres Gráficos Icaro.

(1962) *Túpac Amaru Kumaq taytan-chisman: haylli-taki/A nuestro padre creador Túpac Amaru: himno-canción* (To our father and creator Túpac Amaru: Hymn-song). Lima: Ediciones Salquantay. [Bilingual text]

(1964) *Todas las sangres* (All bloods). Buenos Aires: Editorial Losada.

(1965) *El sueño del pongo: Cuento quechua* (The Indian servant's dream: A Quechua story). Lima: Ediciones Salqantay.

(1966) *La amante de la culebra/L'amante de la couleuvre* (The snake's lover). Paris: Lettres Modernes. [Bilingual text. Spanish/French.]

(1966) "Mar de harina" (Fishmeal sea). *Marcha* (Montevideo) 28:1321 (September 16): 30–31. [First chapter of the incomplete novel *Harina mundo* (Fishmeal world)].

(1966) *Oda al Jet* (Ode to the jet). Lima: La Rama Florida. [Corrected bilingual text.]

(1967) *Amor mundo y todos los cuentos* (Love world and all stories). Lima: Francisco Moncloa. [Includes "Agua" (Water), "Los escoleros" (The school boys), "Warma Kuyay," "El barranco" (The precipice), "Orovilca," "La muerte de los Arangos" (The death of the Arango), "Hijo solo" (Lonely son), "La agonía de Rasu-Ñiti" (The death agony of Rasu-Ñiti), "El forastero" (The stranger), "Amor mundo: El horno viejo" (Love world: The old stove), "La huerta" (The vegetable garden), "El ayla" (Quechua dance), "Don Antonio."]

SELECTED CRITICAL ESSAYS

(1950) "La novela y el problema de la expresión literaria en el Perú" (The novel and the problem of literary expression in Peru). *Mar del Sur* 9, nos. 1/2: 66–72.

(1961) "La soledad cósmica en la poesía quechua" (Cosmic solitude in Quechua poetry). *Idea, Arte y Letras* 48/49, nos. 7/8: 1–2.

(1963) "La misión del escritor en la evolución de nuestra época: El escritor como intérprete de la sociedad actual" (The mission of the writer in the evolution of our time: The writer as interpreter of contemporary society). [Interventions of José María Arguedas] *Humboldt* (Hamburg) 9 (special issue) for "Primer coloquio de escritores íbero-americanos y alemanes"(First meeting of Latin American and German writers): 36–37, 38, 69.

(1965) "Novela, realidad, palabra" (Novel, reality, word). *Yaraví* (Lima) 2:6–9.

(1965) "Sebastián Salazar Bondy." *El Comercio* (Lima) 14, no. 7: 2. [On the death of Salazar Bondy, July, 4 1965.]

(1966) "La literatura como testimonio y como contribución" (Literature as testimony and contribution). In *José María Arguedas.* Lima: Editorial Juan Mejía Baca.

(1966) "Llamado a algunos doctores" (A plea to certain intellectuals). *El Comercio,* Sunday supplement 3, no. 7: 23. ["Huk doctorkuanaman Qayay." *El Comercio,* Sunday supplement 17, no. 7: 23 (Quechua version).]

(1969) "Inevitable comentario a unas ideas de Julio Cortázar" (Inevitable response to a few ideas by Julio Cortázar). *El Comercio*, Sunday supplement 1, no. 6: 34.

(1969) "Poesía y prosa en el Perú contemporáneo" (Poetry and prose in contemporary Peru) (with A. Romualdo). Casa de las Américas. *Panorama de la actual literatura latinoamericana* (Panorama of current Latin American literature) (special edition) 25, no. 3: 144–53.

SELECTED POSTHUMOUS TEXTS AND CONTRIBUTIONS

[1971] *El zorro de arriba y el zorro de abajo* (The fox from above and the fox from below). Buenos Aires: Losada.

[1972] *Katatay y otros poemas* (Katatay and other poems). *Huc jayllicunapas*. Lima: Instituto Nacional de Cultura [Bilingual text: Quechua and Spanish versions of "A nuestro Padre Creador Túpac Amaru" (To our father and creator Túpac Amaru), "¡Qué Guayasamín!" (unedited) (What a painter!), "Oda al Jet" (Ode to the jet), "Temblar" (To tremble), "Llamado a los Doctores" (Plea to certain intellectuals), "A Cuba" (unedited) (To Cuba).]

[1972] *Páginas escogidas* (Selected pages). Lima: Editorial Universo. [Includes literary narrative, poetic, ethnographic, and biographical selections.]

[1973] *Cuentos olvidados y notas críticas a la obra de José María Arguedas.* (Forgotten stories and critical notes on the work of José María Arguedas). Ed. José Luis Rouillón. Lima: Ediciones Imágenes y Letras. [Includes "Los comuneros de Ak'ola" (The peasants of Ak'ola), "Los comuneros de Utej Pampa" (The peasants of Utej Pampa), "K'ellk'atay Pampa," "El vengativo" (The vindictive one), "El cargador" (The porter).]

[1974] *Agua y otros cuentos indígenas* (Water and other indigenous stories). Ed. Washington Delgado. Lima: Carlos Milla Batres. [Includes "Agua" (Water), "Los escoleros" (The school boys), "Warna Kuyay," "Orovilca," "Runa Yupay," "La agonía de Rasu-Ñiti" (The death agony of Rasu-Ñiti), "El sueño del pongo" (The Indian servant's dream).]

[1974] *Relatos completos* (Complete stories). Ed. Jorge Lafforgue. Buenos Aires: Editorial Losada. [Includes "Agua" (Water), "Otros relatos" (Other stories), "Amor Mundo" (Love world), "El sueño del pongo" (The Indian servant's dream).]

[1976] "La narrativa en el Perú contemporáneo" (Narrative in contemporary Peru). In *Recopilación de textos sobre José María Arguedas* (Compilation of texts on José María Arguedas), ed. Juan Larco, 407–30. Havana: Casa de las Américas.

[1976] *Temblar. El sueño del pongo* (To tremble; The Indian servant's dream). Havana: Casa de las Américas. [Spanish and Quechua texts; includes prologue by Alberto Escobar and notes by Sybila Arredondo.]

[1977] "El puente de hierro" (The steel bridge). *Runa* (Lima) 2, no. 5: 3–5 [Incomplete, unedited short story with introductory note by Antonio Cornejo Polar.]

[1983] *Obras completas* (Complete works). Ed. Sybila Arredondo de Arguedas, et al. 5 vol. Lima: Horizonte. [Includes only literary texts.]

[1983] *Relatos completos* (Complete stories). Intro. M. Vargas Llosa. Madrid: Editorial Alianza.

[1984] "Llamado a algunos doctores" (Plea to certain intellectuals). In *Katatay*. Lima: Editorial Horizonte.

[1990] "Documentos Anotados" (Annotated documents). In *El zorro de arriba y el zorro de abajo* (The fox from above and the fox from below), ed. Eve-Marie Fell. Nanterre, France: ALLCA XXe, Université Paris X, Centre de Recherche Latino-Américaines.

[1997] Arguedas: Los Ríos profundos (Arguedas: Deep Rivers). Newburyport, MA: Focus Publishing. [Introduction and notes by William Rowe]

Pedagogy

(1966) *Algunas observaciones sobre el niño indio actual y los factores que modelan su conducta* (A few observations concerning today's Indian child and the factors that shape his behavior). El niño en el Perú, 3: 3–18. Lima: Ed. del Consejo Nacional de Menores.

[1986] *Nosotros los maestros* (We, the teachers). Ed. Wilfredo Kapsoli. Lima: Editorial Horizonte.

English Translations of Arguedas's Works

(1948) *The Tiger's Eye* (New York) 5, no. 10:93–106. [Incomplete translation of *Canto kechwa*, 1938.]

(1957) *The Singing Mountaineers: Songs and Tales of the Quechua People.* Austin: University of Texas Press. [Incomplete translation of *Canciones y cuentos del pueblo quechua*; includes an introductory essay.]

[1978] *Deep Rivers.* Trans. Frances Horning Barraclough. Austin: University of Texas Press.

[1980] "The Agony of Rasu-Ñiti." Trans. Angela Cadillo-Alfaro de Ayres and Ruth Flanders Francis. In *Review: Latin American Literature and Arts* 25/26:43–46.

[1980] "Between Quechua and Spanish." Trans. Luis Harss. In *Review: Latin American Literature & Arts* 25/26:15–17.

[1980] "Child of Sorrow." Trans. Luis Harss. In *Review: Latin American Literature and Arts* 25/26:48–49.

[1980] "The Pongo's Dream." Trans. Luis Harss. In *Review: Latin American Literature and Arts* 25/26:50–52.

[1980] "Suicide Diary." Trans. Luis Harss. In *Review: Latin American Literature and Arts* 25/26: 47–48.

[1980] "Zumbayllu: The Spinning Top." Trans. Frances Horning Barraclough. *Review: Latin American Literature and Arts* 25/26:21–23.

[1985] *Yawar Fiesta.* Trans. Frances Horning Barraclough. Austin: University of Texas Press. [Includes a translation of the ethnographic article "Puquio, una cultura en proceso de cambio," translated as "Puquio, culture in process of change"; also published in London by Quartet Books as *Yawar Fiesta, Bloody Fiesta*.]

Selected Interviews

(1968) Orrillo, Winston. "Arguedas: Premio Garcilaso" (Arguedas: Garcilaso award). *Oiga* 295:26–28.

(1969) Dorfman, Ariel. "Conversación con José María Arguedas" (Conversation with José María Arguedas). *Trilce* (Valdivia, Chile) 15/16:65–70.

[1975] Castro-Klarén, Sara. "José María Arguedas, sobre preguntas de Sara Castro-Klarén" (José María Arguedas responds to a few questions from Castro-Klarén). *Hispania* 10:45–54.

[1983] Christian, Chester. "Alrededor de este nudo de la vida. Entrevista con José María Arguedas" (Concerning this problem called life: An interview with José María Arguedas). *Revista iberoamericana* (Pittsburgh) 122:221–34.

[1992] González, Galo F. Interview with Sybila Arredondo de Arguedas. "José María Arguedas, una recuperación indigenista del mundo Peruano" (José María Arguedas, an indigenous recuperation of the Peruvian world). *Anthropos* (Barcelona) 21.

Selected Publications about José María Arguedas

Books

Arroyo Posadas, Moisés. 1939. *La multitud y el paisaje peruanos en los relatos de José María Arguedas* (The Peruvian masses and landscape in the stories of José María Arguedas). Lima: Compañía e Impresiones y Publicidad. [A second edition appears in 1972 under the title *José María Arguedas: Etapas de su vida* (José María Arguedas: Significant moments in his life). Abancay, Peru: Ediciones Amankay.]

Castro-Klarén, Sara. 1973. *El mundo mágico de José María Arguedas* (The magical world of José María Arguedas). Lima: Instituto de Estudios Peruanos. [Based on the author's thesis, University of California at Los Angeles, 1968, presented under the title "The Fictional World of José María Arguedas."]

Cornejo Polar, Antonio. 1973. *Los universos narrativos de José María Arguedas* (The narrative worlds of José María Arguedas). Buenos Aires: Editorial Losada.

Cornejo Polar, Antonio, Alberto Escobar, Martin Lienhard, William Rowe. 1984. *Vigencia y universalidad de José María Arguedas* (The relevance and universality of José María Arguedas). Lima: Editorial Horizonte.

De Grandis, Rita. 1993. *Polémica y estrategias narrativas en América Latina: José María Arguedas-Mario Vargas Llosa-Rodolfo Walsh-Ricardo Piglia* (Polemic and Narrative Strategies in Latin America). Rosario, Argentina: Beatriz Viterbo Editora.

Escobar, Alberto. 1984. *Arguedas; o, la utopía de la lengua* (Arguedas, or the utopia of language). Lima: Instituto de Estudios Peruanos. [Includes a bibliography of works on José María Arguedas, including citations in other works.]

———. 1989. *El imaginario nacional. Moro-Westphalen-Arguedas: Una formación literaria* (The national imagination: Moro, Westphalen, Arguedas: A literary formation). Lima: Instituto de Estudios Peruanos.

Flores Galindo, Alberto. 1992. *Dos ensayos sobre José María Arguedas* (Two essays on José María Arguedas). Prologue by Cecilia Rivera. Lima: SUR Casa de Estudios del Socialismo. [Published posthumously.]

Forgues, Roland. 1979. *La sangre en llamas: Ensayos sobre literatura peruana* (Flaming blood: Essays on Peruvian literature). Lima: Librería Studium.

———. 1989. *José María Arguedas: Del pensamiento dialéctico al pensamiento trágico: Historia de una utopía* (José María Arguedas: From dialectic to tragic thought: The history of a utopia). Lima: Editorial Horizonte. [Translation of *José María Arguedas: De la pensée dialectique a la pensée tragique: Histoire d'une utopie*. Toulouse: France-Iberie Recherche, 1982.]

González, Galo Francisco. 1990. *Amor y erotismo en la narrativa de José María Arguedas* (Love and eroticism in the narrative of José María Arguedas). Madrid: Editorial Pliegos.

Huaman, Miguel Angel. 1988. *Poesía y utopía andina* (Poetry and Andean utopia). Lima: DESCO.

Kemper Columbus, Claudette. 1986. *Mythological Consciousness and the Future: José María Arguedas*. New York: Peter Lang.

Lévano, César. 1969. *Arguedas: Un sentimiento trágico de la vida* (Arguedas: A tragic sense of life). Lima: Gráfica Labor. ["Documentos" (pp. 67–108) consists chiefly of chapters of an unpublished novel and articles.]

Lienhard, Martin. 1982. *Cultura popular andina y forma novelesca: Zorros y danzantes en la última novela de Arguedas* (Andean popular culture and the novel form: Foxes and minstrels in Arguedas's last novel). Lima: Tarea/Latinoamericana Editores.

———. 1990. *Cultura andina y forma novelesca: Zorros y danzantes en la úl-*

tima novela de Arguedas (Andean culture and the novel form: Foxes and minstrels in Arguedas's last novel). Lima: Editorial Horizonte. [Expanded edition of *Cultura popular andina*; epilogue by William Rowe, Luis Millones, and José Cerna Bazán.]

Marin, Gladys C. 1973. *La experiencia americana de José María Arguedas* (The American experience of José María Arguedas). Buenos Aires: F. García Cambeiro.

Márquez, Ismael P. 1994. *La retórica de la violencia en tres novelas peruanas* (The rhetoric of violence in three Peruvian novels). New York: Peter Lang. [Includes a study of Arguedas's *Deep Rivers*.]

Muñoz, Silverio. 1980. *José María Arguedas y el mito de la salvación por la cultura* (José María Arguedas and the myth of redemption through culture). Minneapolis: Instituto para el Estudio de Ideologías y Literatura. [Reprint. Lima: Editorial Horizonte, 1987.]

Nugent, José Guillermo. 1989. *El conflicto de las sensibilidades: El mercado y el cementerio como escenarios en una novela de José María Arguedas* (Conflict of sensibilities: The marketplace and the cemetery as landscapes in a novel by José María Arguedas). Lima: Instituto Bartolomé de las Casas-Rimac.

———. 1991. *El conflicto de las sensibilidades: Propuesta para una interpretación y crítica del siglo vigésimo peruano* (Conflict of sensibilities: A proposal for an interpretation and critique of Peru in the twentieth century). Lima: Instituto Bartolomé de las Casas-Rimac.

Ortega, Julio. 1982. *Texto, comunicación y cultura: Los ríos profundos de José María Arguedas* (Text, communication, and culture: José María Arguedas's *Deep Rivers*) Lima: Centro de Estudios para el Desarrollo y la Participación.

Ortiz Rescaniere, Alejandro, ed. 1996 *Jóse María Arguedas: recuerdos de una amistad* (Jóse María Arguedas: memories of a friendship). Lima: Fondo Editorial de la Pontificia Universidad Católica del Perú.

Pantigoso, Edgardo. 1981. *La rebelión contra el indigenismo y la afirmación del pueblo en el mundo de José María Arguedas* (The struggle against *indigenismo* and popular affirmation in the world of José María Arguedas). Lima: Editorial Juan Mejía Baca.

Portocarrero Maisch, Gonzalo. 1993. *Las últimas reflexiones de José María Arguedas en racismo y mestizaje* (José María Arguedas's final reflections on racism and *mestizaje)*. Lima: Casa de Estudios del Socialismo.

Prina, Zulma Prina. 1989. *El mestizaje en América: Mito y realidad en José María Arguedas* (*Mestizaje* in America: Myth and reality in José María Arguedas). Buenos Aires: Editorial Encuentro.

Rodríguez-Luis, Julio. 1980. *Hermenéutica y praxis del indigenismo: La novela indigenista de Clorinda Matto a José María Arguedas* (Indigenous hermeneutics and praxis: The indigenous novel from Clorinda Matto to José María Arguedas). Mexico City: Fondo de Cultura Económica.

Rostworowski de Diez Cansesco, María. 1983. *Estructuras andinas del poder: Ideología religiosa y política* (Andean structures of power: Religious and political ideology). Lima: Instituto de Estudios Peruanos.

Rowe, William. 1979. *Mito e ideología en la obra de José María Arguedas* (Myth and ideology in the work of José María Arguedas). Lima: Instituto Nacional de Cultura.

Spina, Vincent. 1986. *El modo épico en José María Arguedas* (The epic mode in José María Arguedas). Madrid: Editorial Pliegos.

Tauro, Talia. 1993. *Psicopatología y amor en la obra de José María Arguedas* (Psychopathology and love in the work of José María Arguedas). Lima: Editorial Universo.

Trigo, Pedro. 1982. *Arguedas: Mito, historia y religión* (Arguedas: Myth, history, and religion). Lima: Centro de Estudios y Publicaciones.

Urrello, Antonio. 1974. *José María Arguedas, el nuevo rostro del indio: Una estructura mítico-poética* (José María Arguedas; the new face of the Indian: A mythical-poetic structure). Lima: Editorial Juan Mejía Baca.

Vargas Llosa, Mario. 1978. *José María Arguedas, entre sapos y halcones* (José María Arguedas, between toads and falcons). Madrid: Ediciones Cultura Hispánica del Centro Iberoamericano de Cooperación.

Vega Cantor, Renán. 1991. *José María Arguedas, Indio de corazón. El legado cultural de José María Arguedas. Antología* (José María Arguedas, an Indian with heart. The cultural legacy of José María Arguedas, An anthology.). Bogotá: El Buho.

Zúñiga Ortega, Clara Luz. 1994. *José María Arguedas: Un hombre entre dos mundos* (José María Arguedas: A man between two worlds). Posto, Colombia, and Quito: Universidad de Nariño and Ediciones Abya-Yala.

Edited Collections

Fell, Eve-Marie. 1990. *José María Arguedas: El zorro de arriba y el zorro de abajo* (José María Arguedas: The fox from above and the fox from below). Nanterre, France: ALLCA XXe, Université Paris X, Centre de Recherches Latino-Américaines.

Haya de la Torre, Victor Raúl. 1977. *Obras completas* (Complete works). Lima: Editorial Juan Mejía Baca.

Larco, Juan, ed. 1976. *Recopilación de textos sobre José María Arguedas* (Compilation of texts on José María Arguedas). Havana: Casa de las Américas.

Murra, John V., and Mercedes López-Baralt, eds. 1996. *Las cartas de Arguedas* (The letters of Arguedas). Lima: Pontificia Universidad Católica del Peru, Fondo Editorial.

O'Hara, Edgar, ed. 1997. *Cartas de Jóse María Arguedas a Pedro Lastra* (Letters of Jóse María Arguedas to Pedro Lastra). Santiago de Chile : LOM Ediciones.

Pérez, Hildebrando, and Carlos Garayar, eds. 1991. *José María Arguedas: Vida y obra* (José María Arguedas: Life and work). Lima: Amaru Editores.

Monographs and Special Issues

Aibar Ray, Elena. 1992. *Identidad y resistencia cultural en las obras de José María Arguedas* (Identity and cultural resistance in the works of José María Arguedas). Lima: Pontificia Universidad Católica del Perú, Fondo Editorial. [Monograph.]

Aleza Izquierdo, Milagros, Isabel García Izquierdo, and Salvador Pons Bordería. 1992. *Americanismos léxicos en la narrativa de José María Arguedas* (Lexical americanisms in the narrative of José María Arguedas). Cuadernos de Filología, no. 5. Valencia, Spain: University of Valencia. [Special issue.]

Arroyo Posadas, Moisés. 1939. *La multitud y el paisaje peruanos en los relatos de José María Arguedas* (Peruvian peoples and landscapes in the stories of José María Arguedas). Cuadernos de Crítica Literaria y Social, no.1. Lima: Compañía de Impresiones y Publicidad. [Monograph.]

Díaz Ruiz, Ignacio. 1991. *Literatura y biografía en José María Arguedas* (Literature and biography in José María Arguedas). Cuadernos del Instituto de Investigaciones Filológicas, no. 18. Mexico City: Universidad Nacional Autonoma de Mexico. [Special issue.]

De Grandis, Rita, and Oscar Quezada. 1990. "Dos estudios sobre textos de Arguedas" (Two studies on texts by Arguedas). Cuadernos CICOSUL, no. 9. Lima: Centro de Investigación en Comunicación Social de la Universidad de Lima. [Special issue.]

Escobar, Alberto. 1981. *José María Arguedas, el desmitificador del indio y del rito indigenista* (José María Arguedas, demystifier of the Indian and of indigenous rites). Occasional Publications. Chicago: University of Chicago Center for Latin American Studies.

Flores V., Julio. 1970. "José María Arguedas y la nueva novela indígena del Perú" (José María Arguedas and the new Indigenous novel of Peru). *Coral* (Valparaíso, Chile) 13. [Special issue.]

Rens, Ivo. 1974. *La fin d'Arguedas: Reflexions sur les dimensions politiques d'un drame psychologique* (The end of Arguedas: Reflections on the political dimensions of a psychological drama). Geneva: Rens. [Monograph.]

Revista de crítica literaria latinoamericana (Lima: Latinoamericana Editores) 12 (2d semester 1980). [Special issue.]

Revista iberoamericana (Pittsburgh: Instituto Internacional de Literatura Iberoamericana) 122, nos. 1-2 (1983). [Special issue.]

Rivera, María del Carmen P. de. 1975. *Aproximación a la obra de José María*

Arguedas (Introduction to the work of José María Arguedas). Santo Domingo: Instituto Tecnológico de Santo Domingo, División de Investigación y Divulgación Científica. [Monograph.]

Rovira, José Carlos, and Carmen Alemany Bay. 1992. "José María Arguedas: Una recuperación indigenista del mundo peruano: Una perspectiva de la creación latinoamericana" (José María Arguedas: An indigenous recuperation of the Peruvian world: A perspective on Latin American creativity). *Anthopos* (Barcelona), Supplement 31: 1130–2089. [Special issue.]

Vargas Llosa, Mario. 1978. *La utopía arcaica* (The archaic utopia). Centre of Latin American Studies, Working Paper no. 33. Cambridge: University of Cambridge.

Westphalen, Emilio Adolfo. 1969. "José María Arguedas (1911–1969)" and "La última novela de Arguedas" (Arguedas's last novel). *Amaru* (Lima: Revista de Artes y Ciencias de la Universidad de Ingeniería) 11 (December). [Special issue]

Articles in Journals and Collections

Adorno, Rolena. 1983. "La soledad común de Waman Poma de Ayala y José María Arguedas" (The common solitude of Waman Poma de Ayala and José María Arguedas). *Revista iberoamericana* (Pittsburgh) 122:143–48.

Arredondo de Arguedas, Sybila. 1990. "*El zorro de arriba y el zorro de abajo* en la correspondencia de Arguedas"(The fox from above and the fox from below in Arguedas's correspondence). In *José María Arguedas: El zorro de arriba y el zorro de abajo*, ed. Eve-Marie Fell, 275–95 Nanterre, France: ALLCA XXe, Université Paris X, Centre de Recherches Latino-Américaines.

Barrenechea, Ana María. 1978. "Escritor, escritura y 'materia de las cosas' en los Zorros de Arguedas." In *Textos hispanoamericanos: De Sarmiento a Sarduy* (Hispanoamerican texts: From Sarmiento to Sarduy), 289–318. Caracas: Monte Avila Editores.

Befumo Boschi, Liliana. 1985. "El escritor y el hombre desde el narrador en

Los zorros. . . de José María Arguedas" (The writer and the man as seen from the narrator's point of view in *The Foxes . . .* of José María Arguedas). *Revista de crítica literaria latinoamericana* (Lima) 21–22:173–92.

Bermúdez, Manuel. 1974. "Una épica mestiza en la narrativa de José María Arguedas" (A mestizo epic in the narrative of José María Arguedas). In *Tradición y mestizaje: Dos ensayos de aproximación* (Tradition and *mestizaje*: Two introductory essays). Serie ensayo. Caracas: Instituto Pedagógico.

Beyersdorff, Margot. 1986. "Voice of the Runa: Quechua Substratum in the Narrative of José María Arguedas." *Latin American Indian Literatures Journal* 2:1 (Spring): 28–48.

Bonneville, Henry. 1971. "Quelques repères pour l'étude de José María Arguedas" (Some references for research on José María Arguedas). *Les langues néo-latines* (Paris) 199:54–70.

Castro-Klarén, Sara. 1975. "Testimonio sobre preguntas a José María Arguedas" (Testimony concerning questions asked of José María Arguedas). *Hispamérica* (Maryland) 10:45–54.

———. 1983. "Crimen y castigo: Sexualidad en José María Arguedas" (Crime and punishment: Sexuality in José María Arguedas). *Revista iberoamericana* (Pittsburgh) 49 (January–March): 55–65.

———. n.d. "Dancing and the Sacred in the Andes: From the Taqui-Oncoy to "Rasu-Ñiti." *Dispositio* 14, nos. 36–38: 169–185.

Contreras, Jesús. 1987. "El lugar de José María Arguedas en la etnología de España y de los Andes" (The place of José María Arguedas in Spanish and Andean ethnology). In *Las comunidades de España y del Perú* (The communities of Spain and Peru; originally a dissertation by José María Arguedas), 15–25. Madrid: Ediciones Cultura Hispánica del Instituto de Cooperación Iberoamericana, y Ministerio de Agricultura, Pesca y Alimentación.

Cornejo Polar, Antonio. 1975. "La imagen del mundo en 'La serpiente de oro'" (The image of the world in 'The golden serpent'). *Revista de crítica literaria latinamericana* 2:51–62.

———. 1990. "Un ensayo sobre 'Los Zorros' de Arguedas" (An essay on Arguedas's *Foxes*). In *José María Arguedas: El zorro de arriba y el zorro de abajo*, ed. Eve-Marie Fell, 297–306. Nanterre, France: ALLCA XXe, Université Paris X, Centre de Recherches Latino-Américaines.

———. 1995. "Condición migrante e intertextualidad multicultural: El caso de Arguedas" (Migrant conditions and multicultural intertextuality: The case of Arguedas). *Revista de crítica literaria latinoamericana* 21, no. 42: 101–9.

Cortázar, Julio. 1969. "Un gran escritor y su soledad" (A great writer in his solitude). *Life en español* 33, no. 7: 44–55.

Curuchet, C. 1968. "José María Arguedas: Peruano universal" (José María Arguedas: Universal Peruvian). *Cuadernos hispanoamericanos* 228 (December): 749–55.

De Grandis, Rita. 1989. "Los zorros de Arguedas: Una traducción mestiza" (Arguedas's *Foxes*: A mestizo translation). *Lenguas, literaturas, sociedades: Cuadernos hispánicos* (Québec) 2 (1st semester): 149–58.

———. 1990. "*El zorro de arriba y el zorro de abajo* de José María Arguedas: Une traduction métisse" (The fox from above and the fox from below by José María Arguedas: A mestizo translation). In *Parole exclusive, parole exclue, parole transgressive* (Exclusive word, excluded word, transgressive word), eds. Antonio Gómez-Moriana and Catherine Poupeney Hart, 481–502. Longueuil, Québec: Préambule.

———. 1991. "Le regard anthropologique d'Arguedas ou l'évacuation de l'Indien' par le 'Métis'" (Arguedas's anthropological gaze, or the expulsion of the Indian by the mestizo). In *"L'Indien," instance discursive* (The Indian: A discursive moment), ed. Antonio Gómez-Moriana and Daniele Trottier. Montreal: Editions Balzac.

———. 1994. "La segunda versión de una crónica mestiza en *Los zorros* de Arguedas" (The second version of a mestizo chronicle in Arguedas's *Foxes*). In *Conquista y Contraconquista: La escritura del Nuevo Mundo* (Conquest and counterconquest: The writing of the New World), ed. Julio Ortega and José Amor y Vázquez, 575–85. Mexico City and Providence: El Colegio de México and Brown University.

De Grandis, Rita, and Oscar Quezada. 1990. "Los Zorros de Arguedas: Una traducción mestiza" (Arguedas's *Foxes*: A mestizo translation). In *Dos estudios sobre textos de Arguedas* (Two studies of Arguedean texts), ed. Rita de Grandis and Oscar Quezada, 9–17. Lima: Centro de Investigación en Comunicación Social de la Universidad de Lima.

Dorfman, Ariel. 1969. "Arguedas y la epopeya americana" (Arguedas and the American epic poem). *Amaru* (Lima) 11: 18-26.

Escajadillo, Tomás G. 1970. "Meditación preliminar acerca de José María Arguedas y el indigenismo" (Preliminary meditation on José María Arguedas and *indigenismo*). *Revista peruana de cultura* 13–14 (December): 82–126.

Escobar, Alberto. 1972. "La serpiente de oro o El río de la vida" (The golden serpent, or The river of life). In *Patio de Letras* [1965]. Caracas: Monte Avila Editores, 211–301.

———. 1980. "José María Arguedas: El desmitificador del indio y del rito indigenista" (The demythologizer of the Indian and of indigenous ritual). *Nova Americana* (Turin: Giulio Einaudi Editores) 3:141–96.

———. 1980. "La utopia de la lengua en el primer Arguedas" (Linguistic utopia in the early Arguedas). *Revista de crítica literaria latinoamericana* (Lima) 12:7–40.

Fell, Eve-Marie. 1979. "José María Arguedas et le probleme du métissage" (José María Arguedas and the problem of *mestizaje*). *Etudes hispaniques* (Tours) 2:89–102.

———. 1982. "Problémes et perspectives de l'indianité péruvienne: Le point de vue d'un témoin privilégié, José María Arguedas" (Problems and perspectives on Peruvian *indigenismo*: The point of view of a privileged witness). *Amérique latine* (Paris) 12:51–59.

Flores Galindo, Alberto. 1990. "Los últimos años de Arguedas (intelectuales, sociedad e identidad en el Perú)" (Arguedas's final years: intellectuals, society, and identity in Peru). *Literaturas andinas* 2, nos. 3–4: 17–35.

Forgues, Roland. 1990. "Por qué bailan los zorros" (Why the foxes dance). In *José María Arguedas: El zorro de arriba y el zorro de abajo*. Ed. Eve-Marie Fell, 307–15. Nanterre, France: ALLCA XXe. Université Paris X, Centre de Recherches Latino-Américaines.

———. 1991. "El mito del monolingüismo quechua de Arguedas" (The myth of Arguedas's Quechua monolingualism). In *José María Arguedas: Vida y obra* (José María Arguedas: Life and work), ed. Hildebrando Pérez and Carlos Garayar, 47–58. Lima: Amaru Editores.

Gold, Peter. 1973. "The Indigenista Fiction of José María Arguedas." *Bulletin of Hispanic Studies* 50 (January): 56–70.

Gómez Mango, Edmundo. 1990. "Todas las lenguas: Vida y muerte de la escritura en 'Los Zorros' de J. M. Arguedas" (All languages: The life and death of writing in Arguedeas's *Foxes*). In *José María Arguedas: El zorro de arriba y el zorro de abajo.* Ed. Eve-Marie Fell, 360–68. Nanterre, France: ALLCA XXe, Université Paris X, Centre de Recherches Latino-Américaines.

Harrison, Regina. 1983. "José María Arguedas: El substrato quechua" (José María Arguedas: The Quechua substratum). *Revista iberoamericana* (Pittsburgh) 49 (January–March): 111–32.

Kemper Columbus, Claudette. 1995. "Grounds for De-Colonization: Arguedas's Foxes." In *Genealogy and Literature*, ed. Lee Quinby, 116–33. Minneapolis: University of Minnesota Press.

Larco, Juan. 1976. Prologue to *Recopilación de textos sobre José María Arguedas* (Compilation of texts on José María Arguedas), 7–20. Havana: Casa de las Américas.

Lastra, Pedro. 1992. "Imágenes de José María Arguedas" (Images of José María Arguedas). *Escritura: Teoría y crítica literarias* 17, nos. 33–34 (January-December): 47–59.

Leon Caparo, Raúl. 1973. "Versión del mito de Inkarrí en Qollana-Wasak" (A version of the Inkarrí myth in Qollana-Wasak). *Ideología mesiánica del mundo andino* by Juan M. Ossio, 473–77. Lima: Ignacio Prado Pastor.

Lienhard, Martin. 1977. "Tradición oral y novela: Los 'Zorros' en la última novela de José María Arguedas" (Oral tradition and novel: The foxes in José María Arguedas's last novel). *Revista de crítica literaria latinoamericana* (Lima) 6 (2d semester): 81–92.

———. 1980. "La última novela de Arguedas: Imagen de un lector futuro" (Arguedas's last novel: The image of a future reader). *Revista de crítica literaria latinoamericana* 6, no. 12: 177–96.

————. 1990. "La 'andinización' del vanguardismo urbano" (The Andeanization of urban modernism). In *José María Arguedas: El zorro de arriba y el zorro de abajo*, ed. Eve-Marie Fell, 321–32. Nanterre, France: ALLCA XXe, Université Paris X, Centre de Recherches Latino-Américaines.

Lindstrom, Naomi. 1983. *"El zorro de arriba y el zorro de abajo*: Una marginación al nivel del discurso" (The fox from above and the fox from below: Marginalization at the level of discourse). *Revista iberoamericana* (Pittsburgh) 49 (January-March): 211–18.

Lockert, Lucia. 1987. "Peruvian Social Realities in José María Arguedas." *Michigan Academician* 19, no. 2 (Spring): 243–51.

López Maguiña, Santiago. "Letras, palabra y escritura en el Inca Garcilaso y José María Arguedas" (Literature, word, and writing in the Inca Garcilaso and José María Arguedas). *Hoja Naviera* (Lima) 2, no. 3 (November): 35–43.

Losada, Alejandro. 1974. "La obra de José María Arguedas y la sociedad andina: Interpretación de su creación como praxis social" (The work of José María Arguedas and Andean society: An interpretation of his work as social praxis). *Eco* (Bogotá): 162 (April): 592–620.

March, Kathleen N. 1979. "Lenguaje y lucha social en *El zorro de arriba y el zorro de abajo* de José María Arguedas" (Language and social struggle in Arguedas's *The fox from above and the fox from below*). *Anales de literatura iberoamericana* 8: 145–67.

Mathews, Daniel. 1994. "La ciudad del silencio" (The city of silence). *Hoja Naviera* 2, no. 3 (November): 44–50.

Melis, Antonio. 1994. "Escritura antropológica y escritura narrativa en José María Arguedas" (Anthropological and fictional writing in José María Arguedas). *Hoja Naviera* (Lima) 2, no. 3 (November): 26–34.

Mitchell, Fergus. 1978. "The Foxes in José María Arguedas's Last Novel." *Hispania* (Journal of the AATSP) 61 (March): 46–56.

Montoya, Rodrigo. 1979. "José María Arguedas y su lección de peruanizar al Perú" (José María Arguedas and his inspiration to "Peruvianize" Peru). *QueHacer* (Lima) 2: 88–95.

————. 1981. *"Yawar Fiesta*: Una lectura antropológica" (*Yawar Fiesta*: An anthropological reading). *Revista de crítica literaria latinoamericana* 12:55–68.

———. 1994. "Arguedas en España" (Arguedas in Spain). *Hoja Naviera* (Lima) 2, no. 3 (November): 16–25.

Moretic, Yerko. 1964. "Tras las huellas del indigenismo literario en el Perú" (Searching for traces of literary *indigenismo* in Peru). *Atenea* 156 (October–December): 205–16.

Moriondo Kulikowski, María Zulma. 1991. "El cuerpo femenino en *El zorro de arriba y el zorro de abajo* de José María Arguedas" (The feminine body in *The fox from above and the fox from below* by José María Arguedas). In *The Body and Sexual Politics in Modern Latin American Fiction*, ed. Ruth Gabriela Kirstein, 113–22. Buffalo: Artur Efron.

Murra, John V. 1978. Introduction to *Deep Rivers*. Trans. Frances Horning Barraclough, ix–xv. Austin: University of Texas Press.

———. 1983. "José María Arguedas: Dos imágenes" (José María Arguedas: Two images). *Revista iberoamericana* (Pittsburgh) 122:43–54. [Reprinted in *Las Comunidades de España y del Perú* (The communities of Spain and Peru) by José María Arguedas, 7–13. Madrid: Ediciones Cultura Hispánica del Instituto de Cooperación Iberoamericana y Ministerio de Agricultura, Pesca y Alimentación, 1987.

Ortega, Julio. 1974. "Sobre la última novela de Arguedas" (Concerning Arguedas's last novel). In *La imaginación crítica: Ensayos sobre la modernidad en el Perú* (The critical imagination: Essays on Peruvian modernity). Lima: Ediciones Peisa, 189–98.

———. 1982. "Texto, comunicación y cultura, en *Los ríos profundos* " (Text, communication, and culture in *Deep Rivers*). *Nueva revista de filología hispánica* 31:44–82.

Ostria, Mauricio. 1980. "Dualismo estructural y unidad textual en la narrativa de José María Arguedas" (Structual duality and textual unity in the narrative of José María Arguedas). *Estudios filológicos* (Valdivia, Chile) 15:81–104.

———. 1981. "José María Arguedas o la escritura contra la muerte: Construcción y desconstrucción de un verosímil narrativo" (José María

Arguedas, or writing against death: Construction and destruction of narrative verisimilitude). *Acta literaria* (Concepción, Chile) 6:39–55.

Oviedo, José Miguel. "El último Arguedas: Testimonio y comentario" (The final Arguedas: Testimony and commentary). *Cuadernos hispanoamericanos* 492 (June 1991): 143–47.

Noriega, Julio. 1989. "'El sueño del pongo': Una forma de liberación utópica" (The Indian servant's dream: A form of utopic liberation). *Imprévue* 2:91–103.

Quijano, Anibal. 1984. "Arguedas: La sonora banda de la sociedad" (Arguedas: Society's resounding band). *Hueso húmero* 19 (October-December): 157–62.

Rama, Angel. 1975. Introduction to *Formación de una cultura nacinal indoamericana* (The formation of a national Indoamerican culture) by José María Arguedas, ed. Rama, ix–xxiv. Mexico City: Siglo XXI Editores.

———. 1976. "José María Arguedas, transculturador" (José María Arguedas, transculturator). Prologue to *Señores e indios: Acerca de la cultura quechua* (Lords and Indians: About Quechua culture) by José María Arguedas, 7–38. Buenos Aires: Arca.

———. 1987. "La gesta del mestizo" (Mestizo gests), "La inteligencia mítica" (Mythic intelligence), "La novela: Opera de los pobres" (The novel: Work of the poor). In *Transculturación narrativa en América Latina*. (Narrative transculturation in Latin America), 173–269. Mexico City: Siglo XXI Editores.

Ribeyro, Julio Ramón. 1976. "José María Arguedas o la destrucción de la Arcadia" (José María Arguedas, or the destruction of Arcadia). In *La caza sutil: Ensayos y artículos de crítica literaria* (The subtle hunt: Essays and articles on literary criticism). Lima: Editorial Milla Batres, 85–93.

Rouillón Arróspide, José Luis. 1966. "Notas sobre el mundo mágico de José María Arguedas" (Notes on the magical world of José María Arguedas). *Mercurio peruano* (Lima) 2, no. 461 (May–June): 121–33.

———. 1973. "El espacio mítico de José María Arguedas" (The mythical space of José María Arguedas). *Nueva narrativa hispanoamericana* 3, no. 2 (September): 161–78.

———. 1978. "José María Arguedas y la religión" (José María Arguedas and religion). *Páginas* (Lima) 3, no. 15: 11–30.

———. 1979. "Arguedas y la idea del Perú" (Arguedas and the idea of Peru). In *Perú: Identidad nacional*, ed. César Arróspide de la Flor, 379–402. Lima: Centro de Estudios para el Desarrollo y la Participación.

———. 1990. "La luz que nadie apagará: Aproximaciónes al mito y al cristianismo del último Arguedas" (The light that no one will extinguish: An introduction to the myth and Christianity of the final work of Arguedas). In *José María Arguedas: El zorro de arriba y el zorro de abajo*, ed. Eve-Marie Fell, 341–59. Nanterre, France: ALLCA XXe, Université Paris X, Centre de Recherches Latino-Américaines.

Rowe, William. 1973. "Mito, lenguaje e ideología en *Los ríos profundos*" (Myth, language, and ideology in *Deep Rivers*). *Textual* (Lima) 7: 2–12.

———. 1978. "El nuevo lenguaje de Arguedas en *El zorro de arriba y el zorro de abajo* " (Arguedas's new language in *The fox from above and the fox from below*). *Texto crítico* 11: 198–212.

———. 1983. "Arguedas: El narrador y el antropólogo frente al lenguaje" (Arguedas: The narrator and the anthropologist face to face with language). *Revista iberoamericana* (Pittsburgh) 49, no. 122 (January–March): 97–109.

———. 1987. "Arguedas: Música, conocimiento y transformación social" (Arguedas: Music, knowledge, and social transformation). *Revista de crítica literaria latinoamericana* 13, no. 25: 97–107.

———. 1990. "Deseo, escritura y fuerzas productivas" (Desire, writing and productive forces). In *José María Arguedas: El zorro de arriba y el zorro de abajo* (José María Arguedas: The fox from above and the fox from below), ed. Eve-Marie Fell, 333–40. Nanterre, France: ALLCA XXe, Université Paris X, Centre de Recherches Latino-Américaines.

Salazar Bondy, Sebastián. 1965. "Arguedas: la novela social como creación verbal" (Arguedas: The social novel as verbal creation). *Revista de la Universidad de México*. 19, no. 2 (July): 18–20.

Spitta, Silvia. 1995. "Jóse María Arguedas: Entre Dos Aguas" (Jóse María Arguedas: Between two waters). *In Between Two Waters: Narratives of Transculturation in Latin Amrica*, 139-76. Houston, TX: Rice University Press.

Vargas Llosa, Mario. 1972. "Tres notas sobre Arguedas" (Three notes on Arguedas). In *Nueva novela latinoamericana* (The new Latin American
novel), comp. Jorge Raul Lafforge, 30–54. Buenos Aires: Editorial
Paidós.

———. 1978. "Ensoñación y magia en *Los ríos profundos* " (Daydream and
magic in *Deep Rivers*). In *José María Arguedas: Los ríos profundos*
(José María Arguedas: *Deep Rivers*) , ix-xiv. Caracas: Biblioteca Ayacucho.

———. 1980. "Literatura y suicidio: El caso de Arguedas *(El zorro de arriba
y el zorro de abajo)"* (Literature and suicide: The case of Arguedas
[The fox from above and the fox from below]). *Revista iberoamericana*
(Pittsburgh) 110–11 (January–June): 3–28.

———. 1981. "Arguedas, entre la ideología y la arcadia" (Arguedas, between
ideology and utopia). *Revista iberoamericana* (Pittsburgh) 116–17:33–46.

———. 1983. "José María Arguedas entre sapos y halcones" (José María Arguedas, between toads and falcons). Introduction to *José María Arguedas: Relatos completos* (José María Arguedas: Complete stories).
Madrid: Alianza Editorial.

Selected Conference Proceedings and Reviews

Cornejo Polar, Antonio, Alberto Escobar, Martin Lienhard, and William
Rowe, 1984. *Vigencia y universalidad de José María Arguedas* (The relevance and universality of José María Arguedas). Panel discussion
sponsored by Editorial Horizonte and coordinated by Sybila
Arredondo and the Biblioteca Nacional de Lima. Lima: Editorial Horizonte.

Del Llano, Aymara. 1992. "La crítica literaria y la zoología: prácticas argu-
mentativas" (Literary criticism and zoology: Discoursive practices). In
Cuadernos para la investigación de la literatura hispánica (Studies for
research on Hispanic literature). Madrid: Seminario Menéndez y
Pelayo 16:219–37. [A review of *¿He vivido en vano?* (Have I lived in
vain?), a roundtable discussion on *Todas las sangres* (All bloods), June
23, 1965, published by the Institute of Peruvian Studies, 1985.]

Escobar, Alberto, ed. 1985. *¿He vivido en vano?* (Have I lived in vain?). Roundtable discussion on *Todas las sangres* (All bloods), June 23, 1965. Lima: Instituto de Estudios Peruanos.

Forgues, Roland, ed. 1989. *Rencontre de renards* (Convention of foxes). Proceedings of the International Conference on José María Arguedas. Grenoble, France: Edicious det Tignhaus (Centre d'Etudes et de Recherches Peruviennes et Andines, Université Stendhal).

Montoya, Rodrigo, comp. 1991. *José María Arguedas, veinte años después: Huellas y horizonte, 1919–1989* (José María Arguedas, twenty years later: Traces and horizon, 1919–1989). Proceedings of the seminar "La Cultura en el Perú" sponsored by the Department of Anthropology, National University of San Marcos, Lima, Peru.

Narradores Peruanos, 1986. *Primer encuentro de narradores peruanos* (First meeting of Peruvian writers). Proceedings of a conference sponsored by Casa de la Cultura de Arequipa, 1965. Lima: Latinoamericana Editores.

Rochabrun S., Guillermo. 1992. "Viviendo en vano: Una relectura de la Mesa Redonda sobre *Todas las sangres* (Living in vain: A reinterpretation of the roundtable discussion on *All Bloods*). *Socialismo y participación* (March): 21–34.

Radio Broadcasts

"José María Arguedas: The Death of a Dancer." In "Faces, Mirrors, Masks: Twentieth-Century Latin American Fiction." Washington, D.C.: National Public Radio. [Audiocassette, 30 min.; program 3; actor Hector Elizondo reads from the journals, fiction, and poetry of Arguedas.]

Biographies and Biographical Sketches

Arredondo, Sybila. 1983. "Vida y obra de José María Arguedas y hechos fundamentales del Perú" (Life and work of José María Arguedas and fundamental events in Peru). In *José María Arguedas: Obras completas* (José María Arguedas: Complete works), 1:xv–xxvi. Lima: Editorial Horizonte.

Arroyo Posadas, Moisés. 1972?. *José María Arguedas: Etapas de su vida* (José María Arguedas: Significant moments in his life). Abancay, Perú: Ediciones Amankay.

Castro-Klarén, Sara. 1992. "José María Arguedas." In *Dictionary of Literary Biography*, ed. William Luis, 113:18–29. Modern Latin American Fiction Writers, first series. Detroit: Gale Research.

Damián M., A. Arguedas, E. Murrugarra, and H. Blanco. 1980. *José María Arguedas: Testimonios* (José María Arguedas: Testimonies). Lima: Instituto Cultural José María Arguedas.

Forgues, Roland, Hildebrando Pérez, and Carlos Garayar, eds. 1991. *José María Arguedas: Vida y obra* (José María Arguedas: Life and work). Lima: Amaru Editores.

Lévano, César. 1969. *Arguedas: Sentimiento trágico de la vida* (Arguedas: A tragic sense of life). Lima: Editorial Gráfica Labor. [Includes journal entries from *El zorro de arriba y el zorro de abajo*, "Inevitable comentario a unas ideas de Julio Cortázar" (Inevitable response to a few ideas by Julio Cortázar), "Qollan, Vietnam llaqtaman," "De Mariátegui al año 1966" (From Mariátegui to the year 1966), and an article published by Enrique González Manet previously published in the Cuban newspaper *El Mundo*, January 23, 1968.]

Merino de Zela, Mildred E. 1970. "Vida y obra de José María Arguedas" (Life and work of José María Arguedas). *Revista peruana de Cultura* 13–14 (December): 127–78.

Sabogal Wiesse, José. "José María Arguedas (1911–1969)." *América Indígena* (Mexico City) 30 (1970): 206–17.

Westphalen, Emilio Adolfo. 1969. "José María Arguedas (1911–1969)" and "La última novela de Arguedas" (Arguedas's last novel). *Amaru* (Lima: Revista de Artes y Ciencias de la Universidad de Ingeniería) 11 (December).

Bibliographies

Castro-Klarén, Sara. 1992. "José María Arguedas." In *Dictionary of Literary Biography* , ed. William Luis, 113:18–29. Modern Latin American Fiction Writers, first series. Detroit: Gale Research.

Fell, Eve-Marie, Ed. 1990. Bibliography in *José María Arguedas: El zorro de arriba y el zorro de abajo* (José María Arguedas: The fox from above and the fox from below), 444–62. Nanterre, France: ALLCA XXe, Université Paris X, Centre de Recherches Latino-Américaines.

Prosdocimi, María del Carmen, Nilda del Valle Palacios, and Olga Oblodiner. 1972. *Reseña para una bibliografía sobre la realidad peruana y su literatura: La obra de José María Arguedas* (Outline for a bibliography on Peruvian reality and its literature: The work of José María Arguedas). Chaco, Argentina: Universidad Nacional del Nordeste (Facultad de Humanidades).

Rowe, William. 1970. "Bibliografía sobre José María Arguedas" (Bibliography on José María Arguedas). *Revista peruana de cultura* 13–14 (December): 179–97.

Contributors

Priscilla Archibald is assistant professor in the Hispanic Studies department at Northwestern University. Currently, she is investigating the renewed political and theoretical interest in the Andean region. She is also working on a feminist analysis of mestizo culture.

Monica Barnes is an editor of *Andean Past*, a numbered publication series published by the Cornell University Latin American Studies Program. She is also book review editor of the *Latin American Indian Literatures Journal* published by the Pennsylvania State University, as well as the author of numerous articles and reviews on aspects of Andean literature, history, and archaeology, including "The Yawar Fiesta of Pampachiri," *NAOS* 10, no. 1–3. From 1978 to 1981 she conducted archaeological surveys in the Peruvian departments of Ayacucho and Apurímac, visiting many of the sites mentioned in Arguedas's novels and essays.

Sandra M. Boschetto-Sandoval is associate professor of Spanish at Michigan Technological University. She has published essays on Hispanic literature in a number of journals and anthologies, including a recent special issue on Third World Women's Inscriptions for *College Literature* (1995). She is coeditor (with Marcia P. McGowan) of *Claribel Alegría and Central American Literature* (Athens: Ohio University Center for International Studies, 1994), and is now at work on a book-length study of Chilean feminist writer Amanda Labarca Hubertson.

Antonio Cornejo Polar is professor of Latin American literature at the University of California, Berkeley and emeritus professor and former president of the University of San Marcos (Lima, Peru). He is also a member of the Spanish Royal Academy. His latest books include *La formación de la tradición literaria en el Perú* (The formation of literary tradition in Peru) (Lima: Centro de Estudios y Publicaciones,1989), *La novela peruana* (The Peruvian novel) (Lima: Editorial Horizonte, 1989), *Clorinda Matto de Turner, novelista* (Clorinda Matto de Turner, novelist) (Lima: Lluvia Editores, 1992), and *Escribir en el aire: Ensayo sobre la heterogeneidad socio-cultural de las literaturas andinas* (Writing in the Air: An essay on the Sociocultural heterogeneity of Andean literatures, 1994).

Rita De Grandis is an associate professor of Spanish and Latin American Studies at the University of British Columbia. A specialist in modern Spanish American literature, she has collaborated in various projects. Her recent books are *Polémica y estrategias narrativas en América Latina* (Polemic and Narrative Strategies in Latin America) (Rosario, Argentina: Beatriz Viterbo Editora, 1993), and (coedited) *Inprevisíveis Américas: Questões de Hibridação Cultural nas Américas* (Unforseeable Americas: Questions of cultural hybridity in the Americas) (Pôrto Alegre: Sagra-duzzatto, 1995). She has also authored numerous articles on Peruvian and Argentine literature and culture.

Luis A. Jiménez is professor of Latin American Literature at Florida Southern College. He has published articles on such authors as Juan Francisco Manzano, Juan Rulfo, Octavio Paz, Rafaél Catalá, and Julia de Burgos. His recent books include *El arte autobiográfico en cuba en el siglo XIX* (Autobiographical Art in nineteenth-century Cuba) (New Brunswick, N.J.: Ometeca Institute, 1995) and *Literatura y sociedad en la narrativa de Manuel Gálvez* (Literature and society in the narrative of Manuel Gálvez) (Buenos Aires: Editorial Peña Lillo, 1990).

Alita Kelley is assistant professor of Spanish and French at Pennsylvania State University, Delaware County. A native of Yorkshire, England, she has published several articles, books, and translations on chicana/o, Peruvian, and other Latin American writers, as well as her own poetry (in English) under her Peruvian name, C. A. De Lomellini. *Target Practice* (Bradford, England: Redbeck Press, 1994) is her fifth and latest book of poetry.

Claudette Kemper Columbus is professor of English and Comparative Literature at Hobart and William Smith Colleges. She is the author of *Mythological Consciousness and the Future: José María Arguedas* (New York: Peter Lang, 1986). More recent work on Arguedas includes an article in *Genealogy and Literature*, edited by Lee Quinby (Minneapolis: University of Minnesota Press, 1995), and *Anthropológica* (Lima: Pontificia Universidad Católica del Perú, 1997)

John C. Landreau is assistant professor of Spanish at Trenton State College. He received his Ph.D. from Princeton University in 1995 with a dissertation entitled "Translation and National Culture in the Writings of José María Arguedas." Currently, he is preparing a manuscript of the same title.

Pedro Lastra is professor-emeritus of Spanish Literature at the State University of New York at Stony Brook. He was named Honorary Professor of the University of San Marcos (Lima) in 1973. He has published several books of poetry, including most recently *Noticias del extranjero* (News from abroad) (1979; 1982; Santiago, Chile: Editorial Universitaria,1992) and *Travel Notes* (Maryland: La Yapa Editores, 1992), a short anthology translated by Elias Rivers. He has also edited *Conversaciones con Enrique Lihn* (Conversations with Enrique Lihn) (1980; Santiago, Chile: Atelier Ediciones, 1990) and *Relecturas hispanoamericanas* (Hispanic-American rereadings) (Santiago, Chile: Editorial Universitaria, 1987).

Martin Lienhard is professor of Latin American and Iberian Literatures at the University of Zurich. His research has focused primarily on the literary practices of plurilingual and pluricultural communities in Latin America (Mesoamerica, Caribbean, Andes, Paraguay, and Brazil). His latest books include *La voz y su huella* (The voice and its trace) (1990; 1991; Lima: Editorial Horizonte, 1992) and *Testimonios, cartas y manifiestos indígenas* (Indigenous testimonios, letters, and manifestos) (Caracas: Biblioteca Ayacucho, 1992).

Antonio Melis is professor of Latin American Languages and Literatures at the University of Siena, Italy, and honorary professor at the National University of San Marcos (Lima). He has published essays on the work of José Carlos Mariátegui, José María Arguedas, Cesar Vallejo, José Martí, Waman Puma, Sor Juana Inés de la Cruz, and Juan Rulfo, among others. With Anibel Quijano, he is coeditor of the *Anuario mariateguiano*, and serves on the editorial board of *Revista de crítica literaria latinoamericana*. Along with other literary and anthropological works by Arguedas, he is also the Italian translator of Arguedas's posthumous novel *El zorro de arriba y el zorro de abajo* (The fox from above and the fox from below).

Julio Ortega is professor of Hispanic Studies at Brown University and the Simon Bolivar Chair Professor of Latin American Studies at Cambridge University. He is the author of, among other books, *Poetics of Change: The New Spanish American Narrative* (Austin: University of Texas Press, 1984), and the editor of *Gabriel García Márquez and the Powers of Fiction* (Austin: University of Texas Press, 1988).

William Rowe is professor of Latin American Cultural Studies at King's College, London, and co-editor of the *Journal of Latin American Cultural Studies: Traveía*. He has published, among other works, *Memory and Modernity: Popular Culture in Latin America* (with Vivian Schelling; London: Verso, 1991); *Rulfo: El llano en llamas* (Wolfeboro, N.H.: Tamesis Books, 1987) and *Mito e ideología en la obra de José María Arguedas* (Myth and ideology in the work of José María Arguedas) (Lima: Instituto Nacional de Cultura, 1979).

Ciro A. Sandoval is associate professor of Spanish and Comparative Studies at Michigan Technological University. His interdisciplinary research includes articles published in *Revista iberoamericana, Philosophy Today, OMETECA (Science and Literature)*, and *The Encyclopedia of the Essay*. Along with Latin American literature, his areas of specialization include the essay; interdisciplinary relations across literature, science, and technology; and theories of linguistics, translation, and language for special purposes.

Monographs in International Studies

Titles Available from Ohio University Press, 1996

Southeast Asia Series

* Southeast Asia Translation Project Group

No. 93   Salleh, Muhammad Haji. Beyond the Archipelago: Selected Poems. 1995. 247 pp. Paper 0-89680-181-0 $20.00.

No. 94   Federspiel, Howard M. A Dictionary of Indonesian Islam. 1995. 327 pp. Bibliog. Paper 0-89680-182-9 $25.00.

No. 95   Leary, John. Violence and the Dream People: The Orang Asli in the Malayan Emergency 1948–1960. 1995. 275 pp. Maps, illus., tables, appendices, bibliog., index. Paper 0-89680-186-1 $22.00.

No. 96   Lewis, Dianne. *Jan Compagnie* in the Straits of Malacca 1641–1795. 1995. 176 pp. Map, appendices, bibliog., index. Paper 0-89680-187-x. $18.00.

No. 97   Schiller, Jim and Martin-Schiller, Barbara. Imagining Indonesia: Cultural Politics and Political Culture. 1996. 384 pp., notes, glossary, bibliog. Paper 0-89680-190-x. $30.00.

No. 98   Bonga, Dieuwke Wendelaar. Eight Prison Camps: A Dutch Family in Japanese Java. 1996. 233 pp., illus., map, glossary. Paper 0-89680-191-8. $18.00.

No. 99   Gunn, Geoffrey C. Language, Ideology, and Power in Brunei Darussalam. 1996. 328 pp., glossary, notes, bibliog., index. Paper 0-89680-192-6. $24.00.

No. 100 Martin, Peter W., Conrad Ozog, and Gloria R. Poedjosoedarmo, eds. Language Use and Language Change in Brunei Darussalam. 1996. 390 pp., maps, notes, bibliog. Paper 0-89680-193-x. $26.00.

Africa Series

No. 43   Harik, Elsa M. and Donald G. Schilling. The Politics of Education in Colonial Algeria and Kenya. 1984. 102 pp. Paper 0-89680-117-9 $12.50.

No. 45   Keto, C. Tsehloane. American-South African Relations 1784–1980: Review and Select Bibliography. 1985. 169 pp. Paper 0-89680-128-4 $11.00.

No. 46   Burness, Don, ed. Wanasema: Conversations with African Writers. 1985. 103 pp. paper 0-89680-129-2 $11.00.

No. 47   Switzer, Les. Media and Dependency in South Africa: A Case Study of the Press and the Ciskei "Homeland." 1985. 97 pp. Paper 0-89680-130-6 $10.00.

No. 51   Clayton, Anthony and David Killingray. Khaki and Blue: Military and Police in British Colonial Africa. 1989. 347 pp. Paper 0-89680-147-0 $20.00.

Latin America Series

Ordering Information

Individuals are encouraged to patronize local bookstores wherever possible. Orders for titles in the Monographs in International Studies may be placed directly through the Ohio University Press, Scott Quadrangle, Athens, Ohio 45701-2979. Individuals should remit payment by check, VISA, or Master-Card.* Those ordering from the United Kingdom, Continental Europe, the Middle East,. and Africa should order through Academic and University Publishers Group, 1 Gower Street, London WC1E, England. Orders from the Pacific Region, Asia, Australia, and New Zealand should be sent to East-West Export Books, c/o the University of Hawaii Press, 2840 Kolowalu Street, Honolulu, Hawaii 96822, USA.

Individuals ordering from outside of the U.S. should remit in U.S. funds to Ohio University Press either by International Money Order or by a check drawn on a U.S. bank.** Most out-of-print titles may be ordered from University Microfilms, Inc., 300 North Zeeb Road, Ann Arbor, Michigan 48106, USA.

Prices are subject to change.

  * Please add $3.50 for the first book and $.75 for each additional book for shipping and handling.

** Outside the U.S. please add $4.50 for the first book and $.75 for each additional book.

Ohio University
Monographs in International Studies

The Ohio University Center for International Studies was established to help create within the university and local communities a greater awareness of the world beyond the United States. Comprising programs in African, Latin American, Southeast Asian, Development and Administrative studies, the Center supports scholarly research, sponsors lectures and colloquia, encourages course development within the university curriculum, and publishes the Monographs in International Studies series with the Ohio University Press. The Center and its programs also offer an interdisciplinary Master of Arts degree in which students may focus on one of the regional or topical concentrations, and may also combine academics with training in career fields such as journalism, business, and language teaching. For undergraduates, major and certificate programs are also available.

For more information, contact the Vice Provost for International Studies, Burson House, Ohio University, Athens, Ohio 45701.